OPEN QUESTIONS

OPEN QUESTIONS

Diverse Thinkers Discuss God, Religion, and Faith

Luís F. Rodrigues

 PRAEGER

AN IMPRINT OF ABC-CLIO, LLC
Santa Barbara, California • Denver, Colorado • Oxford, England

Library of Congress Cataloging-in-Publication Data

Rodrigues, Luís F.
   Open questions : diverse thinkers discuss God, religion, and faith / Luís F. Rodrigues.
     p. cm.
   Includes bibliographical references and index.
   ISBN 978-0-313-38644-2 (hard copy : alk. paper)—ISBN 978-0-313-38645-9 (ebook)
1. Religion. 2. Intellectuals—Interviews. I. Title.
   BL48.R4728 2010
   200—dc22   2010011195

ISBN: 978-0-313-38644-2
EISBN: 978-0-313-38645-9

14   13   12   11   10   1   2   3   4   5

This book is also available on the World Wide Web as an eBook.
Visit www.abc-clio.com for details.

Praeger
An Imprint of ABC-CLIO, LLC

ABC-CLIO, LLC
130 Cremona Drive, P.O. Box 1911
Santa Barbara, California 93116-1911

This book is printed on acid-free paper ∞

Manufactured in the United States of America

Contents

Introduction

Since the dawn of history, much has been made of the existence of God—or gods. Some people believe in many gods; others believe in just one God. For some who believe in a singular deity, that deity is a personal being, like a father figure; for others, God is Nature, embedded in all things and beings, or a kind of universal consciousness. A minority of humans believe in no gods, one God, or even what is conventionally called "the supernatural."

Although I once believed in God, I now count myself in this atheist minority. Still, I have never dismissed the "god question" as foolish or childish. I do not think that nonbelief in God is a claim to intellectual superiority. I am open to the critique that my journey toward atheism is a journey toward a blindness to the spark of the divine. Nevertheless, I hold this principle: I do not embark on my journey in fear; I have deliberately based my choice of path on the objective tools and techniques of rational inquiry and the subjective means by which I interpret the results. (Besides those, what other tools do we have to help us understand the cosmos?)

Born in Portugal, a very Catholic country, I was raised in a liberal religious environment. I did not attend Mass frequently, but I was baptized as an infant and I took my first Communion at the age of 10, and I must say that I had great pleasure attending catechesis when I was young. I am an architect and painter, and I've always had a natural inclination to draw and to paint, so I spent a lot of time at catechesis not only listening to the gospel but also making drawings of my images of Jesus, the apostles, God, and other biblical characters.

It should be clear that I've never resented religion in general or the Catholic Church in particular; these were part of my cultural milieu and education. So it must be firmly stated that I am not moved by any kind of agenda against religion. Religion was not a poison in my life: religion was, and continues to be, part of my cultural heritage—for good and for bad.

It is true that, in some nations (and families), religion is not an option that one can abandon when inclined to doubt. In such cases, religion is true poison and coercion that objectively serves tyranny. Nevertheless, its "truth claims" have nothing to do with the use and abuse of religion. We don't censure soccer because there are hooligans who use sport to manifest their violent attitude, and we don't censure politics in general because some politicians are corrupt. The same goes for God, religion, and faith. If we want to question them, the best way to do so is to inquire not only about their effect in society, but primarily, their truth claims. And that was just what I did.

Alongside my main activity as an architect, I started to read and investigate everything about history and philosophy of religions. In 2008, while investigating the history of atheism in Portugal, it occurred to me how interesting it would be to interview distinguished scholars and intellectuals in the various areas of knowledge—science, history, philosophy, theology—about God, religion, and faith.

I was drawn to scholars and experts from all sides of the religious debate. I sought to have conversations with authors involved in Christian apologetics, with members of the Jesus Seminar, with writers of recent texts against religion. The book you now hold is the result of those interviews.

The kindness, availability, and committed interest that these various experts gave to a project suggested to them by a complete stranger cannot be praised enough. Here are great scholars and sages giving some of their precious time for the sake of sharing their knowledge with others. Some say that religion separates people, but this book demonstrates the possibility of the contrary: Debating religion can bind people and bring them closer to one another—even when they are continents apart.

The question is, how do we debate religion?

As some of my interviewees have pointed out, 9/11 was a decisive date in the history and development of that debate. From that point on, the notion of a "religious other" became more and more prevalent, and that once-forgotten notion of a clash of civilizations proposed by the late Samuel P. Huntington became a frightening reality.

If theists and atheists envisage "the other" as the antagonist (the inhuman, the ungodly, the monster, the damned, the irrational, the heretic, the pagan, the ignorant, the nonscientific), our debate becomes entrenched in conflict. Suspicion will prevail and none will benefit. There will be no "rational" or "irrational" persons, only enemies.

Maybe Hobbes was right: Maybe we should be suspicious of one another because "man is the wolf of man." Nevertheless, suspicion only works as a precaution in a first contact, never as a permanent way of conduct toward "the other." Suspicion feeds on itself and diminishes belief in the value of trust—and trust is a fundamental value for life in this epoch of increasing globalization.

In these interviews, I tried to establish trust and encourage the expression of diverse opinions. You can be sure that, despite my own identification as an atheist, it was with great enthusiasm and delight that I embraced all of these conversations. The main objective is to open questions for both sides (thus the title of the book) and establish empathy between believers and nonbelievers.

The interviews themselves are conversational and accessible. Readers who are not expert in the areas addressed—historical Jesus studies, for example, or Big Bang cosmology—may find their interest piqued and wish to deepen their understanding by engaging more specific and technical literature. I regard this collection of interviews as a light invitation to reflection about religion, God, gods, faith, myth, history, science, philosophy—life in general! As Socrates is said to have remarked, "The unexamined life is not worth living." I heartily concur.

Wherever the journey of life examination leads, there is no need to live a constrained life just because the banners of science or church tell us to. Theist or atheist, we can—and must—challenge and question conventional science, just as great scientists such as Galileo, Newton, Einstein, Heisenberg, and others did before us. We can—and must—challenge and question the churches, just as great philosophers and theologians such as the Cluny reformers, Thomas More, Martin Luther, and many others did before us.

Besides the attempt to discover the "religious other" and engage him or her with empathy, this set of interviews also tries to show that religion and faith are not subject matters reserved for scholars or sages. Everyone should talk about it. Fulfill yourself by searching and debating with others in a critical and skeptical manner. Organize a local debate group; try to put atheists and theists together. Create a "Dead Poets

Society" of religious studies. Invite teachers, historians, philosophers, theologians, and all sorts of personalities from different backgrounds and creeds to talk about these issues. Expand this book by creating your own: Conduct interviews of teachers, priests, friends, or relatives and keep them in a diary. You will be amazed when you come back to them, 1, 10, 20, or even 50 years later. It will be like looking not at an ancient photograph from college or high school days, but rather, at a snapshot of your inner being, your existential quest, at a particular moment in time.

This is not a solo work: This work belongs to all the interviewees who participated in it and contributed to what I hope is a fruitful dialogue. Given the logistical challenges of distributing income generated by this book among all of them, it is my intention to distribute a fair share of my profits to charitable institutions. So, it is not Luís Rodrigues who is offering this. It is they, the interviewees—theists and atheists alike—who, with their enormous generosity in granting me these interviews, are helping to improve the quality of dialogue about issues that are all too often fraught with controversy, conflict, and vitriol. I thank them for their time, support, wisdom, and kindness.

I would like to thank everyone at ABC-CLIO who made this project possible—in particular Michael Wilt, a 24-hour-a-day tireless editor (and a newly acquainted friend) who had to keep up with the transcontinental task of supporting this English-grammar stumbler from Portugal. Without them, these conversations would have been lost in my personal files and never reached you, the reader. I only hope I have met your expectations. If not, you have only me to blame and not my interviewees.

I regret that we did not have the opportunity to discuss everything that any given reader would consider important. Nevertheless, at the end of the day, I think we can take from these conversations one of the most important lessons that a human being must learn: to appreciate and understand the anxieties, the expectations, and the sense of meaning given by theists and atheists alike to something that we all share, something that we all consider the most precious and wonderful thing in the world—life itself.

Stephen M. Barr

Stephen M. Barr is a theoretical physicist at the Bartol Research Institute of the University of Delaware and a frequent contributor to *First Things*. His book *Modern Physics and Ancient Faith* (2008) is "an extended attack" on what Barr calls scientific materialism. Barr has long been interested in the relationship between science and religion. His activities in exploring the links between religion and science also led to his receiving the Benemerenti (good merit) Medal, a papal award for service to the Church, presented by Bishop Michael A. Saltarelli. Barr was cited in *The Dialog*, the Wilmington diocesan newspaper, for his "significant intellectual contributions in promoting Catholic teaching and in Catholic apologetics, the defense of the faith." Barr's writing career on religion and science began with a book review he wrote for *First Things*, an ecumenical religious journal that has Protestant, Jewish, and Catholic members on its editorial board, which now also includes Barr. He also has written for other national magazines and has lectured at William and Mary and Dartmouth colleges, given the 2002 Erasmus Lecture of the Institute of Religion and Public Life and the 2006 Thomas Merton Lecture at Columbia University, plus many talks to churches, synagogues, and other organizations. Most recently, Barr was invited to join the U.S. board of advisers of the Templeton Foundation, which funds many projects involving the relationship between science and religion.

Luís Rodrigues—Instead of speaking about a conflict between religion and science, you talk about a conflict between religion and materialism. Can you explain your idea?

Stephen M. Barr—Scientific materialism is a philosophy that says that matter is the ultimate reality. Some people fail to distinguish science itself from this philosophical stance and therefore come to the conclusion that science and religion are inherently in conflict, whereas it is really this materialist philosophy that is at war with religion. Admittedly, there are many scientists who are philosophical materialists. It is also the case, however, that many scientists are religious. Indeed, most of the great founders of modern science, such as Copernicus, Tycho Brahe, Kepler, Galileo, Boyle, and Newton, were religious believers, and there are eminent scientists of our own day who are religious as well. It is not only arrogant, but also harmful to science, for people to identify science with the philosophical views of one segment of the scientific community. That would turn science into an ideology. One of the glories of science is that it is a community of people of many cultures, backgrounds, and philosophical viewpoints, united by their interest in the study of nature.

LR—Against this materialist view, Christians propose a dualist view—where soul and body are combined. How can a nonmaterial substance like the soul exert its influence and control over the physical body?

SMB—You ask about the "soul." The traditional Christian understanding is that what makes the human soul "spiritual," and therefore not reducible to matter, are the soul's powers of intellect and will, i.e., reason and freedom. So we are really talking about certain aspects of the mind. How matter and mind are related is a profound mystery. Even many philosophers who are not at all religious are baffled by the question of how it is that certain configurations of atoms—brains—have consciousness and are able to have subjective experiences. This does not follow from the equations of physics. Given how very little we presently understand about what the mind is, it seems to me that your question is premature. It also contains a subtle ambiguity. Suppose I ask, "How does a magnetic field bend the trajectory of a charged particle?" At one level, physics has known the answer for more than a century: The Lorentz Force Law describes this bending with mathematical exactness. But, at another level, physics says nothing about the "how." A magnetic field is one thing and a charged particle is another. The laws of physics merely say that if the former is present the latter will do certain things. So, what exactly are we asking when we ask "how" matter affects mind, or mind affects matter? We know that when certain things happen physically there are mental consequences—for example, if some molecules are present in a certain concentration in some part of your brain, you feel depressed. And we likewise know that when certain things happen in minds there are physical consequences. Science advances one step at a time; your question may be 100 steps ahead of where we are today. According to many physicists (e.g., Eugene Wigner, Rudolf Peierls, Henry Stapp, Euan Squires), quantum mechanics may be giving hints about the subtle relation of mind to matter. As Wigner put it, quantum mechanics suggests that the "content of consciousness" may be just as fundamental a part of reality as matter.

LR—When we talk about one's having the capacity to make emotional, ethical, aesthetical, or moral judgments, dualists tend to think of that capacity as something being derived from one's soul. Hasn't neurobiology shown that different brain parts, when damaged, can modify all those behaviors and judgmental capacities? (For example, the famous case of Phineas Gage.) If so, isn't the soul hypothesis jeopardized?

SMB—Neuroscience has indeed shown this; but really we knew this before. For example, people have always known that having a lot of alcohol in one's system can impair the exercise of moral judgment. So can fatigue. In any case, a simple logical fallacy is involved in the conclusion that the dependence of the mind on the brain conflicts with the idea of a soul. The traditional understanding is that something nonmaterial is necessary for some of our mental operations, but not sufficient. Other things—material things—are also necessary. The traditional Christian teaching (explicitly set forth in the Catechism of the Catholic Church, for example) is that a human being is a psychophysical unity, i.e., a true unity of matter and spirit. You used the word dualism to describe the Christian view; but some forms of dualism—specifically those that underestimate the importance or value of the physical—are rejected by Christianity as unorthodox. Christianity is incarnational: We are flesh and blood.

LR—To refute the idea of materialism, theists rely on the Lucas-Penrose argument, which tries to establish that machines can never achieve human-like intelligence. Some mathematicians

have refused this hypothesis by stating that although one cannot prove now that something is possible in principle, that doesn't mean that it will always be impossible as a matter of fact. Surely no medieval knight would ever conceive something like the satellite or the cell phone. What is your answer to that?

SMB—I don't think religious people would "rely" on the Lucas-Penrose argument; rather, they see in it further confirmation of what they already believed on other, more philosophical, grounds. It is true, as you say, that sometimes science finds ways to do what was once thought to be impossible. On the other hand, however, science sometimes shows that things people thought might be possible are not—for example, perpetual motion machines, faster-than-light travel, and the transmutation of "base" metals into gold by chemical means.

LR—Some scientists don't exclude the possibility of the existence of an infinite number of universes generated by other Big Bangs beyond the space-time that spans over the 15 billion years that comprise our own universe. What is your opinion about this issue as a scientist and as a Catholic Christian?

SMB—There are a number of interesting speculative theories that involve what some people call "other universes," though it is more accurate to call them other regions or "domains" of our single universe. Examples are the "bouncing universe" idea, the formation of "bubble universes" in the context of eternal inflation theories, and the "ekpyrotic" universe theory. I find some of these scenarios plausible (especially eternal inflation), others less so. But even if we don't go beyond the simple, standard Big Bang model, it is highly probable that the universe is exponentially larger than the part we can see, i.e., the part within our "horizon," which is about 15 billion light years across. Catholic teaching has nothing whatsoever to say about any of these possibilities. Cardinal Nicholas of Cusa, a leading philosopher and theologian of the Middle Ages, speculated that the universe is infinitely large, as he felt that an infinite universe better reflected God's own infinity. As far as Catholic teaching goes, the only assertion it makes is that the universe had a temporal beginning. Modern cosmology tends to agree with this. It is hard to construct consistent cosmological models in which time had no beginning—though it might not be impossible.

LR—Why is the Genesis hypothesis of a sole universe created by the Judeo-Christian God the best explanation for the existence of the universe?

SMB—The book of Genesis does not say that there is one "sole universe." It describes (though not in a scientific way) the creation of this universe. It says that God is the Creator of everything in this universe, and by implication of all things that exist. It nowhere asserts that God has not created other universes. Is God the "best explanation" of the existence of the universe? Well, what other explanation is there? Certainly, physics does not give an explanation. There are very interesting and, I would say, quite plausible scenarios in which the universe began as a "quantum fluctuation." However, these "quantum creation" ideas really do not explain why the universe exists. They simply say that given certain laws of physics, and given that these laws describe an actual universe or universes rather than merely fictitious or hypothetical ones, then those universes would have (or could have) begun in a certain way. But, as Hawking has well said, all physics does is give you some set of rules and equations, it does not explain why there is an actual universe for those rules and equations to describe. Whatever the correct laws of physics may turn out to be—superstrings or something else—it would have been just as logically self-consistent for there never to have been any universe described by any laws, i.e., just blank nonexistence. So physics cannot answer the old philosophical question "Why is there something rather than nothing?" As far as nontheistic religions are concerned, what explanation do they offer? Does Buddhism say why there is this cycle of return, or why anything exists at all? As far as I can see, the choice is between saying that there is some ultimate cause of being, which leads to some version of monotheism, or saying there is no ultimate cause, and that the existence of the universe is just a brute fact, a given with no explanation, which leads most logically to atheism.

LR—The permanent cycle of creation and destruction occurring in the universe seems to reveal more kinship to Hinduism than it does, for example, with Christianity or Judaism. Can it be that religious doctrines who try to explain the "why" of the cosmos

are just a matter of one's picking and choosing the perspective that suits one best?

SMB—What "cycle"? On Earth, of course, there are seasonal cycles. But the cosmos, as far as anything science is able to say at present, does not have a cyclical history. Rather, it has a storyline that starts at a beginning and moves through unrepeated stages toward some end. There was a beginning at the Big Bang; then the period when matter was generated ("baryogenesis" and "leptogenesis"); then the stage of "primordial nucleosynthesis" when the smallest elements, such as hydrogen, helium, and lithium, formed; then the period of "structure formation," when galaxies and larger structures condensed out of the primordial gas made of these elements; then the stage we are now in, of the birth and death of several generations of stars; and then at some point all the nuclear fuel will be gone, and there will be no more stars, and no more life on planets heated by those stars. Eventually it will all end, either with the universe recollapsing into a "Big Crunch" or with the universe getting ever larger, ever colder, and ever more dark and empty—the so-called "heat death" of the universe. There is no "cosmic cycle" here. Admittedly, there are highly speculative scenarios (for which absolutely no empirical evidence exists at present) according to which the whole story from Big Bang to Big Crunch (or Big Bang to heat death) is endlessly repeated. But even in such scenarios, it is hard to get away from the idea that there was a first cycle. No, it is not just what suits one best. Indications both observational and theoretical favor a beginning at some point in the past.

LR—When we talk about the designer of the universe, God seems to be the ultimate answer. What do you think of Richard Dawkins's argument when he says that it is illogical to refer to God as the designer because an immediate question follows, which is: "Who designed the designer?"

SMB—Dawkins's question is hardly new. Every intelligent schoolchild has probably asked at some point, "Who created God?" The traditional answer is that God is a "necessary being" rather than a "contingent being." A contingent being is one that does not have to exist by any a priori necessity. Its nature or essence does not entail its existence, and so its existence requires an explanation outside of itself. According to the traditional view, however, it is God's very nature to exist. His defining property, one might say (speaking very loosely), is existence or reality. To use a crude analogy, the light that comes from most of the objects around us, and which allows them to be seen by us, is reflected light. But some things, such as the sun, or a light bulb, do not have their light from something else but are sources of light. By analogy, contingent beings have their existence from God, but God is the source of existence.

Now, Dawkins makes the "schoolboy argument" in a slightly different form than is usual. He asks who designed God, not who gave God being. His point is that in our experience the person who designs something is more complex than the thing he designs. For example, the brain of the human architect is much more intricate than the house he builds. So, Dawkins reasons, God would have to be even more complicated than the universe. If complicated things always had to be designed by someone, there would be an "infinite regress" of designers. So either one gets an infinite regress, or one admits that some complicated things don't require a designer at all. Either way, out the window goes the "design argument" for God.

This argument of Dawkins implicitly conceives of God as a kind of machine. The more sophisticated and powerful a machine is, the more intricate and complex. But if we conceive of God not as a machine, but as an infinite Idea or Thought, the picture changes. A thought, by which I mean an act of understanding, is in a sense something simple and indivisible. What goes on when I understand that "$2 + 2 = 4$"—or, even more basically, when I grasp the concept "2"? Well, doubtless this thought is prepared for and accompanied by much activity in my brain. Probably billions of neurons are doing something. But is the concept itself that complicated? Is it not, rather, something very simple? Can you cut up the concept "2" into many little parts? Can you have 57 percent of the concept? Every mathematician and physicist has had the experience of wrestling with a problem over a long period of time—trying to understand why something is true, or trying to prove some theorem—and all of a sudden, perhaps while reaching for the salt, the answer comes to him in a blinding flash of insight. It may take him an hour to work out the details on paper later, and five hours to explain it to the nonexpert. But he has the insight in a moment. It is the nature of understanding to hold many things together in a single insight. The more powerful the insight, the more it holds in its grasp, the more it unifies, the more it simplifies. God, in the traditional view, is the infinite act of understanding that grasps all of reality. It is a doctrine of Catholicism that God is

not complicated nor made of parts, but rather utterly "simple." To someone who thinks only of physical objects, mechanisms, machines, and
organisms, that may sound strange. But God is not something assembled
out of physical bits. God is "spirit," by which is meant that God is a
purely intellectual substance.

My answer has gotten too long, but these are very deep questions
about which much has been written by philosophers and theologians
over the last 2,400 years. One cannot dispose of them in a few sentences. Those who think that Dawkins has found a trivial refutation of the
philosophical arguments for God are naïve. Catholic philosophy and
theistic philosophy in general have produced analyses of these questions
much more sophisticated than Dawkins realizes—as a number of eminent philosophers who are atheists have pointed out.

**LR—If one poses the existence of life in other places of the
universe—or even in other universes—can Catholicism be defended
as a valid universal doctrine? I mean, does the atonement of Jesus
need to happen in those places too?**

SMB—The possibility of life elsewhere in the universe is not a difficulty
for Christian theology. If there are rational and free creatures elsewhere,
then they too are "spiritual" and made in the image of God. God presumably desires them also to be freely united with him and with each
other in a relationship of love. He presumably would reveal himself to
them also, so that they could be in that loving relationship with him.
There is no difficulty at all in supposing that the union of God and
these other creatures happens through incarnations in which their
created natures are joined to the divine nature. Some people worry
whether there could be more than one incarnation. Probably this is
because they do not correctly understand the orthodox teaching on the
incarnation developed in the first centuries of the Church and set forth
in the formulations of the early Councils, especially the Council of
Chalcedon in 451 AD. Would these other creatures need to be redeemed?
That would depend on whether they had fallen into sin. (This may not
affect the question of whether God has become incarnate for them,
however. It is a very traditional idea that the Incarnation of God as
man may have happened whether or not man had fallen into sin.) If
these other races require redemption from sin, as we do, then there
is no difficulty in supposing that this happens through redemptive

sacrifice. I would say that the logic of love, which desires to be united with its object, and which expresses itself in sacrifice and mutual self-offering, does indeed have a "universal validity."

LR—How have you come to choose Catholicism? Aren't your ideas more in tune with a deist perspective of the universe?

SMB—I was raised Catholic. My mother was Catholic and my father had no religious background and always described himself as a Humean skeptic. When he was 79 years old, he became Catholic himself. From the age of 10, I attended a nonreligious private school in which the great majority of students were Jewish, mostly nonbelievers in God who had a low opinion of religion. So I have thought a lot about these issues. Atheism has never made sense to me. The existence of God has always struck me as luminously self-evident. It was the rest of Catholic belief that I struggled with. (With my father it was opposite: The only Catholic doctrine that gave him trouble was the existence of God! So much for genetic explanations of belief.)

I cannot be satisfied intellectually with deism. If God exists, then to me it seems absurd to suppose that he is unconcerned with human welfare. Human beings who care about other human beings are clearly on a higher level than selfish people are; and it makes little sense to me to say that the Creator can exist on a lower level than the beings he creates. Can a character in a play have greater wisdom and be greater of soul than the play's author? How can an author create a character deeper and wiser than himself? This reasoning leads me to conclude that God must care about us. And if God does care, it makes perfect sense that he would reveal himself to us and seek to draw us into a free relationship of love with him. Of the revealed religions, Christianity seems to me to be the most logical, and to have the deepest and most satisfactory conception of the nature of God.

When I was young, various specific doctrines of Christianity seemed strange to me. But many times I would discover, after investigation, that the Church's teaching on some point wasn't actually what I thought it was, but was more profound, more nuanced, and more sophisticated. And many times I had insights that brought me to a higher level of understanding from which I saw that some doctrine which had seemed to me extraneous and peculiar actually fit in with the rest of Christian doctrine in a beautiful, harmonious, and satisfying way. So, over time, I came to see how much more profound than I am Christianity is. After 55 years, I am still learning.

LR—But consider for a moment this analogy: We can "create" and develop in our body cancerous cells that we are unaware of; even if we are the creators on an upper level (with higher intelligence, higher complexity, etc.), nevertheless, we are unaware of those "beings" we create—until they ultimately destroy us. Even posing the existence of God, why can't things happen in the same way? Couldn't we be the unperceived creation of God the same way some of our body's cells are unperceived creations of ours?

SMB—One problem that materialists have in trying to understand the nonmaterialist position is that their imaginations have been contracted to the point where they can only use physical analogies. Everything is thought of as a structure, a machine, a complex physical system. (We saw this with Dawkins and his idea that God as designer would have to be a complicated universe-building machine.) So your question supposes that God's creating us is analogous to a physical structure giving rise to other physical structures. My analogy, which is closer to the traditional understanding, is of God as analogous to the mind of the playwright who invents the minds of his characters.

You are right that physical systems can evolve in the direction of greater complexity—that is what evolution shows us. But can an inferior mind comprehend a superior mind? Could the mind of a six-year-old write a play with fully developed characters who were mature and sophisticated adults? Could a complete fool write a play with characters who evidenced wisdom? Could a shallow person convincingly create a character of genuine depth? We are talking about minds, not physical structures. Of course, the materialist's dogma—for that is what it is—that everything, including every aspect of any mind, is at bottom nothing except matter compels him always to think in terms of material analogies. But as long as he does this, he will never even understand the position he is rejecting. He will always be transposing the ideas of the nonmaterialist into another language that lacks the vocabulary needed to express them.

Perhaps something should be clarified here about the traditional understanding of God's relationship to the world he has created. In a play, events give rise to other events by an internal logic of the play. On the other hand, the entire play, including every event in the play and the internal logic of the play by which these events are related to each other, is conceived in the mind of the playwright. In an analogous way, events in the physical world give rise to other events by an internal logic of the universe that we call the laws of physics. But the whole universe, including all its events and all the natural laws that relate those events to each other, have been conceived in the mind of God from all eternity. So a Creator as traditionally conceived—assuming he exists—must be able to understand everything he has created. He cannot conceive in his mind that which is superior to his mind. He cannot conceive of a loving or wise being if love and wisdom are alien to him. Could love (caritas) and wisdom just be byproducts or "epiphenomena" of the material processes taking place in brains, in such a way that God understood the material processes that he had created, but did not expect and foresee the byproducts? The nonmaterialist position is that wisdom and love are not just epiphenomena of matter.

LR—Why is that, as a Catholic, you are committed to justify Christianity through science when even Jesus didn't seem interested in this aspect of reality? He seemed more concerned about morality, ethics, and cultic observance, didn't he?

SMB—I do not try to justify Christianity through science. I merely try to answer those who say that science and Christianity are in conflict. I do not see such a conflict, but harmony. As for Jesus, I do not think he was primarily an ethical teacher, and he said almost nothing about cultic matters. He was concerned about bringing people to God, and his followers are supposed to do the same. For some people, science—or a misunderstanding of it—is an obstacle to finding God. I would like to help them see that it isn't an obstacle.

LR—How should a Catholic Christian understand the stories of the Bible in which the natural laws seem suspended—and I'm talking about stories like the parting of the Red Sea by Moses, the miracles of Jesus, etc.?

SMB—The miracles recorded in the New Testament were witnessed by the apostles themselves, upon whose testimony the whole of the Christian religion rests. Given their sincerity, proven by their willingness to endure cruel martyrdoms (for example, Peter, Paul, James, etc.) and the deep wisdom, virtue, sobriety, and balance that is evident in their writings, I find them credible witnesses. Certainly one cannot believe that they were fanatics or deluded men, if one reads their writings. I do not find miracles such as those of Jesus at all hard to accept. If God instituted the laws of nature, he may also suspend them.

LR—Were you ever at odds with any of the Vatican's central ideas about science?

SMB—A Catholic thinks not in terms of "Vatican's ideas" but of the Church's teachings, of which the pope is the chief custodian and expositor. The Church (including the pope) rarely makes anything but very general statements about science, and I find those statements to be reasonable. The Galileo case was an aberration of a sort that hasn't been repeated and is extremely unlikely to be repeated in the future. I am very pleased with the attitude of the Catholic Church toward science.

LR—What is your answer to those who say that the Vatican's prejudices against some moral issues—like condom use or homosexuality—are not signs of a progressive and enlightened institution?

SMB—Prejudice is the wrong word. The Church's positions on these issues are deeply consistent and principled. Does sex have a meaning and purpose? Does it have some intrinsic connection to procreation and the rearing of children, and thus to marriage and the family? Is it therefore meant to express conjugal love? Or is it just a matter of having orgasms whenever and however one wants? The latter view is gaining ground, but I consider that neither enlightened nor progressive. On the contrary, I see contemporary hedonistic ideas on sex as degraded and foolish. Studies have shown that believing and practicing Catholics have much lower rates of divorce, depression, suicide, criminality, and social pathology of all sorts, and are generally happier and mentally healthier than the general population. By the way, as far as condoms for combating AIDS, which I take to be implied in your question, the answer is simple: Those who do follow the Church's teachings on sexual morality are guaranteed not to get AIDS by sexual transmission, and those who do not follow the Church's teachings on sexuality cannot be harmed by those teachings. Some have claimed on the basis of studies that African countries that have programs to discourage sexual promiscuity have done better at combating the spread of AIDS than countries that have stressed condom use.

LR—New Age Spirituality thinkers like Deepak Chopra, Eckhart Tolle, and others make a call to some kind of spiritual monism influenced by Eastern philosophical and religious ideas. Is Christianity being threatened by this New Spirituality movement? I'm talking about things like the so-called "Law of Attraction" or the book *The Secret*.

SMB—The Church has always been opposed to superstition, not because it is a danger to the Church, but because it is harmful to those who indulge in it. Of course, Christian belief and worship can also degenerate into superstition, which the Church always has to guard against. As the present pope has stated, science can be of assistance in purifying faith of superstitious elements.

LFR—What is your opinion about New Spirituality "scientific theories"—posed by scientists like John Hagelin, for example?

SMB—I don't know enough about John Hagelin's beliefs to comment on them. I don't think that New Age movements have generated any scientific theories.

LR—What about scientists from the secular side of the spectrum— scientists like Richard Dawkins, Steven Weinberg, or Carl Sagan? With whom is Christianity more at odds?

SMB—I would say that Christianity is more at odds with the New Agers. Scientific materialists are at least committed to reason. Reason is of God, all unreason is opposed to God. Indeed, the Greek word for reason is logos, which is what God is called in the beginning of John's Gospel: "In the beginning was the Logos, and the Logos was with God, and the Logos was God." The Catholic Church is bitterly opposed to every form of unreason.

LFR—When we see so many kinds of scientific theories being proposed to defend different theological, philosophical, or

spiritual ideas, one might ask the following: "Is there really something like Science with a capital 'S'"?

SMB—I am not aware that people propose scientific theories just to defend theological, philosophical, or spiritual ideas. That doesn't happen to any great extent in my field of particle physics and cosmology. For example, though one of the two founders of the Big Bang theory was a physicist who also happened to be a Catholic priest—Georges Lemaitre—he proposed it for scientific reasons, not theological ones. In fact, he got very upset by attempts to merge theology with physics. And similarly, although the "eternal inflation" theory was invented by Andrei Linde, who is an atheist, it wouldn't be taken seriously unless there were scientific reasons.

Yes, there is such a thing as science. But it is not to be confused with the philosophical systems people sometimes build upon it. There is no such thing as Catholic science, atheist science, or Buddhist science. Science is just science, and people should not try to make it into something else.

Swami Bhaskarananda

Swami Bhaskarananda, a senior monk of the Ramakrishna Order of India, is president and spiritual leader of the Vedanta Society of Western Washington in Seattle, an affiliated branch of the Ramakrishna Order. He is also the spiritual guide of the Vedanta Society of Hawaii and the Vivekananda Vedanta Society of British Columbia, Canada. He has authored *The Essentials of Hinduism* (2002); *Life in Indian Monasteries* (2004); *Meditation, Mind and Patanjali's Yoga* (2001); and *Journey from Many to One* (2009). He has translated *The Philosophical Verses of Yogavasishtha* and *Reminiscences of Swami Brahmananda*, and is editor-in-chief of *Global Vedanta*, a quarterly journal.

Born and raised in India, he joined the Order in 1958 after finishing his university education. He was stationed at the Order's headquarters in India for 12 years before being sent to serve the Seattle Vedanta Society in 1974. He and two other religious leaders formed the Interfaith Council of Washington State. He has given talks and conducted spiritual retreats in the United States, Canada, South America, Europe, and Asia.

Luís Rodrigues—What does Hinduism propose for the human being? What is its main message and goal?

Swami Bhaskarananda—Hinduism aims at helping individual human beings to achieve their ultimate spiritual goal, which is none other than experiencing their divine essence or inherent divinity. It prescribes various proven methods and techniques called *yogas* to achieve that goal.

The main teaching of Hinduism is that everything is divine. Not only human beings, but also all subhuman beings as well as nonliving objects. Divinity is equally present in them, but its manifestation differs from one to the other. In human beings divinity is more manifest than in other beings, and in some special human beings who are called "God-men" or "God-women" or "divine incarnations," God's manifestation is maximum. In animals, God's manifestation is much less than in human beings. In plants, the manifestation of divinity is even less than in animals. In nonliving objects, the manifestation of divinity is minimal. From that comes the teaching—"Everything is divine."

LR—What are the most significant differences between Hinduism and the Judeo-Christian-Islamic religions?

SB—We do not think that there is any essential difference. We believe that all the religions are gradually going toward the same spiritual goal, the same Truth, the same Divine Truth. Religions have grown in different countries according to the needs of the people who live there. According to their ways of thinking and conditioning, their religions have developed. Different religions are so many different paths that lead to the same Divine Truth.

Aside from this, unlike the Judeo-Christian-Islamic faiths, Hinduism does not have any known "founder." Many Hindu saints or sages at different periods of time in history experienced God or the Divine Truth. They had no reason to think that they had invented or founded that Truth. They looked upon themselves as so many discoverers of that Eternal Truth and preferred to remain anonymous.

LR—Is it possible to conceive of Hinduism without relying on belief in God?

SB—One does not have to necessarily believe in God in order to be a Hindu. In this context, by the word *God* I mean *Creator* God—God endowed with a personality. This, however, is not the highest concept of God in Hinduism. The highest concept of God in Hinduism is that God is not a person. God is transcendental. God is beyond all kinds of limitation. God is beyond form and the forces of nature. God is beyond time, space, and causation. So, a Hindu need not necessarily believe in a Creator God. He can believe in God as God truly is: Impersonal Divinity.

Aside from this, Hinduism is also able to help an atheist to experience his or her inherent divinity. For such a person Hinduism prescribes a spiritual path called *Jnana-Yoga*. This path may also be called the Path of Knowledge or the Path of Philosophical Inquiry.

LR—When we talk about Hinduism, we have an idea of diversity and complexity—many gods and many schools of thought. How does one choose the right path to the truth?

SB—Hinduism does not believe in many gods. It believes in only one God. What some people perceive as so many gods in Hinduism are, in fact, personifications of various aspects of the One and Only Divinity or Reality in which Hinduism believes. Such personifications are called deities. Each deity represents some powers or aspects of God. When we think of God as the giver of wisdom, then we look upon him as a deity called Saraswati. When we look upon God as the giver of wealth and prosperity, that aspect of God is personified through the deity Lakshmi. But it is not that Lakshmi and Saraswati are essentially different entities; they're only personified symbols of two different aspects of the same God.

Hinduism accepts the fact that human beings differ in their temperament and nature. That's why different disciplines or paths are prescribed for them. Some people are emotional by nature. Their emotion can easily be transformed into love and devotion for God. For such people, Hinduism prescribes *Bhakti-Yoga* or the Path of Devotion. Similarly there are other paths such as *Karma-Yoga* or the Path of Right Action, *Jnana-Yoga* or the Path of Knowledge, and *Raja-Yoga* or the Path of Mental Concentration. According to one's temperament one can choose one or the other yoga and reach the ultimate spiritual goal. Spiritual aspirants can also seek spiritual guidance from genuine spiritual teachers to know which spiritual path or yoga is suitable for them.

LR—The Western tradition relies on material proof and evidence to deal with knowledge—to achieve it. How does Hinduism deal with epistemology? I mean: In Hinduism, how does one "know" that God exists? How does one "know" that reincarnation happens? What are the grounds of "knowing" for Hinduism?

SB—Hinduism accommodates in it several highly developed schools of religious philosophy. It allows all sincere questions to be asked. The word *blasphemy* is not there in Hinduism. That's why one can ask questions about the truths or ideas contained in the scriptures in order to understand them thoroughly and well. Over the thousands of years of the existence of this religion all possible questions—metaphysical or otherwise—have been asked in Hinduism. And valid answers to these questions are also there in Hinduism. Numerous schools of philosophy based on such questions and answers have thus been developed in Hinduism.

That's why Hinduism has highly developed epistemology. Hindu philosophy has as many as six methods to validate knowledge or truths. These methods are what you mention as grounds of "knowing" (the truth). These methods are called Pramanas in Hinduism. In Western philosophy the English counterpart of the word Pramana is the word *proof.* Among these Pramanas, directly experiencing God with the help of a purified mind is considered the most important proof of the existence of God or Divinity.

In Hinduism God is not considered a mystery. A mystery is something we cannot know about. Hinduism emphatically declares that God can be experienced. But such experience can be had only with the help of a purified mind. The testimony of those who have experienced God with their pure minds is considered a Pramana since "reliable testimony" is one of the six Pramanas in Hinduism. The testimony of those trustworthy people who have experienced Divinity—whether that is impersonal God or God endowed with a personality—is contained in Hindu scriptures, such as the Vedas. Such trustworthy people are called Rishis or Seers, because they have directly seen, known, or experienced the divine truth with the help of their purified minds. That's why the testimony of the Vedas is also considered reliable testimony.

Now in regard to your question about reincarnation, I have to say that in many countries some people, even though their number is quite small, have been seen to have claimed their ability to remember their past incarnation. Many of their claims have been verified to be true in India as well as elsewhere. Their testimony helps us to know that reincarnation is not just a theological doctrine; it is a fact.

For example, in Brazil I met a gentleman from a Catholic background who told me a story of one of his relatives, a lady, who remembered most of the things that had happened to her in her past incarnation. Another Christian gentleman, a high school teacher in Canada—and very rational—also could remember his past life and the way he died—in a home fire. He even remembered the name of the town.

After hearing from him the story of his past life, I said, "Why don't you go to that town and look up the records? Maybe you will be able to find something about the event in the newspapers." He went there and was lucky to find from the microfilm version of the old newspapers an account of that event: that a house got burned and the entire family was killed in that fire.

I asked him to write about it, but he said, "Well, I tried to write, but as soon as I write, I remember my siblings, I remember my parents, and I become overwhelmed with grief." So, it is not that only Hindus and Buddhists believe in reincarnation, some Christians also believe in it.

The other reliable source from which we know about reincarnation is the divine incarnations.

LR—How can Hinduism attract Westerners? Does it want to?

SB—Since it is not a proselytizing religion, it is not the aim of Hinduism to attract anybody. Hinduism believes that the divine truth is there in every person, and it will eventually manifest in everyone.

LR—So, it's not the aim of Hinduism to evangelize?

SB—No. When people come to our temple here—Westerners and others—I tell them that there are many "spiritual restaurants" in Seattle, and this is just one of them. If you like the food that is served here, you're most welcome. Keep on coming and enjoying the food. But if you like some other kind of food that is served in other restaurants, please go ahead. I wish you well. Religion is not something that can be forcibly imposed on others.

There are some people who think that they can save others. Well, who can save whom? One should learn how to save oneself first. One has to experience divinity. One has to be a God-realized person first. Only then can that person become a true teacher, a real helper, a true guru. A person fit to help or teach others has to be a God-realized soul. Not all are God-realized souls. Unfortunately, there are so many fakers.

LR—You talk about fakers. How do you evaluate the "guru craze" that spread over America in the 1970s? Didn't it hurt the reliability of Eastern religions to watch some gurus more interested in money and power rather than in spiritual teaching?

SB—By the expression "guru craze" in America in the '70s, perhaps you mean the interest exhibited by the hippies during that period in teachers of Eastern religions. It is unfortunate that some gurus didn't turn out to be genuine teachers, because they were not real gurus. A real spiritual teacher is one who teaches without the vanity of a teacher. He or she does not crave money, name, fame, power, or position. Nor does a genuine teacher ever write an autobiography for personal glorification.

So far as the monks of our Order (the Ramakrishna Order) who are working in America are concerned, we don't come here of our own accord. We come here having been invited by the Americans. For example, our Order sent me here because the people here had requested our Order to send a Swami.

I've been here for 34 years, and since my arrival, I've tried to understand this country, America, and the American people whom I have been sent here to serve. I have also learned to love them. Had I not developed genuine love and sympathy for them, I wouldn't have been able to serve them all these years.

For your information, it is against our Hindu tradition to charge money for giving spiritual help to anybody. Those who charge money violate that sacred tradition. Our Swamis are lifelong, nonsalaried volunteers. They never work for money.

Incidentally, the hippie movement was no other than a mental reaction of American young men and women who were being forced to go and fight and die in a war in Vietnam that they themselves couldn't justify. Why should they go to another country and die fighting somebody else's war? That's why there was strong resentment. These young people had lost faith in the decision-making capability of the grownups enjoying positions of power and authority in their own country. The reaction was so strong that they resented everything that was American. They started hating their own culture as well as religion. This is the reason why they looked for other things, and became interested in other religions and cultures. It is not to be supposed that they all were really eager for "spiritual food."

At that time, our Vedanta temples were not that many in this country. Our Order could spare only a very small number of monks for America, because our various religious and philanthropic activities in India demanded a large number of monks there. Our Order had only some 12 centers in America at that time. Many American young men came during that period and joined our American centers to become monks, but later most of them left. Others had become followers of some self-styled gurus, who unfortunately were not true representatives of our Hindu tradition.

Gradually the situation changed. The Vietnam War ended. So those hippies went back to their homes and started living their usual, every-day lives. As you can see, the hippie movement and the so-called guru craze were just temporary phenomena.

Nevertheless, there are some people in this country who feel that they are not getting what they are looking for in their own inherited reli-gions. Some of them come to our Vedanta temples in search of that. We tell them that they are welcome to learn from Hinduism, but they need not give up their own religions. While they derive benefits from the teachings of Vedanta, they should also learn to develop a respectful atti-tude toward all religions.

We tell them that Hinduism is like a vast library. Wisdom and spirit-ual ideas accumulated over thousands of years are in it. There are many disciplines and techniques in our religion, which are not available in other religions. You are free to take the help of them (these disciplines and techniques), but in so doing you don't have to become a Hindu. All that we want is that human beings should try to become better human beings.

Just as the presence of quacks cannot diminish the importance and need of genuine doctors, so also the presence of spurious teachers or gurus cannot diminish the importance and need of genuine teachers of Hinduism. True seekers of spirituality will surely be able to find such genuine teachers if they search well enough.

LR—Talking about human beings' moral improvement, doesn't *karma* in Hinduism have the same conservative social function that sin in Christianity or *duhkha* in Buddhism has: to justify one's position in life as something inevitable—and therefore, inescapable?

SB—No. No. The idea of karma is based on the recognition of a certain unavoidable fact. It is the recognition of the fact that if I perform an action, it will produce an effect. If I put my hand into fire, my hand will burn. If I sow a seed and take good care of it, that seed will sprout and will become a plant, which in turn will become a tree, and which in turn will produce fruits. The kind of fruits it will produce is dependent upon the kind of seed I've sown: The seed can develop into a tree yielding either poisonous or delicious fruits. We cannot deny the relationship between action and its effect. The doctrine of karma is based on that recognition.

Hinduism does not give too much importance to what you call "sin." Swami Vivekananda, one of the greatest teachers of Hinduism, used to say that sinning is no other than committing mistakes. And committing a mistake is a wrong action that is going to produce an adverse effect on the doer. Action in Sanskrit is called karma. Committing a mistake is no other than performing a bad karma. The effect of such an action, called *Karma Phala*, will produce suffering or *duhkha*.

That's why, in the light of the doctrine of karma, the suffering that one goes through in life is the result of one's past bad karma. God is not responsible for that. Similarly, earthly enjoyment in one's life now is the effect of his or her past good karma. Therefore, we can create an enjoyable future for ourselves if we strive to perform good action. In short, we are the creators of our own future. Suffering for us is not inevitable in the sense that we can counteract it by our good actions.

In my book *The Essentials of Hinduism* these points have all been discussed more or less thoroughly. You may want to take a look at it—it's not a bulky book.

LR—What about the caste system in India and the way it divides society? Do you think that the existence of "untouchables" is condemnable?

SB—The caste system was originally based on people's professions or capabilities. Initially, people belonging to all castes were treated equally. All castes were considered equally essential for the society. Originally castes were not hereditary. But vested interests gradually crept into the system. This brought about degradation in the caste system. Nevertheless, one of our elderly Swamis in America used to humorously say, "In India there is the caste system. In Europe there is the class system. And in America there is the cash system!"

So far as the idea of "untouchables" is concerned, we condemn it. Many Hindu saints also have condemned this idea. But if we want to know why this idea might have originally crept into the Hindu society, we can perhaps discover a possible cause. Imagine a person with Ebola—a virus that is extremely contagious. Tell me, will you hug that person?

LR—No way.

SB—You won't. So, we can say that you treat such Ebola patients as "untouchables," right? There were and are some people in India who make a living by removing human excreta from bathrooms. They are not allowed to enter the kitchen where food is prepared. I think that from similar sentiments those ideas of segregation came into Hinduism. But in today's Hinduism such ideas are disappearing fast. Educated Hindus do not recognize the degraded caste system anymore.

LR—How does a Hindu deal with death?

SB—Death is an inevitable transition. It's a reality. A person is born, comes out of his mother's body as a baby, grows up, and, given proper food and nutrition, keeps on growing. Then he becomes a youth, a middle-aged person, an elderly person, and then eventually he dies. So death is a natural transition. It is not total extinction or annihilation of one's own existence. A person goes on living in a subtle form after his or her death. Only the physical body is given up, but the soul, along with its subtle body composed of the vital energy, senses, and the mind, goes on existing in a different plane of existence. There are many such planes of existence consisting of different sets of vibration. Such a plane of existence is called a *Loka* in Sanskrit. According to the Hindu scriptures, there are innumerable Lokas. To which Loka a departed soul will go is determined by the degree of purity of that person's mind.

All this information is available in the Hindu scriptures. Once I had to give a talk on Hinduism to a group of high school teachers in this country. During the question and answer period one teacher asked me, "Swami, what is the proof that we exist after our death?" I had to give a tactful reply. I said to him, "We can get this proof only after our death!"

A Hindu has to mentally prepare himself for death. The scriptures advise the practice of detachment in regard to one's earthly possessions, relatives, and friends, because attachment to them makes the transition (death) extremely painful. If such worldly attachment lingers on in the mind of the departed, it will cause severe postmortem suffering for the departed souls in the other world.

LR—But some of those feelings and moods can also be induced without one sharing the belief that God—or even oneself—is

responsible for their appearance, for example, when one is under the effect of alcohol or drugs.

SB—No. Not that. Some people may have similar experiences, with drugs for example, but that is not really reliable. A person has to "consciously" know and improve the quality of his or her own mind. We don't believe in permanent improvement of the mind by any experience that has been artificially induced.

LR—Concerning the process of reincarnation, how can you explain that a nonrational being—a dog, for example—can evolve into higher forms of being like a human?

SB—There is no law that only rational beings will evolve into a higher species. It is, of course, difficult to prove that a dog can become a human being, but it has been proved many times that when human beings die, they eventually are born again as other, better human beings. That much we know. But the Hindu scriptures say that the subhuman beings will also eventually incarnate as human beings, not immediately, but through a process of gradual evolution from one incarnation to the other.

LR—How do you think Hinduism will evolve worldwide?

SB—Hinduism has been and is an evolving religion, but if the entire world accepts it, if the entire humankind accepts it, then its quality will surely go down. The quality of any religion is dependent on the quality of the people who live the teachings of that religion. If too many people accept Hinduism then surely it will undergo decadence.

Human society is like milk. Milk contains cream. How much cream does it contain? Only a small portion, isn't it? It is the same with everything. Flowers contain very little perfume. If I subject a lot of rose petals to destructive distillation, then I get only a small quantity of perfume. One gallon of milk will never contain one gallon of cream. So also the entire humankind cannot consist of only highly evolved people. The number of such highly evolved people will surely be quite small since the best is also the least in quantity.

Nevertheless, Hinduism is not an exclusive religion; it is wide open for all to come and benefit from. It has different teachings suitable for people at different levels of spiritual growth. In this sense it can perhaps play the role of a suitable world religion.

Hinduism has no exclusive ownership in regard to its spiritual truths or ideas. Imagine the laws of gravitation: Are they the property of the British, because Newton discovered them? They're not.

Similarly, the spiritual truths in Hinduism are nobody's own. They are meant for the entire humankind. They're there for anyone to use for a good purpose. But not all people will be able to enjoy or benefit from what we may call "the cream" of Hinduism. The cream of Hinduism is what we call *Advaita*, which means the nondualistic concept of God in Hinduism. Only a small number of people will be able to understand and live up to that. They constitute the cream of human beings.

LR—So, you prefer a religion in quality rather than in quantity?

SB—No. I want a religion that will be suitable for all people. It will be like a library in which all kinds of religious ideas and spiritual disciplines will exist side by side, without creating any conflict with one another. For example, you wear clothes. You wear underwear, and over that you wear a shirt, and over that you wear a suit. Your garments include all kinds of clothes. There are people needing different kinds and sizes of clothes. Fortunately, Hinduism is like a store with all different sizes and kinds of clothes available for different users. There is opportunity in Hinduism for everyone to pick and choose the kind of clothes that fits him or her best. Hinduism does not force its adherents to wear garments of the same size.

Nevertheless, those who constitute the cream of humankind can benefit the most from what we call Advaita in Hinduism.

Leonardo Boff

Leonardo Boff was born in 1938 in Concórdia, Santa Catarina state, Brazil. He is a theologian, philosopher, and writer known for his active support for the rights of the poor and excluded. He currently serves as professor emeritus of ethics, philosophy of religion, and ecology at the Rio de Janeiro State University. Boff entered the Franciscan Order in 1959 and was ordained a Roman Catholic priest in 1964. He spent the next several years studying for his doctorate in theology and philosophy at the University of Munich. Boff's doctoral thesis studied in what measure the Church can be a sign of the sacred and the divine in the secular world and in the process of liberation of the oppressed. He became one of the best known (along with Gustavo Gutierrez) of the early liberation theologians. He continues to be a controversial figure in the Catholic Church, primarily for his sharp criticism of Church hierarchy, which he sees as "fundamentalist," but also for his past critical support of Communist regimes. He has always been an advocate of human rights causes, helping to formulate a new, Latin American perspective with "rights to life and the ways to maintain them with dignity."

Luís Rodrigues—Does liberation theology face atheism in the same negative way Roman Catholicism does (for example, in the Encyclical Letter "Spe Salvi," Pope Benedict XVI strongly condemns an atheistic vision of the world)? Or, with affinity for Marxist ideology, does the liberation theologian see positive aspects in atheism?

Leonardo Boff—Liberation theology does not propose to answer all possible questions. Concerning atheism, liberation theology respects people's options. It understands that an ethical atheism can exist because people see churches and religions serving as an opiate of the people. So they deny God in order to remove the fundamentals of those religious institutions—and they do it in an ethical sense, of helping people to come out of their oppression.

LR—The history of divergences in the bosom of Christianity has been the history of divergences between different interpretations of the Bible. Don't you fear that liberation theology is just one more "interpretational mistake"?

LB—The divergences with liberation theology are not connected with biblical questions. The central question is the poor. The traditional vision is charitable and sees the poor as someone who has nothing and must be helped by those who have something. Liberation theology sees the poor as impoverished, someone who was made poor; the liberation comes from the poor when they become organized and conscious of their condition. Therefore, they have historic force. Many people from the traditional Church saw this interpretation as something Marxist—that's why they fight it and try to polemicize against it.

LR—After visiting Rome, Martin Luther reported that he heard people saying, "If there's a hell, the city of Rome is built on top of it." What ethical portrait do you make of the Vatican, its people, and institutions? Do you have the same dark vision portrayed by Luther about the Holy See?

LB—I do not have bitterness or resentment regarding the Vatican. I have an analytical vision. The Vatican is seated on top of holy power and exerts that power in a way that I consider authoritarian, antimodern, antidemocratic, and antievangelical. This is my background critique. Power strangles the charisma. The Catholic Church is one of the last bastions of conservatism and patriarchalism in the world.

LR—Don't you feel a bit like bishop Arius of Alexandria, fighting against the orthodox power of Athanasius? If Rome continues to win, will that "Arianism" die with you, or will you, in some

way, perpetuate it by fostering the creation of a "New Rome" in Latin America?

LB—My concern is not with the Church. It never was. The question is Christianity as a movement of Jesus that, in the process of globalization, has not yet found its place. I believe that Christianity is a proposal of meaning for humanity; it must be offered as a choice and be added up with all spiritual traditions that wish to preserve and feed the spiritual dimension of human life.

LR—Tertullian said that the blood of the martyrs was the seed of the Church. Isn't liberation theology trying to update that same statement by defending the "martyrs" of neoliberal economy—the poor?

LB—The only church that has martyrs today is the church of liberation. Bishops, priests, nuns, and laity were victims of martyrdom because they stood by the poor—just like the nun Dorothy Stang, for example. In the time of the Cold War, whoever defended the poor was immediately connoted with the Communists. That's why they were spied upon, arrested, tortured, and many were killed. They were martyrs of the kingdom of God and the values of justice and human dignity.

LR—For you, what were the most and the least Christian inspirations? And the most and the least atheist inspirations?

LB—Theology has an eye directed to the past and lets itself be inspired by the holy scriptures, by the great masters and saints in the history of the Church. It also has an eye pointed to the future, being sensitive to contemporary problems—and it tries to illuminate them with the help of the eye of the past. This "two eyes" dialectic is—and always was—present in liberation theology and in my own theological production. So, using this dialectic, it prevents a narrow vision of reality—be it extremely progressive or extremely conservative. What is aimed for is an original stance: responsibility concerning the past and concerning the present, always following the preferential perspective of the poor.

LR—Now, imagine that you woke up some day experiencing the absence of any belief in the existence of God (as for example,

Mother Teresa is reported to have experienced). What kind of meaning would you give to your life? What motivation would you find to continue your social solidarity projects?

LB—We should live, as the martyr and anti-Nazi theologian Dietrich Bonhoeffer once said: "as if there is no God." That means, we should live and act according to convictions that spring from within and define one's way of life. It's not because of God that people commit themselves, but motivated by causes that have to do with their offended human dignity. Behind the cause, I think that there's God; but things are not true because Jesus said them—Jesus said them because they are true for themselves.

William Lane Craig

William Lane Craig is a research professor of philosophy at Talbot School of Theology in La Mirada, California. He earned a doctorate in philosophy at the University of Birmingham, England, before taking a doctorate in theology from the Ludwig-Maximilians-Universität München, Germany, where he was for two years a fellow of the Alexander von Humboldt-Stiftung. Prior to his appointment at Talbot he spent seven years at the Higher Institute of Philosophy of the Katholike Universiteit Leuven, Belgium. He has authored or edited over 30 books, including *The* Kalam *Cosmological Argument* (1979); *Assessing the New Testament Evidence for the Historicity of the Resurrection of Jesus* (1989); *Divine Foreknowledge and Human Freedom* (1990); *Theism, Atheism, and Big Bang Cosmology* (1993); and *God, Time, and Eternity* (2001), as well as over a hundred articles in professional journals of philosophy and theology. His Web site is www.reasonablefaith.org.

Luís Rodrigues—Can you tell me a little about your religious background? How did you find Christ?

William Lane Craig—Well, I wasn't raised in a Christian family, or even a church-going family, though it was a good and loving home. We didn't even attend any sort of religious services. But when I became a teenager I began to ask the big questions in life: Who am I? Why am I here? What is the meaning of life and existence? And in the search for answers, I began to attend a church in our local community. The only problem was, instead of answers to my questions, all I found there was a country club where the dues where a dollar a week in the offering plate; and the other students in high school who claimed to be Christians lived for their real God the rest of the week, which was popularity. And I thought, "Here I am, living, externally at least, a better life then they are and yet, I feel so spiritually empty inside; they're all putting up a false front, they're all just a bunch of hypocrites!" And so I began to become very bitter and angry toward the institutional church because of the hypocrisy and the phoniness that I saw there. Pretty soon this attitude spread toward people in general; I thought, "Everybody is a fake, everyone is holding up a plastic mask to the world, while the real person is cowering down inside, afraid to come out and be real." So I was very angry, very alienated from other people. I thought, "I don't need people, I don't want them!" I threw myself into my studies so that I didn't have to be with people. I was really on my way toward becoming a very alienated young man.

Then, what happened to me was that I met a girl in my high school German class, who sat in front of me and who was always so happy that it just makes you sick! Finally one day I asked her what she was so happy about all the time, and she told me that was because she knew Christ as her personal savior. And I said, "Well, I go to church!" She said, "That's not enough, Bill, you've got to have him really living in your heart." And I said, "Well, what would he want to do a thing like that for?" And she replied, "Because he loves you, Bill!" And that just hit me like a ton of bricks because I was so filled with anger and bitterness inside; she said that there was someone who really loved me, and who was it but the God of the universe. That thought just staggered me! To think that the God of the universe loved me: Bill Craig, that worm down there on that speck of dust called planet Earth! So I went home and got a New Testament and began to read it. I read it from cover to cover. As I did so, I was absolutely captivated by the person of Jesus of Nazareth. There was a ring of truth about his teaching that I had never encountered before—and there was an authenticity about his life that wasn't characteristic of these people who claimed to be his followers in this local church that I was going to. I realized then that I couldn't throw the baby out with the bath water.

So after about six months of very intense soul searching, reading Christian books, meeting other Christian students that this girl introduced me to in high school, I just came to the end of my rope one night and just cried out to God and experienced a tremendous infusion of joy; it was as if though the light just went on inside, and God became a living reality in my life; a reality that changed my life. So ever since then, I've sought to know and follow him with all of my being.

LR—Why did you choose an evangelical form of Christianity and not another? Catholic, for instance?

WLC—Well, I suppose it was through the influence of this girl. She wasn't a Catholic; actually, she was a very conservative Christian. When I became a Christian and had this spiritual experience, I said, "I want to go to your church." And she said, "No, no, that wouldn't be a good idea. Our church has too many problems. Here's a good church that I know of." She gave me the name of a church in Peoria where we lived. She said, "They've got a very good minister, a very good youth group of high school students. Why don't you go there instead?" And so I took her advice and started going there; I basically chose the church on the basis of how well it lived up to and taught what I was reading in the New Testament. For me, denominational labels have never been very important. It's just a matter of whether or not the church believes and teaches what I find in the New Testament.

LR—In Portugal we tend to associate "evangelicals" to "televangelists," like those hysterical preachers dramatically asking for viewers' money. What do you think about this way of spreading the gospel? Is it adequate?

WLC—Well, I think it's a blot on the name of Christ. It's an embarrassment. I'm ashamed of it and just find it deeply regrettable and repulsive. I can understand why in Catholic or Orthodox countries, evangelical Protestantism would look cultish or sectarian. But again, as I say, what I believe in is what C. S. Lewis called "mere Christianity"; that is to say, the essence of the Christian faith that I think is affirmed by all of the major branches of Christendom—be it Catholic, Protestant, or Orthodox. The doctrinal "fine-tuning" to me is of secondary importance.

LR—But, for example, in *American Fascists: The Christian Right and the War on America*, the journalist Chris Hedges wrote a manifesto against the procedures of the faith you try to uphold. How do you comment on his accusations that the Christian right wants to seize political power in America, imposing a "theocracy"?

WLC—I think that's very naïve. There are certain persons in the United States saying that the sky is falling and that the religious right wants to take over the United States. Honestly, Luís, that is extremely naïve. I've never met anybody who wants to do that. Most evangelical Christians simply want the freedom to practice what they believe. And they do want to influence public policy morally in certain ways, but there is no significant movement whatsoever in this country to try to take over the United States and establish some sort of a theocracy. This is just alarmism, frankly.

LR—What if an atheist, for example, was elected president of the United States? Would that be unbearable to you as an evangelical Christian?

WLC—Well, I would say this: I learned from the example of Jimmy Carter—who was, or is, I think, a genuine Christian—that it is far more important that you elect someone who has the right political policies, than someone who has religious beliefs that you agree with. I think Carter had the right religious beliefs, but I think he was very weak as a president.

LR—Do you think that is the message that Americans are receiving from their Christian leaders?

WLC—Yes, I do think that. Look at someone like a James Dobson, for example. I don't think Dobson has ever said, "Vote for somebody because he is a Christian." In fact, we had a Christian running [in the presidential primaries]; I mean, a very overtly Christian man—I'm not suggesting that these other candidates weren't Christian, but this one, Mike Huckabee, was overt in the sense that he was an evangelical minister. And yet he did not receive the endorsement of people like James Dobson or other leaders of the so-called religious right. They were for people like Giuliani, and some for Romney, who is Mormon; they were clearly advocating candidates with whose policies they agreed, not with whose religious beliefs they agreed. So that's a very good example that these folks aren't interested in establishing some kind of religious theocracy in the United States.

LR—Concerning other alternative forms of spirituality, how do you see the relationship between Christianity and these "New Age" movements—like quantum healing, power of the crystals, etc.?

WLC—You know . . . it makes me think that David Hume was right: that people really do crave the miraculous and that superstition is very, very alive today. I'm just shocked that people in the 21st century can believe in things like Oprah's *The Secret*, these crystals, vortexes, and things like that. It just astonishes me! I think of these things as very much like Gnosticism in the early centuries of the Christian church. Gnostics attempted to piggyback on the Christian movement by using Christian literature as a means of propagating Gnostic beliefs, even though Gnosticism was very much at odds with Christianity. I think that a lot of these "New Age" cults today are very similar to Gnosticism in that they propose secret knowledge by means of which one can realize one's unity with God; they piggyback on biblical and Christian terminology to try to sound Christian, when in fact they're very deeply anti-Christian.

LR—We have Gnosticism not only on a popular level, but also on an academic one; for example, scholars like Elaine Pagels bringing the study of Gnosticism to the university. What do you think about these alternative teachings of Christian faith?

WLC—I think it shows a dissatisfaction with orthodox Christianity on the part of some of these academics, since they're trying to revive these early Gnostic ideas—which I think are quite incompatible with Christianity. The idea on the part of people like Pagels is to represent these beliefs as alternative forms of Christianity that are acceptable for Christians today, when in fact early Gnosticism was not Christian in origin at all: it was pagan. This was simply an attempt to piggyback on the Christian movement by using Jesus and the apostles as mouthpieces for spouting Gnostic doctrines; these ideas are not alternative forms of Christianity: they're Greco-pagan religious ideas. They're incompatible with what Jesus himself taught and believed.

LR—But according to Walter Bauer, we have the idea that early Christianity evolved from a diverse mosaic of sects and religions, and not from a single common source. Isn't "orthodox" Christianity today that which has survived from a large mosaic of "heterodox" diversity?

WLC—No; I think that, again, is an attempt to try to portray some of these really anti-Christian movements—which had non-Christian sources—as alternative forms of Christianity. But you see, we have the great advantage that we have the primary source documents; we've got the original letters of Paul and the original Gospels—and I don't mean the autographs, the original manuscripts, but we have the writings of the first century from which this early Christian movement was founded. And so, that's why, especially as Protestants, we always go back to the Bible, to the writings of the New Testament, and we weigh any kind of spirituality or Christianity against the teachings of the New Testament and say: "Is this in unison with the writings that we have in the New Testament?"

LR—Some theological questions now: According to Saint Augustine, before creating the universe, God did nothing. Why would God change his mind 13.7 billion years ago by setting off the Big Bang?

WLC—Well, that was not really what Saint Augustine said. When Augustine was asked, "What was God doing prior to the creation of the universe," the answer was not that he was preparing hell for those who pry into mysteries! Rather, he said, the answer is that there is no moment prior to creation. Time begins at the moment of Creation, at the beginning of the universe. Therefore, the question of what God was doing prior to Creation of the universe is a meaningless question. There is no such state of affairs as "one hour before Creation" or "10 trillion years before Creation" because time begins at the moment of Creation. So we shouldn't think of God as sitting around idly for an infinite period of time, twiddling his thumbs, and then he changes his mind and decides to create the world. Rather, we should think that God exists beyond time and space with a timeless intention to create a world with a beginning—and God does that, and the world begins to exist. It couldn't begin "earlier" because there wasn't any "earlier."

LR—Aren't there other alternatives to explain that? I mean: why "one God"? Why not many gods? Why not demons? Why not a "natural force"?

WLC—Well, now . . . what kind of sources of information are you willing to accept as an answer to that question? Biblically, it's clear that the Bible teaches that there is only one God, that it teaches monotheism, that in the beginning God created the heavens and the Earth. Now if you are asking me philosophically, I guess what I would say is that a principle known as Occam's razor says that we should not multiply causes beyond necessity, so that one would be unjustified in inferring any more than a single cause besides the creator of the universe; that would be unjustified. And so, one is justified at most in inferring a single creator of the universe.

LR—But shouldn't we apply the Occam's razor principle also to the Divine Trinity? Why conceive three persons in one God?

WLC—Let me answer that on two levels: First, a God has to be personal in order to explain why anything at all exists, why the universe began to exist, why the universe has the complex order it does, and why the universe has an objective realm of moral values. In all of these cases, the only explanation adequate for these phenomena would be an immaterial being that transcends time and space, has enormous intelligence, and is the source of moral right and wrong and moral duties. That requires that this being should be personal. Now on the basis of those arguments [alone], you would be quite right: One would not be justified in inferring that God is three persons because one person would be enough to meet the demands of why something exists rather than nothing, why the universe began to exist, why the universe is fine tuned for our existence, and why a realm of objective moral values exists. What prompts Christians to believe that God is tri-personal is the message of Jesus of Nazareth. It's on the basis of Jesus' radical claims to be the divine Son of God filled with the Holy Spirit that Christians believe that God is not just only one person but three persons. Since I think we have good grounds to believe that what Jesus taught about God is true, I think we have good grounds for believing in the Trinity on the basis of what he taught and believed.

LR—Prior to human existence, as far as we know, there was no "morality" in the universe. What need would God have to create a moral framework for our puny life form in the universe?

WLC—I do think that insofar as you mean by "morality" moral values and moral duties, these do exist prior to the advent of human existence. Indeed, I would say that many of these moral values and duties are necessary and so hold in every possible world—even in worlds where God didn't create anything at all. God is the source of moral value and, therefore, even in the absence of human beings, his will would express itself in certain necessary truths; for example: the torturing of a child for fun is wrong. And that moral truth is true whether or not any children ever actually exist or not. The truth of the statement "Torturing a child for fun is wrong" doesn't depend upon the existence of any children; that's a necessary truth that applies whether there are children or not. So morality—both moral values and moral duties—is rooted in God, not in humanity. It's not as though God creates this as a framework for our life forms. Rather, this is a necessary and essential attribute of the nature of God himself, and since we're persons like God—we're created in his image as finite persons—we have certain moral duties regarding how we ought to treat other persons because persons are intrinsically valuable.

LR—Do you assume that the morals of God are codified in the Ten Commandments?

WLC—Those would be some of the morals duties that he has laid upon us, yes.

LR—But can you prove that full compliance to the Ten Commandments does not lead to murderous free regimes? Moses himself seems to prove the contrary when he slaughters his brethren just because they didn't comply with the Commandment "You shall not make for yourself an idol" in Exodus 32.

WLC—In Exodus, we have a system in which there was no distinction between the civil government and God's divine government. You have theocracy, in which God is the head of the government; therefore, there was no separation of church and state. Now we don't live in a condition like that. We don't live in a theocracy. There is no state of which God is the head of the government. Israel itself demanded a king, and said, "We don't want God to be our head anymore. We want to have a human king!" And so he allowed them eventually to have that after Moses. So there's no reason to think that the Ten Commandments ought to be civil laws or civil statutes. I think that we ought to have a separation of church and state.

LR—But Dr. Craig, if God's morality must be seen as an absolute value, wasn't that act of Moses absolutely wrong?

WLC—No! What he did was absolutely right: He administered God's justice on those who had sinned. But, you see, God is the one who is going to ultimately administer justice on the Judgment Day when the scroll of human history is rolled up, coming to an end. But in the meantime, we are not under any sort of authority to administer God's justice now because, as I say, God isn't the head of the government. So the government can't administer the justice of God; we have civil laws. Many things are immoral, but, nevertheless, they're not illegal. For example, I think it's immoral to smoke cigarettes because this destroys a person who is intrinsically valuable in God's sight. Therefore, to destroy yourself by cigarette smoking, I think, is profoundly immoral. But, nevertheless, it's not illegal. You have the perfect right to destroy yourself and your body if you want to—as long as you don't hurt anybody else. So don't equate what is illegal and what is immoral. Certain things are immoral, but they're not illegal because we don't live under a divine theocracy.

LR—Concerning God's ruling, we have to be confronted by the characters of Adam and Eve. Due to the Theory of Evolution (Darwinian or not), doesn't the Judeo-Christian "Fall" of Adam and Eve lose its meaning? Why would human beings have to repent if there's nothing to repent? Or do you believe in a "real" Adam and Eve?

WLC—Well, I do believe in a real Adam and Eve. And the Roman Catholic Church—which has endorsed the idea of biological evolution— also believes in a real Adam and Eve. The Roman Catholic Church believes that the human body is a product of biological evolution, but that form, which has evolved physically, doesn't become a human being until it has a soul, until God puts an immortal soul into that body. So the evolution of the physical part of man is not at all incompatible with saying that there was an original human pair who were the first human parents. That's perfectly consistent with modern biology, too, which actually says that every person living on the face of the Earth today is descended from a common human female ancestor—who is sometimes called the "mitochondrial Eve," because she's the "mother" of every living person on the Earth today.

LR—When in time do you think they have lived?

WLC—I don't know. This is one of my unanswered questions. I have a lot of questions that I haven't had a chance to explore and that are still unanswered. That's one of them. I do think that when you look at hominid forms, creatures like Cro-Magnon man, this is clearly a human being, it seems to me, and therefore, we would want to say that Cro-Magnon was human. When you get back earlier than that, then it gets a little harder to tell where the line between primates and real humans is; so, I'm not really sure.

LR—If life is finite, if there is no immortality for human beings after death, why should that be unbearable? Why would mortality be more unbearable than the infinity of nonexistence that preceded our existence? I mean—you don't miss the time that occurred before you were born.

WLC—I've never been able to understand why atheists push this argument! [Laughing.] It seems to me that the clear answer to this is the asymmetry of time. Namely, time is not perfectly symmetrical; time is going forward. Therefore, we celebrate a person's birth because he comes into existence at that point, but we mourn a person's death because he ceases to exist at that moment; and so, the destruction of existence that comes after a person has lived is obviously much more existentially significant than the period of nonexistence that preceded his coming into being. His coming into being is reason for celebration, but the destruction of the existence of a living, intelligent, artistic, loving, human person, I think is a terrible tragedy. Why I think this is unbearable—here I agree with many of the French existentialist philosophers like Jean-Paul Sartre and Albert Camus, who said that in the absence of immortality and of God, life becomes ultimately absurd. In the face of death, there is no ultimate meaning to existence, there is no ultimate value, and there's no ultimate purpose to human being. All of those are reasons to think that atheism really leads ultimately to hopelessness and despair.

LR—But don't you think, as the Christian Dietrich Bonhoeffer did, that one ought to live as if there was no god?

WLC—No. I guess I don't think that, and I don't understand that attitude. That's certainly not the attitude of, for example, the Apostle Paul in the New Testament. Paul lived his life in light of eternity. Because he knew that the grave was not the end, this gave him the courage to face even his own martyrdom—knowing that this was not ultimately the end, that there was hope for life beyond the grave. So it's why we needn't lapse into despair when a person gazes at death or is afflicted with some suffering or pain that we see no good reason for. I think that the hope of immortality is a wonderful hope that can give us strength and courage to live our days here on Earth.

LR—You talked about Paul, and something about "that" Paul was the idea that the "promised kingdom of God," announced by Jesus, would be granted to the faithful and the just by the grace of God in the name of Jesus, after one's death and for all eternity in a supernatural realm. According to authors like Albert Schweitzer, Jesus, as an apocalyptic prophet, was not thinking in the long term; rather, the kingdom of God was near and the dead would resurrect in a pristine physical body to be ruled by Jesus on Earth. When we speak about Christianity, shouldn't we rather speak about "Paulinism"—since it was Paul who was the real force behind missionary activity and the man responsible for spreading this kind of "churchlike" Gospel?

WLC—That has been said in the past, in the 19th century, but I think that it is generally recognized among New Testament scholars today that Paul's religion comes from Jesus of Nazareth, that this is the inspiration for what Paul believed and worked for. With respect to the "coming of the kingdom of God," scholars have noticed that with Jesus, there is a tension between the kingdom of God being already here among us, in his person, but then also, it's not yet here in its fullness: Death, sin, and destruction are still in power. He has not yet established his reign, and so there is a tension between the "already" and the "not yet." When you read some of Jesus' parables, it's very evident in these parables that he thought there could be a long time before he would return again and the kingdom of God would be finally established. He would tell parables, for example, of a landlord who would go away on a long journey and while he was gone, the servants would say, "My master is delayed in returning"; they begin to carouse and not do their responsibilities and so forth. And Jesus warned them that the master will return when they don't expect and will demand an accounting. There's another parable where he talks about how the bridegroom is supposed to come, but he doesn't come on time—he's delayed—and so some of the lamps of the people waiting for him burn out, and they didn't have enough oil for their lamps. Jesus is saying, "You need to always be ready because it might not come when you expect." There are quite a number of parables where Jesus himself teaches that the time may be very long before he returns, and, in fact, he said he himself did not know the date of his return. He said, "Only the Father in Heaven knows the date of my return, not even the Son knows this." So I think every generation should be ready and live as though Christ were going to return in your lifetime; but we don't know really when it will happen.

LR—But being that Jesus is a part of the Trinity—and therefore "being also God"—shouldn't he know the date of the kingdom's arrival?

WLC—You need to understand the doctrine of the Incarnation; that Jesus was both God and man. As a man, Jesus had an ordinary human consciousness. We shouldn't think of the baby Jesus lying at the manger simultaneously contemplating astrophysical cosmology or the infinitesimal calculus. He had a genuine consciousness of a little, human baby, and the Bible says that as he grew older, as a boy, he grew in wisdom and in stature, and it also says that he learned through what he suffered. So in Jesus' humanity there is development, there's growth, and there's no reason to think that he was like some sort of a Superman encased in a human body. He had a genuine human consciousness with all the limitations that would imply. I think if you could go back in time and ask Jesus of Nazareth about modern subjects, he wouldn't know anything about auto mechanics or quantum mechanics because those are not in his field of consciousness. Now insofar as he is God, I believe he had that knowledge as God, but it wasn't part of his human consciousness, not part of his waking conscious life; you could say that would be in the subliminal, perhaps.

LR—Could the "younger Jesus" be less divine than the "older Jesus"?

WLC—No. You have to understand what I'm saying here. I'm saying that he is simultaneously God and man but that in the state of the Incarnation, his human mind had an ordinary human consciousness that grew from being like a little baby to a boy to a man. Now, as God,

I think he knew all things, but this would not be conscious knowledge; it would be subliminal or subconscious. For example, there are lots of things that you know, but you're not conscious of them right now. You probably know the multiplication table, but you're not thinking of it right now, you're not conscious of it. There are probably other memories and things of that sort that are deep in your subconscious that you might not even be able to bring out. Well, in the same way, if we understand that a human personality has these sorts of layers, we could imagine that in Jesus' waking consciousness there would be development, limitation, and growth, even if in the depths of his subliminal or subconscious he had all the knowledge that God has.

LR—So, I think you're proposing a "new quest": not only a "Quest for a Historical Jesus" but also a "Quest for a Psychological Jesus."

WLC—Well . . . yeah! I think that's a very interesting subject, and I've written on this a little bit. It's a very interesting topic.

LR—Concerning that issue, the Vatican seems to diminish the role of the "historical Jesus" in favor of the "Christ of faith." The Jesus "biography" by Pope Benedict XVI is one example of that. How can a "historical Jesus" be more accurate than a "Christ of faith," or vice versa, since both rely on documents about the life of Christ made by his apologists and not by some outside, objective observer?

WLC—I haven't read this biography by Pope Benedict that you mentioned, but this distinction between the "Jesus of history" and the "Christ of faith" was originally made by a 19th-century German theologian named Martin Kähler. I think it was an attempt to try to preserve belief in Christ in the face of adverse biblical criticism of the New Testament—for example, you mentioned Schweitzer: This was the kind of project he was engaged in. I think this is quite a false dichotomy. I think this is a distinction we should not endorse. If the Christ of faith is not identical to the Jesus of history, then he is simply a mythological figure and no more deserves our allegiance than other mythological figures like Zeus, Odin, and Thor. So I don't accept this distinction between the Jesus of history and the Christ of faith; I think that they are one and the same. I also think that when you do treat the New Testament documents—as you could—like other first-century documents, they bear the investigation of history very, very well and turn out to be very reliable sources for the life of Jesus of Nazareth.

LR—Believers tend to see Jesus as the writer of a cosmic script who in a moment in time chooses to enter in his own story—or else, he wouldn't be an eternal God. If that's correct, why does it seem that he didn't know the story very well? Rather, he wouldn't have expressed the doubt about his own divinity in Mark 15: "My God, my God, why hast thou forsaken me?"

WLC—Well, now, keep in mind what I've said before: Jesus had a genuine human consciousness that knew fatigue, worry, doubt, and so forth. We should not think of the Incarnation, as I said, as a sort of Superman clothed in a costume of human flesh; it was a genuine Incarnation. But with respect to that example of the cry from the cross, I used to think that this was the moment at which God the Father had, so to speak, "turned his back" upon God the Son and abandoned him to bear the sin of the world and to die in desolation. But what I didn't realize is, when you read Psalm 22 in the Old Testament, Psalm 22 begins with these very words: "My God, my God, why hast thou forsaken me?" Psalm 22 is the prayer of God's righteous servant in distress; it's the prayer that a faithful Jew would pray in times of distress, feelings of anxiety, and so forth. So, at this lowest point, when Jesus is dying, when he's hanging on the cross, what is he doing? *He's praying to his Father.* So I think that far from showing his doubt, this is one of the most poignant demonstrations of Jesus' faithfulness right to the very end of his life. He's praying to God the prayer of the righteous servant in distress.

LR—You talked about the Old Testament. Some scholars say that the New Testament is nothing but a "copy" of the Old Testament, telling the same stories with other characters and different situations. Doesn't that remove some of the authenticity of the New Testament?

WLC—I don't think that the details of the life of Jesus are built up out of Old Testament stories, if that's what you mean. There have been certain scholars, for example, who have said that the story of the discovery of Jesus' empty tomb is patterned on the story of Daniel in the lion's den in the Old Testament: The king throws Daniel into the lion's den, and then the next day he comes, and they roll away the stone, and he asks, "Daniel are you there?" And Daniel says, "Yes, God has preserved me." That is really a very implausible account of the empty tomb narrative. For one thing, the parallels are not very good; they're very different narratives. But on the other hand, we have very good reasons to believe that the empty tomb story is historical: It's multiply and independently attested in several different sources; it has the earmarks of authenticity in that women discover the tomb empty—which would have been pointless for any kind of Christian invention because the testimony of women had no credibility, so they would have made people like Peter and John—the male disciples—discover the tomb empty; the story is also extraordinarily simple and lacks signs of theological or religious reflection or embellishment. For these and other reasons, the majority of New Testament historians today think that the account of the discovery of Jesus' empty tomb by a group of his women followers early on Sunday morning is historical, that this really did happen. I use that simply as an illustration to say why I think it's much more plausible to think that these documents do reflect the actual historical life of Jesus than are Christian concoctions built up out of Old Testament stories.

LR—If you had to name the books that came to disturb the Christian belief about the historical Resurrection of Jesus, what books would they be? And about those, that from your standpoint, have strengthened the faith in the Resurrection?

WLC—Well, this will be an odd answer perhaps to give, but I think the book that caused me the most serious second thoughts about the historical case for the Resurrection is a book by Dale Allison, entitled *Resurrecting Jesus*. Allison in this book actually argues *for* the historicity of the empty tomb, the appearances of Jesus, and the origin of the disciples' faith in Jesus' Resurrection. But he so thoroughly goes through the evidence that I think it is a very, very powerful presentation of both sides of the argument. The fact that Allison in the end comes out on the affirmative side, I think, shows the power of the evidence for the Resurrection because he really gives the negative side the best run for its money. In terms of positive books on the Resurrection, I think the book by N. T. Wright called *The Resurrection of the Son of God* would probably be one of the most important books on the Resurrection in English today. It's a massive 800-page study of the origin of Christianity and the belief that Jesus had risen from the dead. It makes a very compelling case, I think, for the Resurrection.

LR—Discussing the Resurrection issue, do you think it's important to have something like the Jesus Seminar—a group of scholars dedicated to the investigation of the historicity of the life of Jesus?

WLC—I suppose it's good that you have a spectrum of beliefs; but the Jesus Seminar has angered a lot of scholars by claiming to be the mouthpiece or the spokespersons for contemporary scholarship—when in fact, they represent a very tiny left-wing margin of scholarship and really don't represent where mainstream historical Jesus studies are today. So I suppose they serve a purpose, but they have greatly misrepresented their own importance; they're not the voice of scholarship today, by any means.

LR—Who do you think are the most and the least reliable scholars in the Jesus Seminar today?

WLC—Oh, my goodness! [Laughing.] I don't know all of the members in it, but certainly one of the most notable would be John Dominic Crossan. Now, that's not to say I agree with him—I debated Professor Crossan on the subject of the Resurrection of Jesus, and we disagree—but he is certainly a credible scholar. By contrast, there are some people in the Jesus Seminar that are just kooks! For example, Robert Price is a member of the Jesus Seminar, and he thinks that Jesus of Nazareth never even existed, that there never was such a historical person! The lengths to which he has to go to try to explain away the evidence are just preposterous! He thinks that most of the Jesus Seminar is too conservative. Price just falls off the end of credible scholarship.

LR—What about Paul? Dr. Price also questions the authorship of Paul's Epistles.

WLC—Exactly! In order to defend his view, he has to say that a large section of the 15th chapter of Paul's letter to the Corinthians—his first letter—is a later interpolation; but there's no manuscript evidence whatsoever to support this conjecture! And worse than that, what's really funny is that in the passage that is supposed to be a later interpolation, it has words that have their antecedents or their reference in the part of the chapter that is supposed to be genuine! So that's extremely awkward for that point of view. It shows, I think, that the passage is a seamless whole.

LR—Don't you think he has a point in raising these issues or, rather, do you think he has an agenda?

WLC—Oh, definitely, he does have an agenda. You have to understand that some of the folks who are theological liberals today come out of very fundamentalist backgrounds, and they are in strong rebellion against the sort of dogmatic, conservative, fundamentalism in which they were raised. What I find ironic, Luís, is that some of these people come to embrace positions on the left that are just as incredible and just as unsupported as the fundamentalist positions on the right that they now despise and criticize.

LR—What about unreliability on the "right"? There are right-wing fundamentalists writing preposterous things too.

WLC—Oh, sure! Of course there are! What one has to do is try to read responsible scholarship that is published in professional journals—which is peer reviewed. Therefore, watch out and be very wary of popular level books or stuff that you read in newspapers or see on television. You really need to read work that is peer reviewed by other scholars.

LR—But when we talk about "peer review," we are talking about the supervision of a collegial "authority." For Saint Thomas Aquinas, faith is basically trust in an "authority." In order to claim the sphere of authority for faith, the Christian must deny it to reason or must place faith in the bounds of reason. In the first case, faith is outside verifiability; in the second case, faith remains the "gap" of what is unverifiable. Why rely on "faith" in either circumstance—even on the scholarly level?

WLC—I don't think that that is what Saint Thomas said. What Thomas says is that the Christian faith delivers to us certain things to be believed; and because these come from God, they are authoritative and true. Nevertheless, he said, there are certain truths which faith proposes but which reason can also discover. So he thought, for example, that the existence of God would be one of these: Faith proposes for us to believe in God, but he thinks that you can prove the existence of God by reason alone, quite independently of faith. Now, he thought there are some truths of faith that cannot be proved by reason. An example of this would be the Trinity. He would say, "You cannot prove the Trinity just by mere reason alone; you need divine revelation from God to know the Trinity." But even in that case it's not blind faith because what Saint Thomas says is that God has given certain "signs of credibility" to his divine revelation that show that this is really from God; and what he's thinking of here is miracles and fulfilled prophecy. In the case of Jesus, for example, by raising Jesus from the dead, God miraculously authenticated Jesus' teachings, and by fulfilling prophecies in the Old Testament, it shows that Jesus was in fact who he claimed to be. On the basis of these signs of credibility, Thomas says that is quite rational to place your faith in divine revelation and believe what God says. So I don't see that there is this conflict between reason and faith at all. I think that they work together.

LR—What about theology? Doesn't theology work in a "closed system" as a means of understanding the world? I mean, doesn't theology work in the context of a "specific theology": Christianity, Hinduism, Islam, etc.? For me, theology sounds like Shakespeare speaking about the reality of Hamlet or other authors speaking about the reality of their characters: All of them are fiction and none are real. So, why should we rely on theologies if each one of them only produces fiction?

WLC—I think that, in a sense, the question we just talked about answers that. Theology certainly does have a system, in that, for example, Christianity has a certain teaching about God, man, salvation, sin, eternal life, and so forth; and this teaching is different from Buddhist teaching or Daoist teaching. Each of these worldviews has a different body of teaching, if you will. Now the question arises: Which one, if any, of these gives us the truth about the world? Here the system is not at all closed; as Thomas Aquinas said, reason can discover and show many of these truths wholly independently of faith and therefore show that what faith proposes is, in fact, true. Also there are certain signs of credibility like miracles and prophecies that enable us to know what the truth revealed by God really is. While theology certainly does constitute a system, I don't think it's closed in the sense that you described; on the contrary, it's quite open to verification, proof, and evidence.

LR—When one wants to verify "faith," one is inevitably committed to a certain context. What kind of "faith" can be verified if you're, for example, "prisoner" of a Buddhist worldview, a Hindu worldview, an Islamic worldview, etc.? Also, even in the same religious contexts (for example, in sects and cults), you have different interpretations of what is "the faith." It's a very broad term.

WLC—Yes, it is—and used in different contexts means different things. When I used the word "faith" in the sentence, I was using it in the sense of "religious belief." So I was using it in a very general sense, so that we could talk about "the Muslim faith," "the Buddhist faith," "the Christian faith." Now in another context I might say to you, "You should place your faith in God," and what I mean there is: You should put your trust in God, or the commitment of your heart in God. So we need to be very careful when we use words like "faith," because these are ambiguous and they have a whole range of meaning. When I was saying that faith proposes certain doctrines, I mean that there are certain religious beliefs that claim to be from God, that are proposed to us for belief, and then we can investigate whether or not these are true.

LR—But Dr. Craig, when you commit your faith in God, you're not committing that faith directly since you will always need to use intermediaries for that commitment: a specific church, for example. Nobody says, "I talk to a God that I invent in my head, and that solves the issue." You rely on a specific tradition—whether the biblical tradition, the koranic tradition, etc. Why is one tradition about God more reliable than other?

WLC—In one sense, you're right, in that one does place one's faith in a body of truth, a body of doctrine or teaching, and that one didn't just invent this oneself. I didn't come up with this by my own imagination; so in that sense what you say is true. On the other hand, there is an individual element that you must decide for yourself: "Do you believe this is true?" And if you do, are you going to place your trust in this person? Are you going to love God and commit your life to him? That's an intensely personal, individual decision. Now with respect to your question, "Which one is the truth?," I will reiterate what I've already said before: With respect to Christianity, I think that there are good reasons to believe that the Christian God exists; that God really has created the world; revealed himself to the nation of Israel; brought Jesus of Nazareth into the world as the Messiah of Israel and with a view toward the salvation of mankind. I think that there are quite good reasons to believe this. In my published work and on my Web site, I have lots of articles defending the existence of God and the historicity of the radical claims of Jesus and his Resurrection from the dead. None of those things appeals to faith; these all appeal to objective evidence that any person is free to read and think about for himself—and see if he agrees that there is good reason to believe that the Christian God really does exist.

LR—How do you think Christianity will "evolve" in the United States and in Europe?

WLC—This is a really, really good question. My doctoral mentor in Germany, Wolfhart Pannenberg, once remarked that he thinks that liberal Protestantism in Europe will disappear in the next generation because it really has nothing to offer people: You might as well just be a secular humanist or an agnostic, as be a liberal Protestant. So what he thinks is going to happen in Europe is that evangelical Protestant Christianity will continue to grow and that Roman Catholicism will persist. I think that under the last pope and under Pope Benedict, there's real hope for a revival of Roman Catholicism in Europe that will not be just a kind of dead, institutional church, but a really living and vibrant faith—at least, I hope that's what will happen.

In the United States, I'm not sure what will happen here. Evangelical Christianity is very robust in the United States; it continues to grow, but at the same time I also see disturbing signs coming from the "New Age" movement that you've talked about, a kind of subjectivism, pluralism, and relativism that worries me. I think the one thing that gives me great optimism is that in the Anglophone world—that is, in the Anglo-American realm—there has been a tremendous revival of Christian philosophy going on over the last 40 years. As this intellectual revolution trickles down through the university system to students and to the man in the street, I think it's going to help strengthen the church at large and really, really help Christianity to remain vibrant and strong in coming generations. So in that sense, I'm quite optimistic because of what I see going on at the highest academic levels in philosophy, in New Testament studies, and also, I think now, in the physical sciences as well.

LR—What is the greatest danger for Christianity today?

WLC—That's a good question. I think the greatest immediate danger is religious pluralism: the view that no one religion is true, that religion is just relative—and, therefore, that there are many ways to God, and it doesn't really matter what you believe, that all religions are basically true or that all religions are basically false. I think that this kind of religious pluralism, on a philosophical level, is the greatest danger. Now let me be clear about this: I'm not talking here about pluralism in the political sense; in the political sense, I'm a great advocate of religious pluralism, that is to say, the freedom to believe what you want and to practice your own religion. Every sincere Christian should be an ardent supporter of pluralism in that political sense. I said I believe in a separation of church and state. But I'm talking about pluralism in a philosophical sense: the idea that there is no truth, no objective truth about God. That is the greatest immediate danger, and I think that this is rooted in a more fundamental danger, which is the dominance of scientific naturalism—especially in Western Europe. Scientific naturalism is the view that says that the physical sciences are the sole means of discovering truth; therefore, if something cannot be scientifically proven, then it is just a matter of personal taste and emotive expression. It's out of this scientific naturalism that this relativistic attitude toward religion comes because people think that since you can't prove religion scientifically, then it's just a matter of personal opinion and individual taste—therefore, there is no objective truth about these matters. So I think that on a deeper level, counteracting this scientific naturalism is the pressing task of Christian intellectuals today.

LR—Concerning the relativism issue, do you think that this kind of relativism also permeates the political parties most centered

on Christian faith? For example, you see a very pro-Christian, pro-life Republican Party concerned about abortion, but it is also the party that most actively promotes war policies—for example in Iraq, Afghanistan, Iran, etc. Why should life be more decisive in birth control issues than in war issues?

WLC—Well, I don't think it's more decisive. Just think, Luís: Let's just grant that for the sake of argument, abortion is a form of homicide. If the pro-life position is correct, and the destruction of the human fetus is a form of homicide, that means that in the United States alone, over a million human beings are being killed every year through abortion! The number of people who have lost their lives through terrorism or in the war in Iraq just pales in comparison with those numbers. We're talking millions and millions of people who have lost their lives through abortion—if it is, in fact, homicide. So I think you can see why those who believe in the sanctity of life are so concerned about the destruction of innocent human life that goes on today simply for convenience.

LR—But do you think that it's just a question of numbers? What about principles? What about universal moral values?

WLC—We were talking about the value of innocent life, right? Innocent life is lost through war, for example. Innocent life can be lost through crime; an innocent life can be lost through abortion. When you look at just the numbers involved, I do think that it's like a holocaust! The American holocaust has been going on since 1973; we're talking about tens of millions of persons who have been destroyed in their mother's womb; innocent persons who have done nothing to merit being killed like that. Just in terms of the numbers alone, it dwarfs any sort of atrocity that's been going on.

LR—In that context, how do you see some radical moral philosophies—like those of Peter Singer—proposing a more relatively flexible view about abortion and human life?

WLC—Singer has a funny view because, I think, he is a moral realist; he's not a relativist, he believes in absolute moral values. He just thinks that certain higher animals—like chimpanzees and whales—also have moral rights to life and therefore should not be wantonly hunted, killed, and destroyed. The irony is that he apparently thinks that whales and other animals have more right to life than a human infant does. He thinks that parents, even after the child is conceived, should be allowed several weeks until they decide whether or not they have the child destroyed and killed or whether or not they want to keep the child. Well, to me, that kind of infanticide is just morally unconscionable and untenable! While I appreciate his efforts to protect the life of whales and chimpanzees—I think that's admirable—I think he should have the same concern for human infants and fetuses.

LR—Last message for Portuguese believers and nonbelievers?

WLC—You know, I spoke several years ago at the University of Porto. The reaction of the Portuguese students to me was: incredulity! They could not believe that here was a Christian who had two earned doctoral degrees from European universities and was defending belief in God and in Jesus Christ. They actually thought I was an impostor! Some even phoned the University of Louvain in Belgium—where I was working—to see if I was really a genuine scholar there [laughing]. What I want to say to students in Portugal is: You need to realize that outside of Portugal there's a vast Christian movement that includes some of the greatest philosophers and intellects that exist today. So don't let what is happening—or not happening, perhaps—in your immediate surroundings blind you to what is happening in the wider world as a whole—which is just a tremendous revival of Christian philosophy, thought, and expansion of Christianity throughout the world. Don't think that just because, perhaps, the church seems dead and boring in Portugal that that's true for Christianity at large. I would encourage folks through the Internet, through resources like my Web site, www.reasonablefaith.org, to access some of this material and begin to ask themselves: Could this really be the truth? Could it really be the case that there is a God who created the world, who loves me, and who gave his son to die for me? I think that if they explore this with an open heart and an open mind, they can find it to be a life-changing truth.

John Dominic Crossan

John Dominic Crossan was born in Ireland in 1934. He received a doctorate of divinity from Maynooth College, Ireland, in 1959, and he did postdoctoral research at the Pontifical Biblical Institute in Rome from 1959 to 1961 and at the École Biblique in Jerusalem from 1965 to 1967. He was a member of a 13th-century Roman Catholic religious order, the Servites (*Ordo Servorum Mariae*), from 1950 to 1969 and an ordained priest from 1957 to 1969. He joined DePaul University, Chicago, in 1969 and remained there until 1995. He is now a professor emeritus in its Department of Religious Studies. He was co-chair of the Jesus Seminar from 1985 to 1996 as it met in twice-annual meetings to debate the historicity of the life of Jesus in the Gospels. In the past 40 years he has written 23 books on the historical Jesus, earliest Christianity, and the historical Paul. Five of them have been national religious bestsellers. The scholarly core of his work is the trilogy from *The Historical Jesus, The Life of a Mediterranean Jewish Peasant* (1991) through *The Birth of Christianity, Discovering What Happened in the Years Immediately After the Execution of Jesus* (1998) to *In Search of Paul, How Jesus's Apostle Opposed Rome's Empire with God's Kingdom*; co-authored with the archaeologist Jonathan L. Reed (2004).

Luís Rodrigues—Today, when somebody talks about Jesus, they could be talking about a wide spectrum of different interpretations of Jesus—the faith healer, the revolutionary, the prophet, the savior, the sage, the cosmic being, and even the imaginary myth. Is it still feasible to talk about a "historical Jesus"? Can it be that the "old Jesus Christ Superstar" is now bursting into a myriad of "new Jesus Christ Supernovas"?

John Dominic Crossan—Or a black hole maybe [laughs]. No, I honestly don't think so. I think the claim that Jesus is historically unknowable is a sort of "transcendental subterfuge," you know what I mean? There are people who either don't want him known historically because they don't like Christianity, or don't want him known historically because they are very conservative Christians—but you can certainly know about Jesus as you can any other human figure that ever lived. I'm convinced, as a historian, that Jesus was a real living figure.

LR—What have you to say about the Jesus portrayed by the New Age spirituality interpretations?

JDC—Part of the major problem is that to do proper historical work—and I distinguish that from either apologetical work (which is pro-Christian) or polemical work (which is anti-Christian), you have to put Jesus back into the matrix—and I would use the word *matrix* to insist on the interactive relationship between Jesus and his environment; so I'm not using *background* or *context*, which might be kind of neutral—and the matrix of Jesus is a world in which the emperor—the Roman emperor before Jesus ever existed, and even if Jesus had never existed—was already called "divine," "son of god," "god," "lord," "redeemer," and "savior of the world." These were the claims and titles of the Roman emperor; so, when somebody takes those titles from the emperor—they made a lot of sense after all: he *was* running the world—and applies them to a Jewish peasant, you must be either dealing with a very funny joke or serious high treason. Since the Romans weren't laughing at all, it was clear it was high treason, and therefore you're claiming obviously a very different meaning for all those words. If I was walking around today saying "I'm a king," obviously I'm either loony or I have a different view of what a king is. So, what's wrong with New Age interpretation is that it simply is not historical. They're taking the titles of Jesus and saying, "Oh, I do mean to say he's divine." I don't care what somebody *today* thinks. I want to know, first of all, what did it mean when people in the first century said that. Then I can decide if I'm a Christian, whether I believe it or not. It's as if you were talking to me now in Portuguese. I couldn't agree or disagree with you. I wouldn't know what you're saying; the first thing I would have to do is to learn Portuguese.

LR—But aren't Christians overestimating the role of Jesus in his historical and social context? Reading some records of that time, the Romans seem to completely ignore the role of this insignificant—for them—Jewish character.

JDC—Well, what we have actually, at the end of the first century from Josephus and at the beginning of the second century from Tacitus (one Jewish and the other Roman), is an agreement of four things about Jesus. Now first of all, neither of them are interested particularly directly in Jesus; they're interested in explaining who these weird Christians are. Otherwise they wouldn't be talking about Jesus, not even a blip on their radar screen. But they're explaining what Christians are, they're trying to explain to their people that in the same way that Platonists follow Plato and Aristotelians follow Aristotle, Christians follow Christ. And they say four things: (1) there was a movement over there in Judea; (2) the founder, Jesus, was executed by Pontius Pilate to stop the movement; (3) it didn't work; (4) the movement now is spread all over. So, we really do know from the Romans, not about Jesus but about the success of Jesus' movement; otherwise of course, they wouldn't be talking about him—in the same way we would not be talking in America about Barack Obama if he had lost [laughs]. So, it's only by the success of his movement—by success I don't mean anything theological, I just mean numbers—that it is becoming a large blip on the radar screen, and they had to explain: "Who's this weirdo who caused all this trouble?"

LR—This movement started to rely upon centralized religion (Roman Catholicism) and doctrinal legislation (the adoption of canonical scripture). From this standpoint, is it possible to refer to "Christian orthodoxy" as the product of a successful bureaucracy and "Christian heresy" as the failed attempt to oppose it?

JDC—Well, if you put it like that, I'd say that's not a historical statement. What we had in early Christianity clearly was a wide divergence of interpretations focused on Jesus. I think of it something like dropping a match into gunpowder, something blowing in all directions. So, you have a wide spectrum even within the New Testament—most people know there are four different versions of the Gospel, different interpretations of Paul within the New Testament; very different interpretations of Jesus, say, from the nonviolent Jesus in the Gospel to the violent Jesus in the Apocalypse. If you go outside the New Testament, you find the diversity multiplied. So I don't presume, as a historian, that everything inside the New Testament is right—however you judge that—and everything outside is wrong, or vice versa. I would have to say, looking at these diversities of Christianity, you might say bluntly, do you think the orthodox people got it basically right? And saying that, in a way we might ask: Do you think Bonhoeffer got it right about Hitler? [Laughs.] Well, maybe he did, maybe he didn't. Among these options, even as a historian, can you tell which might be in better continuity with Jesus? Or do you simply say all are in continuity with Jesus and you have to then make a theological judgment, as a Christian, about which of them do you think you're going to live by? So, I don't particularly like when people condemn one another, let alone burn one another at the stake. I do recognize—I recognize it very much in America at the moment—that there are some visions of the future that are really just bad, and you don't want to say, "Well, there's Cheney's vision and there's Obama's vision and everyone has the right to their vision. . . ." Hmmm—sometime you might have to say, "No! We've tried that one, and after eight years we see that it doesn't work."

LR—Concerning the different visions of history, don't you think Albert Schweitzer is right when he says that the quest for an historical Jesus only brings into the light the wishes and aspirations of those who embark on the quest?

JDC—Well, if you really read Schweitzer, that's not quite what he said—otherwise, there would be no point in his writing a book and going out to Africa. What he really says is that there is nothing that so reveals the searcher as the search for the historical Jesus. At the end of his book on the historical Jesus, he has that great peroration that Jesus is known as your response to a vision. What he does is not leave the church—he leaves Europe for Africa; so he really doesn't say that you see nothing but your own face in the bottom of a deep well. Schweitzer really said that nothing so reveals the searcher, in the searching for the historical Jesus. So when you look at the wide diversity within scholarship today, even the hard core of agreement can be sort of hard to see because when two scholars debate one another, they will not talk about the 98 percent they agree on: they will fight to the death for the 2 percent they disagree on [laughs].

LR—Talking about scholarly debate, what is your assessment of the achievements obtained by the Jesus Seminar?

JDC—I think the major achievement of the Jesus Seminar is to make ordinary educated laypeople—out of the huge number of educated laity in this country at least who are really interested in this subject—to make them aware that in addition to the sort of "the-gospel-vision-of-Jesus-take-it-or-leave-it" alternative, there is also an historical vision of Jesus that has to make sense of how you get from that (i.e., the history) to the Gospels. It's never been just about the historical Jesus. It's really about saying, "Wait a minute; if you can say this is wrong in the New Testament, then can you say the pope is wrong when he just said this?" And the answer is "Of course!" That's the importance, really, rather than simply saying "They've discovered this, they've discovered that."

LR—In your opinion, why is Christianity a religion capable of critically reflecting about the historicity of its religious characters and events? Why do you think we don't have a Buddha Seminar, a Muhammad Seminar, a Moses Seminar, etc.?

JDC—Well, I think because, first of all, Christianity has always strived to be a historically grounded religion; it was always made that way. It could have said "Well, Jesus is like a parable." You could tell the parable of the good Samaritan—which Jesus just made up—and at the end, Jesus says, "Go and do likewise." So, you could say, "Okay. The early Church created a parable of an imaginary person called Jesus." The challenge is: This is how you live; this is how you should live; this is how God wants you to live. That would mean that historicity really didn't have anything to do with Christianity; it would be only as important as you and I arguing over whether the good Samaritan actually existed, and then saying, "I don't think so; maybe Jesus made him up, or he could be a mythical figure who reincarnates again and again like a Bodhisattva in Buddhism." What happened was Christianity made a claim and the mortgage has come due on that place: If Jesus is an historical figure, then he must be subject to the same "ifs and whats and maybes" of all historical investigation—otherwise, he's quarantined beyond all investigation.

LR—In your writings, you seem to emphasize the metaphorical. Are the metaphorical interpretations of the atonement,

Resurrection, and other deeds of Jesus motives enough to justify Christianity? Doesn't a religion presuppose "real" resurrections, miracles, and the exaltation of the supernatural?

JDC—I use again the analogy with Augustus: The Roman emperor at the time of Jesus was a real person, but what surrounds him is a whole conundrum of majesty and divinity. Do I think, for example, that the god Apollo and his mother Atia conceived him? No. But I understand that the claim that's being made there is that his political control of the Roman Empire is willed by the gods and it probably would be unwise to have told Augustus: "You do understand you're a metaphor?" I'm sure he didn't think his mother conceived him as a god, but that was their way of saying, "This person is the greatest thing that happened to the human race." And you have a counter-claim by Christians about Jesus: "No; the best thing that happened to the human race was not the Roman emperor but this Jewish peasant." So, if I'm a first-century, open-minded, pre-enlightenment pagan who believes that all sorts of wonderful things can happen—and I'm listening to Paul—my question to Paul is not going to be: "Excuse me, Paul, I don't believe that stuff; I just don't believe in divine conceptions, divine resurrections, and ascensions into heaven; that's all pre-enlightenment rubbish." I can't say that because in pre-enlightenment world, I believe that stuff is possible. I'm going to say to Paul: "Okay, tell me why I should give a hoot about your Jesus? Sure he could be resurrected from the dead. Good for him! I don't care. Augustus has never done anything for me and he's up in heaven; tell me why your Jesus will do something for me?" Now, if I can persuade enough people in the first century that my Jesus will do more for them than their Augustus, I've got a community. If I don't, I'm finished.

LR—Jesus brings a message of personal immortality that is much better than Augustus's message to serve him on Earth?

JDC—No, I don't think so. That might persuade people today, but that would never, ever have got a religion going in the first century, because there were all sorts of other people guaranteeing that same deal. The only reason that some people believe in your vision of the next life was that they could see it already in this life. For example: "Okay, your god heals the sick, is that right?" "Yes." "Does your god charge for healing the sick?" "No." Okay, now I'm listening. I'm not yet convinced, but I know that Aesculapius is very expensive; I can go to his temple, but that's going to cost me; so, you're telling me that your Jesus heals and it's free? So, I'm thinking, "Okay. I've got nothing to lose. If your Jesus heals me, good! If not, I can always fall back on Aesculapius." So what you're really dealing with is a ruthlessly pragmatic people quite at home with god's intervening, coming down from heaven, messing up the world for good or evil, and the only reason that makes your god interesting is what your god is going to do for me. Now, if I see what I'm getting from your god in this life, okay, I'll trust that god for the next life. But otherwise, it's what I call transcendental snake oil—if you buy this sort of oil from me, it will cure whatever you've got; if you send me 10 dollars, I will send you an ointment and it will cure whatever you've got.

LR—It's like the televangelist cure by TV . . .

JDC—Exactly! You send in the dollars, I send out the oil and . . . well, maybe your disease will go away in any case and then you're happy. My point is that if all early Christianity said was, "Augustus fixes up the world; come to us, and we'll fix you up in the next life," I don't think it would have gotten off the ground.

LR—Reading about the healings and miracles of Jesus, one does not seem to denote a particular affection or love for those who are healed—Matthew 17:15–18 is a good example of that. The subliminal message of Jesus seems to be: "Okay. I'm healing you just because I have to fulfill the prophecies of the Old Testament; when I'm done, I can finally proceed to my greater mission in Jerusalem—to rule over you and become king." Doesn't he seem like a doctor who wants to make his reputation more than he wishes to devote himself to the deep concerns of his patients? Being that his mission seems so individualistic, do you think Jesus is embarking on a program of social reform?

JDC—I've talked about the Roman matrix; you have to put that into the Jewish matrix, and the promise was that someday, God was going to heal a broken world. So it really was not about what you and I might call "social justice" or "social reform"; the Romans would not have been the least bit annoyed by somebody who was going around just healing people. That was fine. They got annoyed when you raised the issue: "Who had the right to run the world? Should it be run their way or some other way?" Those were the bigger issues. It wasn't just that Jesus healed bodies: He raised the issue of who controls bodies; he raised the issue of whether they might be sick not because of, for example, their own sins but because of injustice, overwork. And with that, the whole discussion of God's kingdom—the way God wanted the world run—comes in.

LR—But in the Gospels, Jesus shows some lack of concern for his mother (Matthew 12:46–50), rebukes Peter and calls him "Satan," rebukes his disciples (Luke 9:54–55), rebukes the vendors in the Temple (John 2:16), doesn't miss a chance to rebuke the Pharisees (for example, in Matthew 23), removes blessings of peace (Matthew 10:13–15), and so on. With such harsh behavior, how can nonbelievers find a "moral Jesus," an inclusive and righteous man in the New Testament? Comparing moral behaviors, even Buddha seems to be a better character than Jesus, don't you think?

JDC—Well, the way I would address this is: We have four versions of the Gospel. After 200 years of study, we know that Mark was used as a source by Matthew and Luke—let's just keep it simple like that for the moment. Therefore, it's very simple to start by reading Mark and then see what happens to the same incident in Matthew and Luke. The process you're going to see with Jesus—that's going to end up in the Apocalypse, in the whole second coming of Jesus—is that Jesus consistently gets nastier. You find Jesus saying in the Sermon on the Mount that you're not supposed to use violence because God is nonviolent and sends rain on the just and the unjust, and the sun is there for the good and the bad. But pretty soon you'll find the sort of thing you're mentioning. Matthew is going to have those terrible talks with the Pharisees; they're not in Mark. As the early followers of Jesus get opposition, you can almost calibrate the degree of opposition by the nastiness of the language of Jesus—I'm not talking about Jesus' own experience, I'm talking about depictions 10, 20, 30, 40, 50, 60 years after Jesus. By the time you get to John's Gospel in the 90s, when it looks pretty clear that most of his fellow Jews have said "no," then you've got John talking about "the Jews did this" and "the Jews did that," as if Jesus himself wasn't one. So, there's what I call a "violent kosher" being added to Jesus steadily, all the way to the book of the Apocalypse. It doesn't just appear there suddenly out of the sky. These Christians have invented something that is nowhere in the Jewish tradition, namely a second coming, because they will not accept a coming of the Messiah that does not recall the type of vengeful and punitive God who basically is threatening you—and if you don't accept, you're going to be punished. That doesn't seem to be the teaching of Jesus at all.

LR—So we can see, in the evolution of the Gospels, a power struggle occurring within the Jewish community and between its various sects?

JDC—Well, yes. The first century makes the situation in Israel today look like a picnic. Every major group has a vision for the future; every group has a different way to handle the Romans. You have people who have armed resistance against them, you have people who have nonviolent resistance against them, and you have people who have withdrawn into the desert to ignore them. All of the options are there in the first century. What I'd call Christian Judaism, Pharisaic Judaism, Sadduceean Judaism, Essene Judaism—to mention the main ones—they're almost like theological political parties, or theologically motivated political parties, all of which are really struggling with one major issue: What to do about the Romans? It's not simply a colonial question; it's a question of how can it be God's will that this people run our country? It's really a theological question for them.

LR—How much were early Christians influenced by these different sectarian Jewish groups?

JDC—I would think profoundly. I think that part of the nastiness, the especial nastiness between—let me use these terms carefully now—Christian Judaism and Pharisaic Judaism, is that they're just the closest together, not the farthest apart. You don't hear Jesus and his followers talking about the Sadducees; they're up there in Jerusalem, they're not meeting them everyday. I think before the war of 66–74, all of these are options within Judaism, and one of the things we used to think before the Dead Sea Scrolls were discovered was that the Christian Jews are way out there on the left wing, they were so far out, how could anyone even listen to them? Then we read about this group down at the Dead Sea, who no longer attend the temple, who don't have the same calendar as their people, and all of the sudden, Christians seem almost somewhere in the middle, with the Essenes way out in the left wing—so far out in the left wing that you don't even find Christians talking about them. But they argue like mad with the Pharisees and call one another names—hypocrites, and every nasty name you can come up with.

LR—It's like a love-hate relationship.

JDC—Well, it's too close within the family; you find that out in Christianity. Some Christians can be very urbane about Buddhists, let's say, but when they talk about the Southern Baptists and the Northern Baptists, then it gets really nasty! [Laughs.] The important thing I'm saying is that there is a clear line within the New Testament—I'm staying simply within the New Testament—that the coming of Jesus, the Incarnation, is inadequate; that Jesus doesn't do what he's supposed to do: Where's the violence? Where's the condemnation of all evil people? So early Christianity invented the second coming, which would be violent and punitive, and all the evildoers would be destroyed. That's a desecration of Jesus. It would be like bringing Gandhi back with a machine gun or something.

LR—If I'm not mistaken, you tend to see the Gospels not as fragmented documents with distinct origins, but rather as a succession of updated layers coming from a single source, is that correct?

JDC—Well, yes. That's simply mainstream thinking, but it's crucial for understanding the Gospels because if you simply knew there were four versions in there, and you've never read them, you could easily think of these like four witnesses in a court of law trying to tell exactly what happened as best they could remember and each of them doing their very best to be accurate—and if there's any difference, it is just memory, a mistake or something like that. But when you realize that Matthew and Luke have deliberately used Mark and changed Mark—and since we do still have Mark, you can watch it being done—you realize they're telling us the truth. They're writing gospel, not history. They're telling histories of history as good news and they feel much freer to adapt and interpret and change than you would in transcribing what I am saying now.

LR—With all that information coming from a single source, can we establish an analogy between the New Testament and a "snowball effect"—something that starts at one insignificant and mundane point becoming progressively larger and larger? If that's so, why must one rely on such an insignificant initial trend to inform us about a wider worldview of the cosmos?

JDC—Well, I don't know why. I think if you were just doing it in the pure imagination and saying: "Do you think a peasant from Galilee, from the village called Nazareth, could ever influence the world?" I would say, "No; come on! He doesn't even know how to speak Latin, for God's sake. He's not even literate." So for that to happen, I think you can see certain other things had to happen.

LR—But did Jesus really influence the world, or was it the followers and the interpreters of Jesus that influenced the world using his name?

JDC—You're quite right; if nothing had been written down, everything would have been forgotten. Let me give you a simple example: Supposing the followers of Jesus decided to stay in Galilee. When the war of 66 and 74 came, I think that will be the end of the Christian movement. But in the early 30s, they had already moved to Jerusalem—I think because they expected the second coming there—but Jerusalem is a pilgrim city in contact with all the other cities of the Mediterranean. I don't know whether that was design, genius, or providence, but all of the sudden, we know they're in Damascus, they're in Antioch, they're rolling. So it's not the snowball effect, and it's not actually that nothing could stop this movement. This movement could have died out quite easily, but it got into the bloodstream of the cities of the Roman Empire, so that if you're counting numbers—I'm making this up—let's say we agree there were 1,000 Christians by the year 100, the big question is not: "Are there 1,000 Christians in Galilee?" but "Are there 10 Christians in each of a hundred Roman cities?"

LR—For you, what were the main motives for the survival of the early Christian movements?

JDC—Well, that would be the first one: The first one was the move to the cities, and Paul simply followed that by focusing on the capital cities of the Roman provinces. He doesn't simply work along the Roman road to stop at every town: He goes for Thessalonica, the capital of Macedonia, Corinth, the capital of Achaia. He goes for Ephesus, the capital of Asia, he's a capital-ist! [Laughs.] And that's very important because if you get the capitals, you will get the others cities and then, the countryside; that's a huge strategic decision. So, that's the first thing: to go urban. The second one, of course, is that Christians opened their mission to gentiles; they bring them in as full members. The third one would be, I think, the Roman wars: If there hadn't been those two huge wars which destroyed the temple and devastated the Jewish homeland, we really don't know what would have happened if in the year 150 the Sadducees were still running the temple, offering sacrifices and everything was going on fine. The Pharisees, the Essenes, and the Christians might have got together and created a common anti-Sadduceean front. We really don't know, we really don't have a clue of what would have happened. So, cities, gentiles, wars, and a final thing: What if the Romans had decided in the year 64—when Nero persecuted Christians—the following: "Okay! We've had enough of you guys. Every time we keep running into you, you're causing trouble. You're now a forbidden religion." In other words, genocide instead of martyrdom. I don't think Christianity would have survived that. It survived precisely because the Romans did exactly what they should not have done: They created martyrs.

LR—So it is as Tertullian said: "The blood of the martyrs is the seed of the Church"?

JDC—Yes, but notice that this is not yet genocide. If the Romans had said, "Being Christian is a crime in and of itself, you don't have to prove wrongdoing," I don't think the Christians would have survived something like that. That's a very different thing from what the Romans actually did.

LR—All that capacity to spread the message of Christianity and to thrive seems to denote a missionary vocation that is expressed by "the Great Commission" in Matthew 28; that, however, seems to be contradicted by the teachings of Jesus in the same Gospel—Matthew 15:24. What are the most reliable accounts of Jesus' teachings about missionary activity? Was Jesus thinking globally or locally?

JDC—Well, he was thinking locally with a global message—to be honest with you. The Jewish tradition of the prophets has always been local and global. Let me put it this way: It was a global vision operating locally; it didn't simply say, "Well, we're supposed to live a just life and the rest of the world can do whatever it wants." It pretty much said, "It's supposed to be a just world, and it certainly should be—at least in Israel."

LR—But wasn't Jesus sent only to "the lost sheep of Israel" (Matthew 15:24)?

JDC—Notice that you're using Matthew; you don't find anything like that in Mark. Matthew's understanding is that during the life of Jesus, the concentration was on the Jews, but that after the death of Jesus, it was to go global. So, there's a kind of a rhythm: Jews first, gentiles second in Matthew.

LR—In your opinion, how relevant is Paul's contribution to the thriving of Christianity?

JDC—In one sense, I think that the most important contribution of Paul was that he wrote! He actually wrote! He could have the most magnificent oral theology that you and I could ever imagine, but I think that he introduced something in Christianity which made it all of the sudden move into the big league: he *wrote.*

LR—Nevertheless, some scholars, even in the Jesus Seminar, question the authenticity of Paul's writings.

JDC—There's a pretty massive consensus among scholars that there are only seven authentic letters of Paul—and I agree completely with that: Romans, Galatians, First Thessalonians, First and Second Corinthians, Philippians, and Philemon. These are certainly authentic. From the other six, three of them are probably not authentic: Colossians, Ephesians, Second Thessalonians. The other three are certainly not authentic: Titus, First and Second Timothy. About these, there's a massive consensus that I think is right. What I would add to it is this: It's not simply that those are post-Pauline, are pseudo-Pauline—like, people writing in Paul's name; they are deliberately trying to deradicalize and sanitize Paul back into a more complacent vision with regard to social things—like slavery and patriarchy in the Roman world—so, they're almost anti-Pauline.

LR—In order to establish the historicity of those documents, scholars rely on criteria like religious dissimilarity, coherence, multiple attestation, etc. What if the main sources on which these criteria are applied have been corrupted or forged? Aren't we all mistaken in the sense that we might be deriving our religiosity from fake documents such as the Secret Gospel of Mark, for example?

JDC—As a historian, you have to lay out your evidence, what do you think comes from where, what do you think comes from Jesus, what do you think happens to it. I think we have certain trajectories that help you to see what's happening: It is not going from a violent Jesus and they're trying to quiet him down; it's going from a rather peaceful Jesus and they're trying to make him more punitive. So, like any historical data, I think you have to go over all of the stuff and make your decision, and that's why I insisted that you cannot separate history and faith and say, "Well, we got the Gospels and you just believe in them." That doesn't tell you anything—there are four of them. That's a warning: We probably have four interpretations.

LR—Was your personal religious faith based upon scripture, a reflection about the cosmos, or both of them?

JDC—I really think both of them. I think that if I was getting a totally different vision from just personal experience, there might be a disconnect, but if I look at human evolution—say, the last 6,000 years, since the Neolithic Revolution—I do see that violence has escalated to the point that endangers the world. That's also a message I get from within the Bible—which comprises its own violence, by the way. So, yes, I suppose if I were getting messages, it probably could be best described as a dialectic between experience and faith. I don't think you can simply operate by one alone. If somebody had a vision of Jesus and Jesus told him to go out and kill somebody—and I was convinced the person was absolutely sincere—I would simply call the police. I wouldn't say, "Well, it's faith and we just have to believe it." I would say, "No, I'm going to call the cops."

LR—In what conditions do you conceive yourself becoming an atheist—if that's in any way possible?

JDC—It wouldn't be possible because an atheist depends on the theist—linguistically. If somebody's definition of atheism depends on, say, the idea of God as a being out there, separate from the universe, who is controlling everything like a puppet master, well, that's not the way I imagine God at all. So if somebody, like Christopher Hitchens, rejects God on that basis, I just don't find him interesting. He has an antivision of something I don't even accept. If you take of all this literally, then, taking it anti-literally is just as silly.

LR—So, what do you think about these New Atheists like Hitchens, Dawkins, or Harris?

JDC—I think they're remarkably silly. Honestly! I mean—it's the only word I can use. I can't even read them because most of the time I say, "Yeah, yeah, sure. . . ." They're a reaction to the ascendancy of the right wing in this country where right-wing Christianity—literal Christianity—was given far more profile than it deserves. All of the sudden, people for whom all of this was just bunk, who would never have bothered refuting it, let alone discussing it, in the past, now say, "Wait a minute! There are people who believe that God has given this whole land to the Jews and we can't have peace in Palestine because God has forbidden it." So we now have an atheism that presumes, that depends on, a specific theism. But if you've never accepted that theism—which I never did—I don't find the atheism particularly interesting. It's like attacking trenches in a war after they have evacuated.

LR—Are you more "condescending" with a philosophically grounded atheism such as that proposed by philosophers like Anthony Flew or Michael Martin, for example?

JDC—No, because the issue for me is: I do not think that human beings can live without meaning. That's an historical statement; I don't need to dignify it by calling it a philosophical statement, it's just empirical. Human beings need meaning, and meaning seems to involve a chain of cause and effect: I do this because of that; okay, why do you do that? Because of this; and you keep getting deeper into people's motivation and intentionality. It doesn't seem to me that we can live the happy way that our household pets do—you know, waiting for the next meal!

LR—But can't you conceive meaning in a finite life? You've mentioned Bonhoeffer and he said that we should live like there is no God.

JDC—No, what I said is: "Atheism" for me would mean the state of being completely convinced that there was no meaning in this life—the state of being of a sociopath or a psychopath—with no reason to do this rather than do that. Let me repeat: Including people like Flew, the vision of God they're opposing is pretty much the literalistic Christian vision of God and that's why it is such an easy target. If you're talking about ultimate meaning, I can't imagine living without it. But if you would presume a different type of humanity, I suppose you could; if I could find it, I suppose it could be done.

LR—What do you think will be the future of Christian studies? Do you think there are ways to explore it even further, or do you think everything has been all dug up?

JDC—I think there are two things going on: materials and methods. Methods do keep changing, they really do. I see no reason why we won't get more materials, although realities like the fact that the Aswan High Dam is lifting the water table in Egypt and are making it less and less likely that we will find huge collections of documents that are uncontaminated—but that's simply an accidental thing. In theory, there's no reason we couldn't find other Nag Hammadi, Dead Sea Scrolls, and everything else, but it's getting trickier and trickier. In 1966 and 1967, I went all over Iraq and Iran. I'm trying to think what southern Iraq must look like now. In that time, the whole plane was littered with tells, you knew there were ruined cities there. Maybe they're all bomb craters now. So, I don't know what chances we have of discovering more materials, but there are also more methods—sociology, anthropology, archaeology—that do let us look at exactly the same things with different eyes.

LR—What line of investigation—or what investigators—are capturing your attention now?

JDC—I think what I'm mostly interested at the moment is following the line of the Jesus Seminar and talking to laypeople in this country. I'm least interested in doing biblical exegesis and just debating with my fellow scholars. That's great fun, but in the meanwhile, large numbers of people in this country are using the Bible as a basis of our foreign policy. I don't think we can simply go on chatting about the Bible as if it has nothing to do with our foreign policy. Now, it might well be the same in countries in Europe, I don't know about Portugal . . .

LR—Well, I don't think there are any problems with the Bible in Portugal because I doubt that even a small amount of my fellow countrymen have ever read it. By the way, I suppose the same happens in the United States.

JDC—You're right, they don't read it; they just shake their hands in the churches.

LR—But I think you have one thing we don't have here: You have spiritual religious leaders. We don't have that; people go to church if they want, but we don't have those media stars that make their radio and television appearances in the United States—like Billy Graham, Jimmy Swaggart, or Joel Osteen.

JDC—It may well be that, after the next election [2008]—if the Republican Party is beaten as badly as I hope it will be—they will be looking for a scapegoat; and the scapegoat they may well find is their right-wing religion.

LR—Since you've mentioned the Republican Party, it seems rather strange that a party that once had religious liberal ideals, and even deist or agnostic ideals—I'm remembering Abraham Lincoln and Robert Ingersoll, for example—has now chosen a religious hard-line philosophy. How to explain that?

JDC—Well, I think what happened was it began to realize that there was a huge constituency out there, and if you talked the right language and used the right terms they would buy it. So you had to mention God quite often in your speech, you had to talk about biblical terms, and nobody would question.

LR—What do you think about the pervasiveness of religion in the political discourse?

JDC—I think what we have to learn to do, actually, is to figure a dialectic between religion and politics—I'm using politics now in the best sense; not partisan politics but politics in its original meaning: how the city should be run.

LR—Is there critical thinking to do that?

JDC—I think that's what we're going to have to learn. Most people learn this when they're young and then everything else grows up and they don't grow up in this one. But I don't think for a second that we're going to be able to handle Islam with secularism. I think that's the great thing that we have learned, that the delusion at the end of the 19th century, the 20th century, that religion was a personal matter, sort of like hairstyle, that it had nothing to do with economics, politics, or society; I think that was a terrible delusion. It's like with feminism; we now have to figure out how the two sexes negotiate from equal points of view.

LR—When we have radicalization in religious discourse, each part seems to barricade itself in a harsher and more inflexible religious worldview—even talking with one another. This can reinforce the fundamentalism.

JDC—Yes, and that's what's really up for discussion in this country for the moment. If we're going back to the point when we say, "Okay, religion is just a private matter and it's of no social concern," I think that's very naïve. I think there's an obvious need for vision, for the future; most of the problems that we're facing now are global problems and they really need a vision of some type. It's not enough just to react to this and that. You can't just react to global warming and say, "We will do this." You need to have a total vision for the world, and whether we like it or not, religion supplies total visions for the world—some of them good, some of them bad. So we're going to have a dialectic in which religion has to be able to speak in the public square, but with language that other people can understand. If I'm talking in the public square about Jesus, I don't talk about Jesus: I will talk about justice, or I will talk about violence or nonviolence. I don't have to use the name at all. If somebody asks, "Where did you get that from?," I have no prob lem with saying where I got it from.

LR—Concerning violence, my last question: Have you ever received death threats for belonging to the Jesus Seminar? Have you been harassed in any way by fundamentalists because of the opinions you have concerning Jesus? [Laughs.]

JDC—No, no, not at all! [Laughs.] Nothing like that at all. Not even anything like demonstrations or anything like that. I talk over half the weekends in the year in churches. From the middle of September to the middle of December this year, every single weekend—by weekend I mean from Friday to Sunday—I'll be talking in churches. You can prob ably see it on my Web site, it has my schedule from this year onward. I talk in churches all the time, which means there's a huge number of people, not all churches, not all denominations, but in every denomina tion, people who are quite willing to listen to this. That's the most hopeful thing we ought to be doing, scholars not simply talking to scholars but with laypeople too.

Daniel Dennett

Daniel Dennett (born 1942 in Boston, Massachusetts) is a prominent U.S. philosopher whose research centers on philosophy of mind, philosophy of science, and philosophy of biology, particularly as those fields relate to evolutionary biology and cognitive science. He is currently the codirector of the Center for Cognitive Studies and the Austin B. Fletcher Professor of Philosophy at Tufts University. Dennett is also a noted atheist and advocate of the Brights movement. His first book, *Content and Consciousness*, appeared in 1969, followed by *Brainstorms* (1978); *Elbow Room* (1984); *The Intentional Stance* (1987); *Consciousness Explained* (1991); *Darwin's Dangerous Idea* (1995); *Kinds of Minds* (1996); *Brainchildren, A Collection of Essays 1984–1996* (1998); *Sweet Dreams, Philosophical Obstacles to a Science of Consciousness* (2005); and *Breaking the Spell* (2006).

Luís Rodrigues—In your book *Breaking the Spell* you consider religion as a "natural phenomenon." Philosophically speaking, can there be types of phenomena other than "natural" ones? Establishing the dichotomy between natural/supernatural, aren't you conceiving the possibility of a supernatural realm existence?

Daniel Dennett—The only way to provide grounds for believing in supernatural phenomena would be by trying to explain the phenomena as natural phenomena and failing utterly. Of course, there would be the very real prospect that some unimagined naturalistic explanation had been overlooked, but by the time we've resorted to positing radical new laws of physics which we don't understand, we're conceding that the phenomenon is supernatural (by our existing standards of what is natural). It is not hard to describe imaginary trains of events that would convince most naturalists that there were some supernatural events (miracles).

LR—But does atheism necessarily entail an adherence to physicalism (a philosophical view defending that everything can be reduced to a physical/natural explanation)? If not, how can other philosophical views be compatible with an atheist worldview?

DD—Certainly atheism is compatible with nonphysicalist views. For instance, David Chalmers is a well-known dualist, and I am quite sure he is an atheist, though I've never asked him.

LR—When the Vatican, through the Pontifical Academy of Sciences, says it "promotes the progress of the mathematical, physical, and natural sciences and the study of epistemological problems related thereto," how do you see this attempt by religious institutions to "promote science"? Is it real? Is it productive? Is it necessary?

DD—I think the Vatican has genuinely promoted science in a number of regards. So have tobacco companies, for instance. But when supporters of science have an agenda that rules out the widespread publication of certain answers to the questions being raised, you have to be skeptical. Pope John Paul II said evolution is a fact, not just a theory—but then he spoiled the effect by explicitly exempting the mind (soul) of *Homo sapiens*. That is like saying that levitators are exempt from the law of gravity.

LR—Do you think Intelligent Design (a "made in the USA" theory), has the conditions to be exported worldwide and become a part of Catholic doctrine?

DD—I certainly hope not, since it is transparently dishonest, intellectually. I used to think that ID was only an American problem, but recently they have been exporting it rather effectively. The silver lining on this cloud is perhaps that Europe will be less scornful of American credulity when they encounter it among their own citizens.

LR—With the tremendous success of self-help books, the spreading of sects, cults, and a myriad of superstitions related with ancient and recent ideas (astrology, quantum healing, etc.), supernaturalism is on the rise. How can dialogue be established with the growing number of people who wish to enter Plato's cave only to be entertained by the shadows of hope and delusion?

DD—I don't think these people want dialogue. That is, they aren't, as a rule, prepared to do some hard work to find common terms and understanding. Most supernaturalism is quite obviously just an excuse for *not* thinking carefully about one phenomenon or another. So trying for dialogue is often systematically fruitless.

LR—You have a book called *Darwin's Dangerous Idea*. After Darwin's dangerous idea (namely, natural selection), what other ideas and novelties coming out of biology (and also, philosophy) do you think can reinforce atheist arguments? And what ideas can jeopardize them?

DD—The tremendous success of naturalism, in all the sciences, not just biology, makes it an unrivaled foundation for all knowledge claims. Think of how our knowledge of astronomy and cosmology undermines traditional religious ideas. Would God have made billions and billions of galaxies with billions of stars and planets, just for the sake of a few tens of thousands of years of human experience? Our species is unlikely to be eternal, and even if we last for 10 million years more, this will be an insignificant eye blink of time on one tiny planet in one minor galaxy.

LR—Nevertheless, most human beings aren't willing to accept that there isn't a higher purpose in life, or a higher being, bigger than themselves. Where can you find the root and justifications to this unshakable need for "beyondness"? Will it forever be a human trait?

DD—"Bigger than themselves" is nicely ambiguous; I find higher purposes bigger than *my* self, but not bigger than the collective purposes of the best of humanity. We are not wrong to desire the existence of something more important than our own minor individual existences. The idea that this must be something supernatural is simply a mistake.

LR—What do you think prevents people all over the world from questioning their own religious beliefs, even in the face of the diversity of religions, spiritual cults, and philosophies that permeate each culture?

DD—I think a combination of a sense of loyalty, often buttressed by a concern for elders whose lives we don't want to blight with our "betrayal," plus a modesty about one's own powers of inquiry, are enough to make many, if not most, people deeply conservative about what they will profess in public about religion. Their private thoughts are another matter.

LR—Do you think it is preferable to have a society in which social peace is provided by religious bonhomie and unanimity, or a society where conflict is always rising due to the diversity of religious and irreligious points of view?

DD—This is a good question, to which I don't have a confident answer. Might it be better to cloud our vision and live in a comforting stew of hypocrisy and obfuscation, if that way we can avoid emotionally draining conflicts? Maybe it would be! It depends, I guess, on how large a price we pay for our insincere lip service. That is hard to measure.

LR—When some people talk about the deity today, they no longer talk about a deity physically intervening in the world—like the ancient gods of old who intervened in the growing of crops, in child-bearing, in health issues, in battles, etc. The "topology" of the divine seems to reside, today, in the inner self (one of the arguments used is that "Hell is not a place, but a state of mind in which we live when we refuse God or practice evil deeds"). Is this "retreat" of God (and gods), from the objective natural world to the subjective inner world of the self, a more challenging aspect for atheism to deal with? I mean, with no way of confirming or refuting the physical presence and existence of God (since he "lives" inside us), isn't the debate between the theist and the atheist jeopardized by subjectivity? How does one overcome this difficulty?

DD—Maybe, as the concept of God is further eroded in this way, the whole issue of the existence or nonexistence of God will have all the interest and importance drained from it. I certainly spend very little time in *Breaking the Spell* even considering the evidence and argument one way or the other.

LR—How do you think the "New Atheism" movement will evolve, namely in Europe?

DD—I have no idea. It is already possible to be elected to high office in Europe without declaring one's "faith in God." There may be no need for a New Atheist movement in Europe. I'd certainly prefer not to have to talk about atheism for the rest of my days! (Like talking about ESP or tarot cards.)

LR—Can you recommend a small bibliography for the religious neophyte who's interested in knowing more about this "strange idea of atheism"?

DD—Certainly start by reading the other "horsemen of the Apocalypse"— Richard Dawkins, *The God Delusion*, Christopher Hitchens, *God Is Not Great*, and Sam Harris, *The End of Faith* and *Letter to a Christian Nation*.

LR—Most people try to be believers due to their fear of death and the wish to live forever. How do you deal with the expectation of death and the possibility of living forever?

DD—Forever is a long time! I wouldn't want to live forever, and the fact that an eternity with no *me* in it will start in a few decades (or sooner) is no more troubling to me than the fact that an eternity with no *me* in it preceded my birth in 1942.

David Deutsch

David Elieser Deutsch (born 1953 in Haifa, Israel) is a physicist at the University of Oxford. He is a visiting professor in the Department of Atomic and Laser Physics at the Centre for Quantum Computation, Clarendon Laboratory. He pioneered the field of the quantum theory of computation by being the first person to formulate a specifically quantum computational algorithm, and he is a proponent of the many-worlds interpretation of quantum mechanics as a possible physical definition of reality in coherence to the development and perception of the universe(s) and the human being. Politically, Deutsch is known to be sympathetic to libertarianism and was a founder, along with Sarah Fitz-Claridge and Kolya Wolf, of the Taking Children Seriously movement. He is also agnostic. He was awarded the Dirac Prize of the Institute of Physics in 1998 and the Edge of Computation Science Prize in 2005. His book *The Fabric of Reality* (1997) was shortlisted for the Rhone-Poulenc Science Book Award in 1998. He is also the author of *The Beginning of Infinity* (forthcoming).

Luís Rodrigues—What is your response to theists who say that the fine-tuning of the universe for human life could only be the work of a benevolent God?

David Deutsch—I think the fine-tuning is an interesting and not-yet-solved problem. But the trouble with trying to solve it by proposing that an intelligent being caused it is that it just makes the problem worse because we then have to ask: What caused that being to come into existence? You know, this is an old counter-argument to the argument from design, namely that if the solution to the argument from design is that God designed the universe, then we have exactly the same problem with God as we have with the universe: God is also then a complex entity whose attributes are unexplained. I call this an unsolved problem because I think that trying to solve it through things like the anthropic principle has basically the same problem—although it doesn't look as though it does. It cannot be the case that the only explanation for fine tuning is that all values of all parameters exist; that is actually a flawed hypothesis. My guess is that there are different universes with different laws of physics, but that is not the explanation for fine-tuning.

LR—You can conceive that in different universes there may be no fine tuning?

DD—Yes, I can certainly conceive that. What I can't conceive, though, is that God is the sole explanation for the fine-tuning in our universe.

LR—The multiverse hypothesis is somehow connected with a notion of infinity. Can the Kalam cosmological argument undermine an atheistic conception of the universe? I mean, if you have an infinite number of universes, can an actual finite one exist?

DD—First of all, I don't think any unsolved problem undermines a rational view of the universe, because if it did, you would be saying that "unless we know everything, we must accept the supernatural"—and that's silly. That's one issue that you raised. As for the infinite, I think people make too much about the infinite. One thing to bear in mind is that the "physically infinite" is a different concept from "mathematically infinite." If you just for simplicity imagine that the classical laws of physics are true for a moment, it's then the case that if I walk across the room, I've passed through an infinite number of points. The ancient Greek philosopher Zeno was actually very worried by this; in fact, a lot of philosophers have been worried by this sort of thing ever since, because they think, "Well, in order to get across the room you have to do an infinite number of things, but a physically realized infinity is impossible, and therefore you can't walk across the room—in fact, you can't walk a millimeter." This is a mistake. This is simply confusing mathematical infinity (which is something like the number of points in a continuous line) with the physical infinite (which even a physical infinity arguably also can exist); a room that simply has a continuum in it is not physically infinite in any important way.

LR—Theists refer to mathematical infinity to justify the theories that cannot be justified in physical terms?

DD—Yes, I think so. In any case, even if there were a problem with infinity, appealing to the supernatural again wouldn't solve it because we would then have to try to understand an infinite being instead of an infinite universe—which is just that little bit harder, not easier.

LR—Some trends of religious and spiritual thinking tend to associate the deity with concepts of cosmic ordinance and mathematical regularity. What do you think about this idea of a deity transformed into a "scientific metaphor," one that justifies an apparently regular universe?

DD—Arthur C. Clarke said that any sufficiently advanced technology looks like God. If one is willing to redefine God in terms of physical objects, like for instance Frank Tipler does in his *Omega Point* theory—an earlier example of this is Spinoza, who tried to redefine the universe as God—if one does that, then, trivially one can say that God exists because God is the universe and the universe exists. But the thing is that those concepts of God do not have the attributes that religious people want their God to have. Those things are not supernatural; those things are not transcendent, and those things are not explanations of inexplicable things. So, those things aren't the God that religious people are looking for.

LR—What is the physicist's explanation for miracles?

DD—As Hume said, there can't be such a thing as miracles, because everything is controlled by laws of physics—which is another way of saying that everything that happens is in principle comprehensible. Now, the reason we want to believe that is that as soon as you say that not everything that happens is in principle comprehensible, then you're allowing things that don't make sense into your worldview—and if you allow that, then you may as well allow anything. If you want to retain a disciplined respect for reason, then you can't allow inexplicable things and so, miracles would count as that. But miracles in the sense of very unlikely events—for instance if it turned out that the world narrowly escaped being hit by a comet a hundred years ago and we were very lucky—you could call that a miracle. But that's not a miracle in the religious sense because it is fully comprehensible; we know that it happened, why it happened, what the probability was, and so on.

LR—The miracle tends to be seen at a personal level rather than at a cosmic scale.

DD—Let's say I'm in an airplane crash and I'm the only survivor, then I might say, in informal language, "Oh! It's a miracle that I escaped!" But actually, that's no miracle at all; that's not even an unlikely thing, because whoever escaped, if one person in a hundred escaped from the plane crash, they would be saying, "It's a miracle!" But if it was likely that one person out of a hundred would escape, then it wouldn't be a miracle at all.

LR—Looking at the "quantum world," is it still feasible to speak of materialism in the common sense of the word? What prevents a theist from refuting materialism based upon the difficulties concerning the ambiguous definition of "matter"?

DD—I'm not sure which difficulties you mean. I think a lot of the reputation of quantum theory as being slightly mystical, or even slightly mysterious, is caused by wrong interpretations that unfortunately are still prevalent; basically the attempt to deny that there are parallel universes has unfortunately led physicists into some very, very bad philosophy—including giving credence to all sorts of irrationality. But if you adopt what I think is the rational view of quantum mechanics (which is the parallel universes view) then matter, although it behaves in an unfamiliar way, still behaves in a completely materialistic way. It might be odd and unfamiliar to us to think of a particle being in more than one place at the same time and being in different universes and so on, but that is still fully material. The multiverse is still a fully material entity—even though it's an unfamiliar one. So, I don't think there are those difficulties and therefore I don't think there's reason to say that the materialistic worldview is wrong because of quantum mechanics—quite the contrary.

LR—But by opening a door allowing the theory of a multiverse, isn't it possible that we could see God as an entity outside our universe? So, could a deity control our universe from another universe—or universes?

DD—Our whole reason for believing that there are other universes is the laws of quantum mechanics and the experiments that corroborate them. So, if you wanted to postulate that there's a God in another universe that is controlling our universe, then you would have to postulate that the laws of quantum mechanics as we know them are being violated because the actual laws of quantum mechanics only allow certain very limited influence of one universe and another—certainly nothing that could amount to control, let alone supernatural control. So, the very theory that leads us to believe in parallel universes in the first place rules out that there could be an entity in one universe controlling stuff in another universe.

LR—Do you think it's impossible to establish a connection between different universes? Is it possible that, some day, a new theory or a new technology would allow that?

DD—It's very difficult to say what a "future theory" might say but, if we understand the multiverse in the best way that we can today, then there are very limited ways in which the different universes affect each other. The most that we could reason about them would be via something like the anthropic principle; as I said, I don't think that the anthropic principle by itself is enough to explain anything, but fortunately in quantum mechanics, we do have some slight effects of universes on each other—which are interference effects—and those provide, in my opinion, unanswerable evidence that those universes exist but they don't allow things like control. Once you start asking: "What if quantum mechanics is wrong?" then again, you're opening the door to absolutely anything. Then you don't need quantum mechanics. You could say, "What if the whole universe is a dream?"

LR—What is your opinion about a theistic vision of string theory? Let's imagine the hypothesis that our universe is a brain created by an intelligent supreme being living in the bulk space, a space outside any brains . . .

DD—String theory isn't really essential to the vision you've just described. What's essential there is that there is an outside of physical reality in which there is a complex being. If that were so, then a rational worldview would require a theory of how that being works in terms of something, some kind of explanation of it, in the same sense that we have an explanation of things like matter, in terms of atoms, subatomic particles, an explanation of life in terms of evolution, and so on. So, in the same way we would need an explanation of this supernatural entity outside the multiverse or whatever, in terms of something by which it can be understood. If the reply by the people who postulate this entity is, "Well, that entity can't be understood," then we don't need the entity. Like I said, we don't have to go to such lengths to adopt an irrational view if that's what we want to do. We can just say, "Nothing exists except my dream." Once you stop using reason as a criterion—and that implies using science as a criterion for what physically exists—then you may as well postulate anything.

LR—What kind of scientific works now in progress do you think are most capable of undermining a theistic conception of the universe, reinforcing the notion that science is permanently removing God from the picture—the well-known idea that God only serves to justify the gaps in scientific knowledge?

DD—There will always be gaps. I don't believe that the scientific project can ever be completed—by the way, it would be pretty much a disaster if it were. So, I think there will always be gaps. Therefore, it's impossible for science to rule out a God of the gaps. But then, I think that the issue of whether God does or doesn't exist is a philosophical issue, not a scientific one. I'm opposed to trying to use science to resolve philosophical issues—for example, moral issues. What science does is give facts about which we can, for instance, moralize. It can provide facts about which philosophical, metaphysical theories can be formulated.

LR—But, for example, Darwin has provided some answers about the origin of human life that prior to him, only religion was authorized to provide. Doesn't physics have the equivalent of Darwin?

DD—It could happen that, for instance, a multiverse view explains the numerical coincidences; definitely hasn't happened yet, but that could happen. If it did, there would still be gaps, and so the theists—the argument for design—would then change to "Well, yes, but why is the universe constructed in such a way that there are many universes in some of which intelligent life arises?," because it could have been constructed in such a way that there were only three universes and in none of them life arose. So, why was it done one way rather than another? Science would have no explanation for that at that point and so a theist could always say, "Well, that was done by God." I think that the answer to that is not so much to say, "Hey! Look how much of the gaps of previous generations we have now closed," because that's not really a very convincing argument. That's like guilt by association. What we ought to do is first of all say, "The trouble is that the God hypothesis doesn't fill the gap." That's the first thing, and secondly, it's the argument by success: the worldview of science and reason is simply successful not just in the sense of discovering new theories, but it's successful in the sense of it being a good way to be. I think that is the ground on which, in real life, people decide to be that way rather than decide to be the religious way.

LR—Some have the opinion that science is reaching its limit—mainly due to general difficulties posed by the impossibility of overcoming certain physical and technological boundaries. Do you corroborate a pessimistic vision for science or do you believe in an indefinite progress for scientific research and development?

DD—I think that scientific progress is going to go on forever, but that's a philosophical view that I can't represent as my professional opinion. What I can tell you as my professional opinion is that the idea that science, especially fundamental science, fundamental physics, are somehow reaching the end—either because everything is nearly known or because everything from now on is going to be unknowable—has much less evidence to support it than ever before in the whole history of science. John Horgan wrote a book just before the year 2000 called *The End of Science* in which he tried to argue that everything fundamental has already been discovered and that all that remains now is to investigate things like complexity and to find details. He himself pointed out that this was also said in the late 19th century by the great physicist Michelson—the one with the Michelson-Morley experiment. He said that very thing in the end of the 19th century and Horgan said, just because Michelson was wrong at the end of the 19th century doesn't mean that I'm wrong in the end of the 20th century. The funny thing is that there is overwhelmingly more evidence now that we have only just begun to scratch the surface of fundamental physics and science in general than there was in the end of the 19th century. Now, for the first time in the history of physics, we know from our two deepest theories—namely, quantum physics and general relativity—that we have a fundamental discovery yet to make because the two of them conflict in a profound way; not just in a trivial way but in a way where it is obvious, at least to me, that a fundamental new set of concepts is needed to resolve the conflict between them and that the existing way of doing physics won't solve the problem. Science itself is telling us— unlike at the end of the 19th century, where reasonable people might believe that Newton's laws plus Maxwell's equations and so on were already 99 percent of everything there was to be known—that there is no such appearance. It really does look as though we're scratching the surface. I think that is the case—quite apart from the philosophical issue that, even when we discover this, we'll still have an infinite way to go.

LR—Isn't a "theory of everything" the worst nightmare of a scientist?

DD—Yes—if it really were the theory of everything, that would mean that everything that there was to be discovered, had been discovered; that would mean that the whole basis of science—an open human activity, which for instance entails tolerance and whose values have informed Western values in general—that whole enterprise no longer has a justification. The same would be true of politics. If I express that sentiment in terms of political philosophy instead, if the problem of how to make a good society was solved, then all the arguments for tolerance would go away. We would be in exactly the situation that the utopians think they are in, and utopianism always leads to tyranny, intolerance, violence. There is nothing so conducive to authoritarianism as an authority about knowledge.

LR—An authority about knowledge also comes from religious literature. Concerning other kinds of literature, what is your opinion about the rational and mathematical justifications for the existence of God present in some works produced by theologians with a scientific background—Stanley Jaki, for example?

Are they in any way refuting an atheistic conception of the universe by bringing God into the scientific field?

DD—I haven't read Jaki, I'm afraid, nor have I read John Polkinghorne. I think the closest that I've come to reading something in favor of God or religion from a reputable scientist is the work of Don Page. Don Page is someone whom I greatly respect as a physicist and when he writes about religion, he does not write nonsense. But I think what he and the other scientists I've seen from time to time who don't write nonsense on this subject—what they're really trying to do is establish a rational place for religion within philosophy, not within science. They are trying to show that existing scientific knowledge doesn't rule out their philosophical conception of religion. I think they're making a mistake, but it's not a scientific mistake, it's not a mistake that science—or even the scientific worldview—can rule out. I think, basically, it has to be addressed on philosophical grounds, really, I suppose, on the same grounds that I've been mentioning throughout this interview, which is that even in philosophy, postulating the supernatural doesn't solve the problem it purports to solve. It only transfers it to a place where the religious person hopes criticism can be excluded. But, in philosophy, like in science, if you postulate a place where criticism is excluded, you don't need to go to those enormous lengths. You can just believe anything you like.

LR—So, theists are using a kind of "science of the gaps" for their theology?

DD—One can put it that way.

LR—Do you envisage a bright future for human civilization in the cosmos or do you think we are condemned to be nothing more than a little temporal spark of life and intelligence in a vast hostile environment destined to vanish in the "heat-death" of the universe?

DD—I envisage humanity—or at least, thinking beings—basically taking over the universe and becoming the main content of the universe in the long run. Whether that's the human race or not depends on decisions that we make. I believe that we're not going to be so stupid as to wipe ourselves out. Martin Rees recently wrote a book in which he said that he thought that civilization has only a 50 percent chance of surviving the 21st century. First of all, I think he's too pessimistic; certainly there is a chance that civilization could destroy itself, but I think it won't. But more importantly, I think that probability is the wrong category in which to discuss this issue because as soon as you say that something has a probability, you're saying that it is independent of our decisions; you're saying that what we choose doesn't affect things. It's like a coin toss with a 50/50 probability: What you mean by that is that no matter what you do, no matter how hard you wish or whatever measures you take, provided you leave the coin alone, provided you follow the rules of the coin toss, you can't change it. And similarly with roulette; so long as you follow the rules of roulette, nothing you can do can change the probabilities of the outcomes. With things like "destroying civilization," it's the other way around: Here, so long as we follow the rules of physics, it's not the case that the outcome is independent of our decisions. Quite the contrary. The outcome depends 100 percent on our decisions. Therefore, it's a category error to speak about such things in terms of probability.

LR—But isn't it a little bit disappointing to look at the world and realize that a binding "universal project" of science, exploration of the universe, and so on, doesn't exist? It seems that only political conflicts between nations, environmental degradation, starvation in poor countries, and religious intolerance prevail.

DD—Well—Adam Smith said there is much ruin in the nation [laughs]; there is much ruin in the world, but I think there is no question . . . I seem to be quoting a lot of people today [laughs] but, quoting Karl Popper, he said that there's no question that what you might call the "Atlantic community" or the "Western world" is the best society that has ever existed. It's considerably better today than it was even 50 years ago. So, it's the best that has ever existed but on the other hand, it is full of appalling irrationality, violence, tyranny, and potential for disaster, but less so than ever before. We have more of the means than ever before to put ourselves on the path to infinity. My next book is called *The Beginning of Infinity*; "the beginning of infinity" refers to about a dozen different things, which all relate to each other.

LR—It's a very optimistic book I see [laughs].

DD—Indeed, indeed.

LR—With the Large Hadron Collider experiment, everybody's talking about the hypothetical Higgs boson particle—the so-called God particle. What's so important about this experiment—and especially about this particle? What does it have to do with God?

DD—Nothing, I'm afraid. Or rather, no more than the laws of physics in general do. It's a very interesting experiment, for physicists. But when it is represented as being about to reveal something exceptionally deep—or even ultimate—about nature, that is, in my opinion, largely hype. Nor, consequently, is it of much philosophical significance.

LR—What have you to say to all those opposed to scientific progress with the argument: "We must stop playing God with dangerous scientific experiments; the Babel Tower story in the Old Testament teaches us not to be too arrogant about our knowledge"?

DD—If I were a religious person, I would be shocked at the arrogance—or even blasphemy—of likening such puny tinkering as the Large Hadron Collider, or our DNA technology, etc., to the powers and acts of God himself. Furthermore, religious or not, I believe that humans have a moral duty to improve the world, and that this can be achieved by no other means than through reason and science, which in turn requires experiments.

LR—Do you think we still have time to develop a "universal project," or is the human race contributing to accelerate dysfunctions on a planetary scale that may be too late to stop—for example, global warming?

DD—I think global warming doesn't have the potential to halt civilization; at worst, it will have some economic cost and cause some human suffering, but I don't think it has the potential to put the—as you called it—the "universal project" at risk. I gave a talk at the TEDGlobal conference in 2005. There, I say that the global warming thing—I don't like the prevailing attitude toward it. I think we ought to be spending much more effort at undoing the harm than at trying to prevent the harm in the first place. I think that the reason that we're trying to prevent it has more to do with some kind of pseudo-religious morality that has become popular maybe as religion has declined, that it's really our fault and that we should be punished and therefore, anything we do to try and fix that is trying to evade our supernaturally ordained punishment. I don't think there's a rational reason for putting 99 percent of the effort into prevention, as we are doing. But I'm glad to see that since I gave that talk, quite a number of other people have taken up the same theme; so, maybe we'll do the rational thing after all. But even if we don't, I think that global warming is not the kind of catastrophe that can stop civilization progressing.

LR—But doesn't that discourse remove responsibility from the back of politicians, allowing, for example, the continuous prevalence of lobbies backed by the oil industry and others?

DD—Our political system is flawed in various ways, but like I said before, it's still the best political system that's ever existed. Although it has a lot of friction in it—which can prevent good ideas from being implemented until after a lot of harm has been done—it's still the case that after a lot of harm has been done, we do have the means to implement the better policies. We try all the wrong things and then we switch to the right thing and that will get us through. The only thing that could stop us is some catastrophe of the kind of magnitude that would actually destroy civilization; in other words, the kind of magnitude that would destroy these means that we have of improving policies. If they were to destroy the political culture of the West, or destroy the scientific community, then we would be in for either extinction or a new dark age at least.

LR—Do you think scientists are committed to publicize this enlightenment project of clarification, purging wrong concepts and ideas about the world that are used, for instance, by religious fundamentalists?

DD—They are not committed to it. Scientists have all sorts of views, most of which I disagree with, many of which I consider disastrous, and the only good thing I can say about it is: again, this is better than it's ever been before. The enlightenment was never a majority opinion in the world, or in the West, or among scientists: It has succeeded and survived because it is true, not because it has ever had popular support, or majority support, or big battalions on its side, or anything like that. It's only because it's true. Whether you're a capitalist, a communist, or a fundamentalist, if you want to build a suspension bridge, you must use Newton's laws. And a similar thing is true about science in general: Whatever it is you want—even if it is something horrible like better weapons or instruments of torture—in the long run you need science, otherwise your project will fail. Science needs tolerance and openness to new ideas, openness to change and rationality; those things are moral values entailed by science.

LR—But we saw that, in the Nazi experiment for example, one thing was not attached to another: We had an enlightened European country producing science for an evil purpose.

DD—Yes, and that was a terrible disaster which lasted only a couple of decades, after which it was wiped out. We also had the communist experiment, which lasted a few more decades and was then wiped out in a completely different way. These things, if they had succeeded in conquering the world, then they might have prevented the universal project. But as it was, they only succeeded in causing a lot of suffering; They didn't actually impede the long-run outcome.

LR—Don't you think some messianic movements are recurrent? For example, in the United States we are now witnessing an increasing fervor around religious beliefs: lots of people believe in the Rapture, no president is elected if he or she does not profess a religious creed, and so on.

DD—My view about American religion is that—this may be just my optimism—I really don't take it seriously. I think that what is happening in America is actually much more rational than it looks to us, Europeans. When Americans are asked questions like: "Do you believe in God? Do you believe in angels? Do you believe in the devil?," the reason that they answer "yes" is not because they have an especially supernaturally based worldview; it is because they interpret the question in a moral/philosophical context. When someone says, "Do you believe in God?," what they hear is the question, "Do you believe in right and wrong?" I think that when they answer "yes," they're answering that question. I think most public atheists concede too much to the religious point of view; they have far too much in common with it, to such an extent that I sometimes think that atheism, as it is usually practiced, is actually just a branch of Christianity. Most of the public atheists collaborate with religious people in propagating the idea that an objective conception of right and wrong is only possible on the basis of God or the supernatural. The only difference between them in that respect is that the religious people then conclude they must have God regardless of reason and the atheists conclude they must reject morality regardless of reason.

LR—Do you think these public atheists are fueling a dualism of opposition between the supernaturalist worldview and a naturalist one?

DD—I'm not sure whether they are fueling it by agreeing with it, but I think that they are agreeing with it, and I think that's wrong. I think this is possibly a reason that a lot of the well-meaning people are resisting becoming atheists.

LR—In your opinion, what would be the most constructive attitude for an atheist in the public sphere? How to dialogue with religious people, especially if some of them don't want to? What do you think would be the most constructive way?

DD—Well, I don't know. But my general view about "dialogue with bad theories" is that—as you say—first of all, one should have a dialogue with people who want one. But, more than that, I think the way you persuade somebody is not by proving them wrong—it is by succeeding in your way of doing things. Like I said, the reason that the enlightenment has survived, the reason that the scientific worldview has survived—despite hardly anyone ever having been passionate in favor of it, and a lot of people having been passionate against it—is that it is a good way to be. It has succeeded on its own terms and maybe, ultimately, ideas are judged in their own terms. So, I think scientists, scientifically-minded people, atheists, should make progress, not in atheism but in whatever it is they're doing: building quantum computers, writing novels, doing science, whatever. People then can see that's a good way to be, whereas people who deny this are constantly in the position of having to dig their heels in, having to make up silly arguments to maintain their position, having to deny obvious facts, having to force their children to do things that they don't want to do. Those things aren't nice ways to be; people only do them because they feel they have no option.

LR—It can be counter-productive, then, to ridicule believers.

DD—I think it depends on the context. There is also the fact that young people who are rebelling against religion for the first time, they may feel really bad about what they're doing, and if they see religion being successfully ridiculed, it might help them to feel good about it. But I think one has to be careful in what the ridicule is supposed to do; ridicule is not an argument. So, to use ridicule as an argument must be counter-productive because it isn't an argument, it's an invalid argument.

LR—Now a question on a personal level: Facing mortality, don't you get "depressed" by thinking that you will miss large amounts of discoveries and events that will happen after your death?

DD—Well, I don't "literally" get depressed by it—in the sense that I don't have a reduction of serotonin levels in my brain by thinking about it. I do regret that that may happen, although you never know—maybe it won't happen! There are medical improvements happening all the time, there are various scientists who are trying to extend the human lifetime. Some people say that the only possible stance for a rational person is to work on those technologies, which is a bit like Pascal's Wager but in an atheistic setting: If you really believe atheism, then you would be doing nothing except research into longevity [laughs]. I have to say I don't have much of a defense against people who tell me I should be doing that except to say I rather spend my life somehow doing something that I enjoy—namely physics and trying to understand those deep issues—and I don't think I would enjoy biochemical research, but maybe that's foolish of me.

LR—So, maybe one of the goals of an atheistic philosophy would be the search for immortality on a biological level.

DD—But certainly that's a worthy and desirable thing to do; clearly biologically immortality will be achieved in the next 500 years, let's say; it's just an engineering problem. In the long run, the argument for religion based on death will also go away, and since it will go away in the long run, it can't be valid in the short run either.

LR—How can it be possible to manage a planet with the prospect of immortality for all human beings?

DD—Oh! That's not a problem. This is the ultimate resource issue you're talking about here. The ultimate resource is creativity. There's no limit to how much control we can exert over the physical world given that we have the creativity needed to solve the problems that will come up. If we stop solving problems at any point, we're doomed. If we had stopped solving them a hundred years ago, we would be doomed then; if we stop solving them now, we're now doomed. But if we don't stop solving them, then there's no way we can be doomed because there isn't any boundary on the amount of knowledge that can be created.

LR—You think that the best solution for those who believe now in such optimistic prospects of science is to rent a cryogenic chamber? [Laughs.]

DD—That's for each person to decide for themselves [laughs]. No, my argument was a bit different; my argument was designed to refute the argument that God must exist because otherwise there would be no consolation for death. My refutation of that argument is as follows: Let's go forward 500 years to when there is no death. Then, that argument would not be true then. The argument that "there must be a God because of that" would then be false. But if there isn't a God 500 years from now, then there still isn't a God today.

LR—Then, God is just a matter of time . . .

DD—Belief in God would then be a matter of time. If a rational person knows what the belief is going to be in 500 years time, he adopts it.

Dinesh D'Souza

Dinesh D'Souza was born in 1961 in Mumbai, India, and graduated from Dartmouth College in 1983. He served as a policy analyst in the Ronald Reagan administration, as the John M. Olin Fellow at the American Enterprise Institute, and as the Karen Rishwain Fellow at the Hoover Institution at Stanford University. Referred to by the *New York Times Magazine* as one of America's most influential conservative thinkers, his books include *What's So Great About Christianity* (2007); *Illiberal Education, The Politics of Race and Sex on Campus* (1991); *The End of Racism* (1995); *What's So Great About America* (2002); *Letters to a Young Conservative* (2002); and *The Enemy at Home, The Cultural Left and Its Responsibility for 9/11* (2007); His articles have appeared in major magazines and newspapers, and he is a frequent guest on network and cable news programs.

Luís Rodrigues—What led you to be a believer—mainly, a Catholic Christian believer?

Dinesh D'Souza—I was born in Bombay (now Mumbai), India. My family is from Goa—which was, until 1961, a Portuguese colony. The Portuguese missionaries converted my ancestors to Catholicism and so, I was raised as part of that Catholic minority within India. That was the origin of my religious beliefs.

LR—How does it feel to be a part of a religious minority? Have you felt any cultural clash?

DD—Well, India is predominantly a Hindu country with about 80 percent Hindus; the second largest group are the Muslims; Christianity is third, and there are some other small minorities as well (the Sikhs and so on). I think it was, perhaps, a little different being a Christian in

India because, on the one hand, it's a spiritual country—there's a lot of awareness about spiritual issues and the concept of transcendence seems to be part of the culture. On the other hand, I was raised Catholic at a time when there was tension between the Hindus and the Muslims; sometimes the Christians became caught in the middle—in the cross-fire, so to speak—but nevertheless I had a peaceful upbringing. I think, for India, that Christianity—at least, that which I was exposed to—was not very devout; it was mainly "social Christianity." I think I had a good sense of the social, political, and cultural benefits that the West—and specifically, the Portuguese—have brought to India, but I can't say I was a very devout Christian. When I went to college, here in the United States, I found my faith began to fall away a little bit because of the influence of secular education and secular culture.

LR—You talked about the conflict between Muslims and Hindus. Did you feel that religion was a part of the problem in that conflict?

DD—The Hindus and the Muslims have, by and large, gotten along pretty well in India for some centuries. That's particularly striking when you see that the Muslims came as conquerors—there were a succession of Muslim armies that came from Afghanistan, from Persian, the Arab countries and the Mongols established kingdoms in north India. But nevertheless, Hindus and Muslims have fought together to push the British out of India. A little before I was born—and when I was a child—there were pretty good relations between the Hindus and the Muslims. I think that has changed more recently. Part of it is because we're seeing a phase of militant Islam in our time—that has influenced Islam in India—and second, there have been some particular political clashes between the Hindus and the Muslims—over Kashmir, and so on—and that has aggravated the situation. I don't deny that Islamic radicals have been mobilized in the name of religion and sometimes do terrorism and other things in the name of religion. So, religion can be a force used for bad as well as for good.

LR—Is the existence of many religions, sects, and spiritual cults a powerful argument that all of them are untrustworthy? Who should one believe if there are so many to believe?

DD—I don't think so. The presence of different nationalities can be a source of conflict among people but doesn't prove that patriotism is a harmful or a bad emotion. The loyalty to your country seems natural, and in many cases, seems utterly appropriate as a gesture of gratitude for what your country has given you. At the same time, that feeling, interpreted the wrong way, can become chauvinism or nationalism and can lead you to look down on other people. Similarly, when it comes to religion, my thought about it is that God is invisible; since God is invisible, human understandings of God are going to differ (they differ partly because cultures are different). There's a Muslim scholar who once described the understanding of God as sort of different streams that are coming down a mountainside: Each is a human effort to apprehend God. It's the same source, the same God, but you shouldn't be surprised that the understandings differ. They don't differ as much as people sometimes assume, by the way. If you look at Judaism, Christianity, and Islam, there are huge similarities among those. I just completed a study of life after death and, even though there are differences in the way, for example, that Hindus and Christians understand life after death, to me it's very interesting that all these different cultures (even those that have not been in contact with one another), over a very long period of time, would affirm something jointly that is not obvious to our senses. I'm not surprised that different cultures believe in rocks or trees, because you can look outside the window and you see them. But why would all these cultures, collectively, affirm that this life is not the only life? People die and they don't seem to come back. So it's very interesting that you have this universal religious affirmation of life after death. It almost seems like that must be something that is built into human nature; otherwise, why would it have independently developed?

LR—That takes us to the way different religions deal with the unknown. In that regard, isn't the commitment to a particular form of religion—in your case, Catholic Christianity—a more secure way to defend oneself from the inherent uncertainty that permeates all the symbolic, and often incoherent, sets of ideas and texts that constitute the core of different religious traditions? How can we be sure that a particular religious institution represents the truth about reality or even the true message of its founder?

DD—We cannot; but I think that, first of all, it is not surprising that people tend to worship, not as isolated individuals, but in religious communities—and even, traditions. Not only does this appeal to the human desire for solidarity, but even more than that, it tends to give continuity and coherence to religious practices and arguments—in the same way that, for example, in a country, someone might be a liberal or a conservative. Now, you're a liberal or a conservative because you subscribe to a set of beliefs that hang together and, as a consequence of being a liberal or conservative, you may join a liberal or a conservative party which tends to reflect those beliefs. You still may not agree with every particular item in that party platform, but, in general, you are a follower—or you are in agreement—with the ideology or the program, and so you feel comfortable describing yourself—in America, say—as a republican or as a democrat. Similarly, as a Methodist, or as a Catholic, or as a Sunni Muslim, you're placing yourself in a tradition, you're finding some continuity with your own parents, grandparents, and so on.

Now, in Catholicism—and Christianity in general—the idea is to maintain the continuity of the teachings of Christ—and even earlier, the tradition of the Old Testament—but it's not to have a static tradition; it's not to mindlessly reproduce those practices and beliefs from one generation to the next, because there's also an idea in Christianity of the development of doctrine. It's a little bit like with the American Constitution: it's a Constitution, we get it from the Founders, but it does change, modify, and even grow over the decades and over the centuries—and the same with Christianity. Not that the Bible changes of course, but our understanding of it does. If you look at the history of Christianity, it's far from static; it rather reflects, you may say, organic development through the centuries, and the idea is not to live exactly as the early Christians did in 35 AD, but rather to maintain a spiritual and historical continuity with them.

LR—Although the Bible does not change, that continuity is often confronted with opposed interpretations. In the Gospel of Luke 6:29, for example, Jesus tells us that "If someone strikes you on one cheek, turn to him the other also"; but in Matthew 10:34, he tells us that he did "not come to bring peace, but a sword." These contradictory statements, supposedly made by the same person, can be used to legitimate two radical and different worldviews about Christianity. What is your criterion for choosing one instead of the other?

DD—I think that the best way to read those passages is simply to rec-ognize that they articulate principles that are valid in different situa-tions. When I was a child, I learned a series of very useful proverbs. Yet, as I got a little bit older and I began to think about them, I realized that these proverbs contained very useful advice about human nature, but the pieces of advice were contradictory. One proverb says: "Look before you leap." Another proverb says: "He who hesitates is lost." Now, if you think about it, one proverb is telling you to act and the other is telling you to be cautious. Which one is true? Both are true. There are certain situations in which you should be careful, and there are certain situations in which you should be brave. When you're an adult, you also realize that no maxim can be applicable to all situations, and if you're looking for one, you're looking for the wrong kind of Christianity, the wrong kind of advice.

Concerning the teachings of Christ, he will say "turn the other cheek," and yet when he's rounded up himself by the Roman guards and one of them strikes him, he does not turn the other cheek. In fact, he says "Why did you strike me?" So, when I was five years old, I learned what I call "crayon Christianity"; when I was 17 years old, if you have said these things to me, I would say, "These things seem irrec-oncilable!" But now I say to myself, "Look! I'm trying to defend, to articulate, a more adult Christianity in which we're not just taking the sayings of Christ in isolation and saying, 'Okay! These are universal principles and apply to this situation.'" Rather, we have to read the Bi-ble with nuance and draw explanations and insight from it, but also recognize that the insight may apply differently, not only in different situations, but in our world today, which is very different from the world of the Old Testament and the New Testament. Something that was allowed then may not be okay now.

The early Christians knew this. The moment they had to take Christi-anity outside of its original Jewish precincts, they had to face the ques-tion of what to do with the old Jewish laws and regulations. There was a debate among the apostles and the prevailing view—which was articu-lated by Paul—was the idea that there are certain core principles, and those have to be preserved, but we don't expect new converts to Christi-anity to follow Jewish laws: another sign of the adaptability and fluidity of Christianity, even though the core principles remain the same.

LR—Nevertheless, the four Gospels are related in the manner of a story. They have that type of context. For a "proverb-like

Gospel," wouldn't it be more suitable to point out a text like the Gospel of Thomas?

DD—I think that we all have to decide what is the best way to live, but I'm not a "cafeteria Christian" whereby I say: "Okay! I'm going to decide whether I like this saying of Jesus but not that one." I take it as a whole. If you accept the validity of the revelation, if you think it makes sense to believe, not only in God but specifically in Christ, then you have to do your best to understand what he was trying to get at—recognizing that that message will be distorted and filtered through the centuries. But still, that doesn't mean we have no access to it: The message of lots of other people, from Socrates and so on, has been filtered through the centuries, but we still study them and think we have a reasonably good understanding of what they were trying to say. So, similarly here, I'm interested in the "other Gospels," so to speak, but I don't treat them as sacred texts—I just read them as historical documents that help to illuminate ancient Christianity.

LR—Most Christians would assert that Christianity brought dignity and worth to human beings, regardless of their economical or social status. If so, how can that hard-earned dignity be compatible with the idea of hell? Can human beings achieve respect in this life only to find that they can lose it and be eternally punished if they don't behave properly?

DD—My understanding of hell—which is a very traditional one—I think answers this objection if you think about it: What do we mean by the word "hell"? The premise of Christianity is that good things come from God; in other words, God is the author of Creation and everything that is good in the world comes from God—that's the conventional view. Now, that means that, even good things that occur in nature, even good things that are done by people who don't believe in God, come from God. What follows is that, if we reject God, if we say "no" voluntarily to God, then we are basically rejecting what God is and what God offers. So that, to me, is hell. It is not that God is grabbing you and flinging you into some bad place that he has carefully manufactured for you; rather, heaven is the place where there are all good things. There are all good things not because God designed the place; rather, because all good things come from God. To accept God is to be part of that; to reject him is to say no to all that. When you say "eternal torment"—and again, my understanding of eternity is not forever and ever and ever, a kind of life sentence that doesn't terminate, but rather, eternity is understood in the Christian way of being outside of space and time—eternal punishment is nothing more than the human being, in a sense, punishing himself or herself by saying no to God, and thus, depriving himself of what God is and what God has to offer.

LR—The problem of evil ("why do good people suffer and bad guys win") constitutes one of the major stumbling blocks for the belief in an all-good, all-knowing, and all-powerful God. What, in your opinion, is the best answer to this problem?

DD—I do think it constitutes a difficult problem. Now, the difficult problem occurs mainly because we are judging God purely by the standard of terrestrial life. In other words, if you expand the scope of vision to include eternal life, then the argument collapses completely. If your life is one second in the long expanse of eternity, then what complaint do you have? You can't say, "Oh God! The tsunami blew away my hut! Oh God! I lost my left arm in an accident!" The point is, well, yes, but if you hold fast to God's truth and you believe in God, you have an eternity of compensation and blessings waiting for you. So how powerful is this complaint that you were "mistreated" for one second when this is not even an important duration in the long expanse of eternity? In one sense, one can answer the argument very easily by just stepping back and saying, "Wait a minute; in the Christian perspective, this life is not the only life." If it were, then the argument would be much stronger, because it would say we all are given one shot, we live on the Earth for 30, 50, or 80 years and we would expect God to be handing out rewards and punishments in proportion with virtue—but he evidently doesn't, and the reign of both blessings and punishments seems to fall equally on the good and the bad and God is a horrible manager and ruler of the universe. But again, in Christianity, God is not directly ruling the universe; he is the author of it, but we are the architects of it too. We have freedom, and moreover, nature has freedom.

Now, that's a concept that's a little harder to understand; what I mean by "nature has freedom" is not that nature can act voluntarily—a tsunami doesn't have the will to say, "Okay, I'll go and hit Atlanta tomorrow"—but that nature is given autonomy through law. God has created a lawful universe that follows regularities and fixed rules, and we are given autonomy in the universe as free actors within it. So, once you look at both those factors as part of the wisdom of Creation, then you can see how a lot of suffering—and also, a lot of good—comes out of them. God could have created a different universe, a not-lawful universe, a miraculous universe in which he intervenes all the time and nature has no regularity. But then, in that kind of universe, we have to remember there would be, for example, no science, no knowledge of the universe, and human development would be very difficult to envision in that kind of universe. Just as if God had created us unable to sin, we would also be unable to do good things and virtue would be impossible if it were not for free will. I can envision alternative universes that God might have created, but it's not obvious to me that they would be better than the one we have. I'm not saying we live in the best of all possible worlds, but we actually may live in the best of all actual worlds—worlds that could be created by a god according to freedom and according to law.

LR—But if God is going to provide a perfect world—the best of all possible worlds—after one's death, why not provide it here, right now?

DD—That is a question we may never know the answer to. My best way to understand it is simply to say that our lives on Earth are necessary because God wants to create free beings that are made in his image and that can reciprocally love him—and that could not be done the other way. If you look, for example, at the Garden of Eden, and if you look at it symbolically, what is really going on here is that God is trying to say to his creatures, "Look, I'm giving you all this, but I'm looking to see if you love me enough, or have enough gratitude for this, that you will follow this one easy rule I'm going to give you; everything is yours, but just don't do this one thing." Such is the way that we use our freedom, even today—not just Adam and Eve—that even these prohibitions that seem quite gentle in the context of the expected reward, nevertheless, we have to go ahead and eat the apple. In Christianity, for example, it says that the essence of salvation is not even all our great human accomplishments but merely saying "yes" to a sacrifice already performed on our behalf by Jesus Christ. All you have to do is say, "Okay. I accept the gift." That's it, and yet, many people refuse to do even that. We're made in the image of God. What does that mean? Well, God is a free creature; he created freely. If we are created in God's image, it means that we bear a spark, or a stamp of that divine nature, and that is the essence, to me, of human freedom: It reflects that little spark of the divine. God could take it away from us and make us like flies or like stones, where we wouldn't have that. We might have a contented existence, but I don't think it would be a meaningful existence in any sense that we humans understand meaning today.

LR—Granting that God gave human beings free will—whether to do good or evil things—it seems to me logical that this free will will end as soon as the "good person" chooses paradise and the "bad person" chooses hell (because good people can't do bad things in paradise and bad people can't do good things in hell). If an absolute free will cannot logically exist in the Christian notion of an afterlife, why should it have to exist here and now?

DD—This question was very effectively answered by the theologian Anselm in the 11th century in an essay called "On the Fall of the Devil." Anselm pointed out that the reason people do bad things is because they seek happiness in the wrong way. No one does a bad thing for its own sake; no one commits a murder for the sake of murder: You commit murder to rob the bank. Or you commit murder because you have anger at somebody who you think has wronged you. We are all in this life in search of happiness, and the reason that we do evil is we want happiness at the cost of everything else. So we are willing to sacrifice justice, or goodness, or obligation in the name of this happiness. Now, here's the point made by Anselm (he's making it in connection with the angels, but it's just as applicable to human beings): In heaven, you already have happiness, and therefore, there is no reason to do wrong. The only reason we do wrong down here is because we don't have full happiness and we are seeking more happiness and so we say, "Okay! If I get more money I'll be better off and I'll be happier, or if I pull this guy down, it's in effect pulling me up and so, I'll be happier." Anselm's point is that in heaven, we don't have that reason to sin, so even though we have the freedom to do it, nobody wants to do it.

LR—By obtaining total happiness in heaven, we have nothing more to aspire to; everything has been achieved. Therefore, wouldn't eternity be tedious?

DD—We can't conceive of it because, in this world, we are finite and frustrated creatures moved by restless desire. Even if we achieve one thing, our desires move almost effortlessly to the next objective. We pursue the beautiful woman and the moment that she's ours, our sights then start beginning to rove to others. The same with money: We never have enough. But what is that telling us? All it's telling us is that the human fulfillments are not complete fulfillments; they are merely partial fulfillments. In many cases our aspirations reflect nothing but the restlessness of our desire, and it's the unquenchable nature of that desire that's responsible for the frustration. So, in a way, novelty is the only exciting thing: We've achieved "X," now we have to try for "Y," and it's merely that pursuit that's giving us that sense of "being in the game" or having something to live for. On the one hand, that is our human nature, but it's short-sighted not to see that that's not the best way to operate. That's actually a rather low and frustrating way to live. It is our way, and we can't envision a much better one, but I think we simply have to trust that heaven isn't going to be operating exactly according to those principles, and I think it's not that hard for us to envision a different zone of existence where we don't move from one partial fulfillment to another, never satisfied and always seeking what's beyond the horizon.

LR—Concerning morality, should we accept the unchangeable universality of God-given moral laws if, even in Christian countries, the perception of what is right and wrong has changed over time? For example, slavery, crusades, or the burning of witches was once seen as righteous by biblical standards, and now it is not. Have God-given moral laws always existed, though we do not know or apply them in their entirety? Or do they not exist, and human beings define what is moral according to a particular *zeitgeist*?

DD—Moral laws, I think, do exist universally, are recognized to exist universally by all human beings, and have not changed by one iota through history. Now, this requires a little bit of explanation and the key point is this: We have to recognize that we live in a world that, while the moral law may be universal, situations vary enormously. And moreover, there are times when one moral principle appears to conflict with another: the conflict, for example, between justice and mercy, or the conflict between the desire for liberty and the desire for equality. So there are conflicts that will cause individuals—or even groups—to go with principle "X" over principle "Y," but that doesn't mean that both sides don't recognize the universal principles. They are merely interpreting them or applying them differently. Now, look briefly at your example regarding witches. What has really changed? Has the moral law changed? No. The moral law is the same. If today we believed, as a matter of fact, that there were human beings who were inspired and controlled by the devil, who were engaging in nefarious schemes to basically ruin our happiness and destroy our souls, we would burn them ourselves! In other words—and this was a point made by C. S. Lewis, I'm merely relaying it—Lewis's point is it's not that morality has changed: It is the factual belief that there are such things as witches. Our disagreement with our ancestors is we think they were wrong, that these were not women possessed by the devil. They were wrong about the facts. They were not wrong about their morality—their morality was fine—and if we had the same view of the facts that they did, we would do pretty much what they did also.

Slavery is a good example of a clash between human self-interest—very powerful on the one hand; not a moral law but a human fact about our nature—and the kind of moral appeal to compassion and human dignity on the other. Now, here's the point: The Southern slave owners in the United States knew perfectly well that humanity and compassion were inconsistent with slavery. It was simply that slavery was essential to their livelihood, to their plantations, to the growing of cotton, and so, you might say they suppressed that part of their conscience that said, "Look, don't treat people this way; you have no right to take their labor for free." The Southerners knew all that. It's not that they were defective in morality; they recognized the universal morality. They simply shut their eyes to it. Why? Because they were benefiting so much by ignoring it.

Answering your question, I don't think that the human race has a different morality now than it did 2,000 years ago—or even at the time of Socrates. The moral principles remain the same. True, we have to engage in moral reasoning and debate sometimes, to excavate the finer principles and articulate them. In different places and cultures, they apply differently. For the Romans, for example, "honor and glory" is emphasized. Now, with that, comes the danger of committing atrocities, cruelty, and harshness; Roman culture was very manly, it was a glorious culture, but it was also cruel. Spanish culture in the 15th and 16th centuries emphasized piety but also, on the other side, was prone to fanaticism and superstition. Indian culture has certain strengths, but with it come certain weaknesses. So, moral debate would be impossible if we didn't acknowledge a hidden core of moral ideals. I think that those ideals exist now, are universally recognized, and that's what enables people to argue about them.

LR—Some religious institutions have had, for centuries, some problems complying with such universal moral principles. Concerning the specific institution of the Catholic Church, the failure of some popes to speak out against mass murders committed by Catholics (for example, in Belgian Congo and Croatia), the silence of Pius XII regarding European Catholic dictators—such as Mussolini, Salazar, Franco, Pavelic—and the Holocaust, the tolerance of John Paul II regarding South American dictators (like Pinochet), and most recently, the silencing of cases concerning child abuse in Catholic parishes all over the world, give us a picture of the Holy See as an institution not so holy, living by the same secular rules of self-preservation and *realpolitik*, like any other country. Isn't there something morally wrong and condemnable here? Shouldn't the church be more active in the denunciation of worldly wrong deeds, whatever the consequences?

DD—This is one question to which I have a one word answer: Yes! [Laughs.] Historically—for the first 300 years after Jesus' death—the church was an institution independent of politics. That's because it was operating in a Roman state where the Roman rulers were hostile to Christianity, and this danger that you describe was really not there because the church was separate from the government—was essentially operating locally and it was divorced from power. When Constantine converted in the fourth century, the church became part of the ruling apparatus of power and government—it became a human institution like any other (and that created problems right away because the church is supposed to be unlike any other). So, what we have now, the Roman Catholic apparatus, is both a religious institution and a secular institution, and therefore we shouldn't be totally surprised: It is driven by secular rivalries, power interests, property interests. So, for example, here's the Church that is trying to maintain an institutional allegiance of Catholics worldwide. Then you have a South American conflict in which the dictator is allied with the bishops and the Church and professes—however insincerely—to be a pious Catholic, but he is besieged by pro-socialist—or even communist—guerrillas who are trying to overthrow him. The pope and the Vatican realize that the overthrow of, let's say, Pinochet in Chile is going to result in a left-wing anticlerical and anti-Catholic regime in the country, and so, they have a choice of evils. Do we put up with this bad guy Pinochet—who proclaims to be a Catholic, even though he's an autocrat—or, do we condemn him (and thus assist in his overthrow) and bring to power a regime that's going to be openly hostile to Catholicism? What should we do? Interestingly, that is a political question and there is no ultimate answer that the Church gives in a given situation. In some cases, the Church has supported the independence movement. For example, it was a fairly easy decision for Pope John Paul II to support Solidarity in Poland. Why? Because the interests of morality and the political interest of the Church were the same: You are against a communist regime—the Jaruzelski regime—and so, it was an easy choice. It was a harder choice with Franco in Spain, a harder choice with the Sandinistas in Nicaragua. Those were more difficult situations.

LR—What are, in your opinion, the greatest challenges that Christianity—and Christians—must face today?

DD—I think that, in the past, it seems like the biggest challenge to Christianity came either from other religions or came from interdenominational conflicts within Christianity. Today, I think that is not so. Today, I think perhaps the most serious challenge comes from secular modernity, which is the idea of trying to live a life in which values and morals are perceived as secular creations, evolutionary developments if you will; in other words, to live a life that is a life of dignity, but nevertheless, one that is divorced from God. This secular outlook hasn't really existed before; it's a modern phenomenon and it started out only in the West but now is beginning to spread to other cultures—and poses a threat, not just to Christianity, but to all religion. I think what gives this new outlook prestige is that it marches in the name of science; it claims that it is scientifically motivated and points a skeptical eye at all religion. In some ways, I think it is the challenge of Christian apologetics—the defense of Christianity—to answer this secular outlook, and some of my recent work is aimed at doing that.

LR—What other works, what other books, have brought you closer to your faith? Also, what were those that most disturbed it?

DD—The books that pulled me a little bit away from the faith have tended to be books that exposed the arrogance and hypocrisy of the church—the kind of books that could be written today very easily about the scandals in, not only the Catholic but the Protestant churches as well. The charge of hypocrisy is one that any institution that aspires to virtue is inherently vulnerable to. We have to remember that the church, like any other institution, is ruled by fallible men. So when I look, for example, at why much of Europe revolted against the faith, initially I used to think it was because Europe turned against Christianity. But historically, that's not really the case: It's not that the Renaissance, or the Reformation, or the Enlightenment were motivated by atheism. No. What happened in the Enlightenment was that people were outraged by what they perceived to be an oppressive alliance between Throne and Altar, between, if you will, the aristocratic and monarchical powers on the one hand, and the ecclesiastical powers on the other. So this was a political revolt not against Christianity, but against what the church was doing at that time. Whence I begin to understand that some of my own hostility to the church was motivated by that— by what have been done by the bishops, by Henry VIII, by opportunistic popes and figures in power—in some senses, I was able to separate that from Christianity itself.

What are the books that have brought me closer to the faith? Certainly the works of Augustine, Anselm, and Pascal (particularly his book *Pensées*). As my hero—or my model—in modern Christian apologetics, I look to the example of C. S. Lewis because he began his life as a secular writer—in his case, a scholar of medieval literature—but then he became interested in Christian apologetics and began to bring that secular mind to bear on writing about religious questions. My case is somewhat similar. For almost 20 years I've been a secular writer, writing about culture, politics, and international relations. Only in the last few years have I turned my attention specifically to writing about religious issues and, in a way, I bring a very secular mind to writing about them. In my debates with atheists, I don't use religious assumptions and I never quote the Bible: I rely on reason, science, history, and evidence to make my case. In a sense, I'm fighting on the same ground as the atheists do and using the same weapons that they do.

LR—Why did you feel the need to embark in this religious— and Christian—apologetics project? In this phase of your life, what led you to write about it?

DD—Well, initially, when the books of the New Atheists began to emerge—books like *The God Delusion* by Dawkins, or the *End for Faith* by Sam Harris—remember that these books came out in the wake of 9/11 and a unifying theme in these books was the idea that religion is not merely false, but also dangerous. It's dangerous because it leads to terrorism—as in the case of radical Islam—or it leads to conflict and war. A lot of people were very receptive to that message in the wake of 9/11 because "Hey! Look what Bin Laden and his friends were doing in the name of the Koran, in the name of God." Yet, coming as I was out of the political world, and having a sense of history—and having grown up in a culture with Hindus, with Muslims, and so on—I realized right away: "Wait a minute! Yes, Bin Laden is doing what he's doing in the name of God, but there are tens of millions of Muslims and Hindus and religious people who come from those same traditions but they are completely different. They are not inherently fanatical, they live in a democracy—in the case of India, for example—and they run for office—the Muslims do—and if they're voted out, they leave." In other words, I saw that the world was a bigger place, that what the atheists were saying was, quite apart from the religious issues, politically wrong. So I felt a desire to jump into the debate and challenge them just historically and politically. But as I got into the debate, I began to take more and more of their themes. For example, the questions "Is there a creator?" or "Did nature create itself?" or "Does the existence of the world and the universe require a creator?" These kinds of questions, initially I didn't get into them, but as I got into the debate, I became more and more interested in these larger issues. I didn't start out completely that way, but I'm in it now.

LR—What if someone gave you the absolute certainty that God does not exist and you believed it? What would you change in your life?

DD—Well, I don't know if it would change the way I live my life, but it would shrink it enormously. If you remove the idea of God and say, in effect, that we are merely evolved creatures in the world, then, at some sense, you have to say we are passengers on the *Titanic*. Our past actions, our present programs, and all our future plans are kind of pointless. Death is waiting for everyone around the corner, the ship is going down under the sea, and nothing we can do is going to make a bit of difference to that. We can rearrange the deck chairs, we can ask the orchestra to play louder but . . . for what? I think that philosophers who have really thought about this—such as Jean-Paul Sartre—have said that our situation is one of despair, our situation is hopeless. And that's the keyword: hopeless. Not just in a sense that we can't do anything about it, but it removes significance and meaning and hope in an ultimate sense from life. Now, it doesn't remove what you could call "immediate purpose"—I still might want to save money to send my daughter to college, or I might still want to make a new addition to my house. So, I have purpose in that short-term sense, but if I were to step back I could say, "Who cares if my daughter goes to college? She's going to end up in a six-foot box like I am? What difference is it going to make ultimately?" Or "Why do I want to make a new addition to my house?" Or "Why do I care about anything at all? Shouldn't I just selfishly grasp and try to make my way in the world and not really give a damn about anybody else because there is no moral law, no moral giver? What's the point of anything?" I think that that temptation would always hover around human beings if we were to remove the idea of God from the world.

LR—My last question has to do precisely with the meaning of purpose: What purpose could be compatible with an idea of an eternal existence? What do you intend—or wish—to do in the afterlife? Do you think God will provide it?

DD—To me, the interesting thing about the afterlife—and I think I'm typical of the religious people in this sense—is not that I sit around making plans for the afterlife, because I recognize it's going to be a different dimension of existence. Rather, the importance of the afterlife is how it reshapes the way I deal with this life. Look at it this way: If you consider virtue, or doing the right thing, we have a reason to do the right thing right now—and that is that if we don't do it, we might get caught. So, we don't want to cheat in our taxes, because the government will come after us and put us in jail. But what if I could do bad things and never get caught? Then I would have to think seriously about "Why not?" If there is no moral law, if there is no life after death, I will never be held accountable. And if I'm not going to be caught, there's absolutely no reason not to go ahead and do it. Moreover, I'm an evolved creature in the world, my main "job," if you will, is to survive and reproduce—that is my biological imperative—and no one can say different. Now, the moment you introduce transcendence, and God, and life after death, the idea becomes: "Wait a minute . . . no! Even though I do something and I may get away with it, I'm not going to get away with it ultimately. I am accountable." So, the point here being that, in every religion—from Hinduism, to Judaism, to Christianity—the afterlife is the arena of cosmic justice. That's the real meaning of karma and reincarnation: "You lived a terrible life? Sorry buddy, you're going to be punished, you're going to see the consequences of your actions in the next life." The idea of the afterlife is to give us a grounding, and a belief, and a hope that, ultimately, good will be rewarded and evil will be held accountable. So, that provides the horizon for justice in this life and that's really the way that I think about life after death. I think about the fact it makes this life different, infuses meaning and significance into this life, it gives me a reason to act morally, it gives me a way to teach morality to my children, and it makes me look at death a little differently. All creatures fear death, and for me, death is something to be avoided, but it's not a final defeat. Rather, it's a gateway from this life—this valuable, important, and precious life—but nevertheless, a gateway to a different existence.

Nicholas Everitt

Nicholas Everitt is a retired senior lecturer of philosophy at the University of East Anglia (United Kingdom). He is the author of *The Non-Existence of God* (2004), coauthor of *Modern Epistemology* (1995), as well as the author of many articles on epistemology, philosophy of mind, and philosophy of religion. After taking a first degree at Cambridge in moral science, as philosophy was then called, and a postgraduate degree at Oxford, he taught for a short time as a tutorial fellow at the University of Sussex before moving to the University of East Anglia. During his years at UEA, he also taught briefly in the United States (at Fairfield University, Connecticut) and in Singapore (at Ngee Ann Polytechnic). Over a number of decades, he also taught extensively for the Open University, as an associate lecturer, on a wide variety of courses. After retirement, Everitt moved to the Lake District to pursue his passion for fell-walking. He continues to teach for the Open University and writes articles and reviews of philosophy books.

Luís Rodrigues—"Why is there something rather than nothing?" God has always been used as an answer to this question, to fill our lack of understanding concerning the fact of mere existence, of why things and beings exist. Theology then refines the answer, developing theories (for example, original sin, *samsara*, etc.) and practices (the sacraments, ascetic retirement, etc.) around this enigmatic "why," connecting it to God. In your opinion, will God prevail as an eternal symbol of unsatisfied human curiosity or will there be a point in time when our knowledge about the world makes belief in God untenable—or, by the contrary, confirms it?

Nicholas Everitt—It may be that some things exist because they *have* to exist—because it would be self-contradictory to suppose that they did not exist. So the explanation of why they exist is internal to their nature—to understand *what* they are is to understand *why* they are. Prime candidates for such necessarily existing entities are numbers. Since the explanation for the existence of such necessarily existing entities lies within themselves, any supposed creative activity by God is redundant. They are self-explanatory—not in the sense of being obvious, but in the sense that they provide their own explanation of why they exist.

However, there are other kinds of entities which do exist but which apparently might not have existed, such as planets, stars, galaxies, and indeed the entire physical universe. Can there be an explanation for the existence of the totality of such contingently existing things? If there can be an explanation, it clearly cannot be provided by some other contingently existing thing, since there can be no other contingently existing thing outside the totality of such things. But nor could it be provided by any of the self-explanatory entities referred to above. For if they have a necessary existence, anything they explain would also have a necessary, not a contingent, existence. But if the totality of contingently existing things cannot be explained in terms either of necessary or of contingent things, it cannot be explained at all. The question "Why is there something rather than nothing?" is thus potentially deceptive. There isn't a reason why the universe exists, because there *could* not be a reason why it exists.

In short, I think that what is needed to "solve" this question is careful philosophical reflection, not increased scientific knowledge. Provided that the fruits of such reflection are widely known, there is no reason why people should retain a belief in God as an ultimate explainer for what is otherwise mysterious.

LR—Why is it so difficult for people to deal with the "unknown"? In your opinion, why do they need to fill this epistemological vacuum with God, the supernatural, or the divine?

NE—I think that people may have an innate desire to find everything around them intelligible in one way or another. To say that they have no idea why something exists, or has the nature which it does, is thus repugnant to them. If they live in a prescientific society, or if they find proper scientific explanation antipathetic, they are likely to turn to supernatural explanations, including those which invoke God. But I do not believe that there is an innate desire to believe specifically in God.

LR—The general attitude of the mystic, when expounding God, consists in transmitting the divine message in veiled ways (parables, symbols, metaphor, poetry, etc.), emphasizing that these means are better able to communicate the ungraspable in a more comprehensible manner. For example, a poem has more to say about the nature of love than physics or chemistry. How do you evaluate the conflict between knowledge and feeling when one talks about religiosity?

NE—"A poem has more to say about the nature of love than physics or chemistry." True—but that is because the concept of love is not a concept of either physics or chemistry. The concept does not pick out a natural kind which either physics or chemistry studies. But equally, physics and chemistry say nothing about, for example, economic phenomena such as unemployment, inflation, the balance of trade, etc. This does not mean that there are some difficult-to-grasp truths about economics, truths that can be communicated only metaphorically or indirectly. Nor should it make us think that economics deals with some nonphysical supernatural phenomena. In a similar way, if God exists, there is no reason why a range of truths about him should not be formulable in clear and unambiguous terms, even if it is not the language of physics or chemistry. In general, I do not accept that there are any "ungraspable" truths. And if there were, I don't believe that "veiled" ways of speaking would be better able to communicate them. To paraphrase Frank Ramsey, what you cannot grasp, you cannot grasp, even by metaphors.

LR—The word *reason* is always on the mouths of atheists in order to refute what they consider the irrationality of theist beliefs. But irrationality is something that we don't find in sophisticated theist arguments like those of Aquinas, Descartes, Leibniz, Swinburne, and many others. Where is the frontier between what's reasonable and unreasonable in a discourse about God or religion?

NE—On the contrary, I believe that we do find irrationality (in the sense of errors of reasoning) in even the most sophisticated theist arguments. It seems clear, for example, that Aquinas's Five Ways are full of logical errors—either in using question-begging premises, or in drawing conclusions from them which the premises simply do not support. Similar remarks could be made about both Descartes' cosmological argument and his ontological argument, and also about Leibniz, Swinburne, et al.

LR—Imagine that someone says to you, "I have faith in God the same way that someone has faith that Australia and quarks exist, even if they never went to Australia and even if they never saw a quark." How does each kind of faith differ from one another? And what makes one more reliable than the other?

NE—The term *faith*, like the term *reason*, is used by different people with different senses. There is good empirical evidence for the existence of Australia and of quarks, and if someone has that evidence, it would be strange for them to describe their belief as a matter of faith. But if they did, they would clearly be using "faith" to cover cases in which a person has good evidence. If they then say that they have faith in God *in the same sense*, then they are saying that they have good evidence (presumably empirical evidence) for the existence of God, and they need to say what that evidence is. The atheist will then seek to show that the evidence is seriously flawed in some way that the theist has not taken into account. I don't think that there are two *kinds* of faith here, faith in Australia/quarks, and faith in God—indeed, that is ruled out by the questioner saying that their faith in God is just like a faith in the existence of Australia. It is simply that some beliefs are well supported by evidence, such as the belief about Australia and quarks, and other beliefs are poorly supported, such as a belief in the existence of God.

LR—Theists have the tendency to conceive the existence of God in a supernatural realm (and therefore, not subject to scrutiny by observation and experimentation). They grant, nevertheless, that God manifests himself in the real world in the form of miracles, mystical revelations to some individuals, and in other ways that are also regarded as difficult to prove on an experimental basis. What logical basis prevents one from thinking about God in this inscrutable fashion?

NE—It would be a form of intellectual confusion to believe in the existence and nature of something, X, and also to believe that X's existence and nature were wholly inscrutable. So if theists believe in a God who is in any way inscrutable, his inscrutability must have limits. At least some facts about him must be discoverable if someone is to have any reasonable beliefs at all about him. I think that theists implicitly accept this by appealing to nonexperimental evidence, such as alleged miracles, religious experience, etc. My own view is that this evidence is all flawed, and that a belief in God cannot be protected by claiming that he is inscrutable.

LR—Contrary to Freud, Carl Jung didn't seem to see religion as pathology: Humanity's interaction with the symbolic and the sacred had something appealing in itself; it was a web of meanings and codes that connected each individual with the world and his community in a special kind of way. In your opinion, does atheism bring destruction to these archetypes of meaning? If so, is it worth it?

NE—I don't believe that Jung had any useful insights into truths about the relation between individuals on the one hand, and their communities and the world on the other. So if atheism resulted in the discrediting of his ideas, I do not believe that this would be a bad thing. On an atheist account of the matter, fully satisfactory webs of meaning can be constructed, but they are constructed by individuals giving meaning and purpose to their own lives, and they do not require any supernatural scaffolding.

LR—There seems to be a special connection between art and religion. They both pursue the sublime, the untenable platonic perfection.

NE—I don't think that this is true. Some art pursues the sublime and some does not, and the same is true of religious thinking.

LR—But one objection of the believer to the atheist in this regard can be as follows: "You atheists are less capable of having an emotional response to art—and are consequently less capable of having an emotional response to life. You should

prefer art deprived of moral content and emotional pathos; you should stick with Marcel Duchamp's urinal entitled *The Fountain*, while we keep our Michelangelo's *Pietà*. To be coherent, an atheist should reject all spiritual gravitas embracing a pure materialistic approach to art and to life." Is there any point in this set of objections by the believer?

NE—No, this set of objections is unjustified. There is no reason why atheists should be any more emotionally restricted than anyone else, and no reason why their response to art should be emotionally restricted. Equally, there is no reason for them to reject a moral content in art. There are a number of secular accounts of morality (contract ethics, utilitarianism, Kantian ethics, virtue ethics, etc.), all of which are a good deal more plausible than a God-based ethic. In that sense, the atheist is better equipped to take morality more seriously than the theist. I'm not sure what a "materialistic" approach to art is, but if it is meant to exclude, for example, an aesthetic approach, then atheism is simply not committed to that sort of materialism.

LR—Is atheism—or even for that matter, religious indifference—the prelude that announces a different kind of humanity, a cold-hearted humanity that most theists envisage in the regimes of Mao and Stalin?

NE—There is no denying that regimes that were officially atheist have perpetrated atrocities on a large scale. Equally, however, atrocities have been perpetrated by regimes that were deeply religious. I don't think that the evidence indicates that the track record of atheist regimes is any worse than that of religious regimes. But suppose that this is wrong, and that atheism does lead in some way to undesirable outcomes. That would be wholly irrelevant to whether atheism is true.

Even in relation to religious art, like the Michelangelo *Pietà*, I do not believe that the atheist is under any handicap. The theist may well think as he looks at the painting that it is the Son of God who is being sacrificed. But this metaphysical belief about the scene depicted is irrelevant to an aesthetic response to the painting. The atheist can appreciate the organization of the painting, the palette the artist has chosen to use, the expressiveness of the portrayal, the way the artist has developed or perhaps subverted the genre of crucifixions, and so on. Think here of the way in which both theists and atheists can have full aesthetic responses to art featuring the Greek gods. There is no reason to suppose that those responses would be in any respect better if they were accompanied by a belief in the reality of those gods. Similarly, fully aesthetic responses to Christian art do not need support from any metaphysical beliefs about a Christian God.

LR—While atheists can now say that science has never been so accurate in disproving the existence of God and the supernatural by pointing out all the material data that explains the world in a materialistic fashion, theists sometimes counter that science now proves the existence of God even more—pointing to the anthropic principle, for example: Even a slight alteration in the cosmological constant would make the universe lifeless. Therefore, there must be a God behind all this fine-tuned universe. In this rhetorical battle, what is your position about the role of science with regard to supernatural and theistic beliefs?

NE—In forming our beliefs about a subject matter, we need to be guided by good evidence, and this applies whether the beliefs are about, for example, whether it will rain tomorrow, what black holes are like, whether there is an abominable snowman, or whether God exists. It would be a mistake to think that beliefs about God need to satisfy lower evidential standards than other types of beliefs. If there were a God, why would he want our beliefs about him to be intellectually sloppy as compared to our other legitimate beliefs? And even if he did want this, it would still be intellectual sloppy of us to do what he wanted. I do not think that all this evidence needs to be specifically *scientific*, because I think that there are kinds of good evidence, for example, produced in historical studies or in law courts, that are not scientific. But the term *science* and its cognates can be defined in several ways, and perhaps in one of those senses, all good evidence qualifies as scientific. So, I do not think that the distinction between, on the one hand, supernatural and theistic beliefs, and on the other hand, all remaining beliefs, is the important one. The important distinction is between beliefs that are well supported (or perhaps best supported) by available evidence, and those that are not.

In relation to the "fine tuning" argument, I do not believe that it shows the existence of any fine tuner. But even if it did, this would have nothing to do with God. There would be no reason to think that such a fine tuner was omnipotent, or omniscient, or perfectly good, or eternal, or worship-worthy, or had any other of a range of central divine attributes.

LR—History, whether rooted in myth and legend, whether rooted in real facts, has always been the basis for justifying most religious beliefs: Christianity, Buddhism, Islam, Judaism, etc. are all rooted in history. From a philosophical standpoint, what is the role of history in discovering what most resembles "the Truth"? Isn't this epistemological enterprise jeopardized by interpolations, false claims, mythic tales, forged documents, engaged historical accounts, and so on?

NE—Insofar as religions make historical claims, they commit themselves to certain empirical assertions. To be credible, these empirical assertions have to pass the same critical tests as any other claim about the past. In relation to most, perhaps all, of these claims, the evidence available to the historian will be fragmentary, biased, and contradictory, and the historian has to exercise critical judgment to construct from them the account which is best supported by the evidence as she sees it. This applies just as much to historical claims made by religions as to secular claims. It may be that in relation to religion, the evidence is more biased. But I do not see a difference in principle between religious and secular claims about the past.

LR—For theists, the "self" is essentially that which can be shaped and defined by morality, one that emanates from God: A good self goes to heaven, a bad self goes to hell. If for most people their moral codes are imbedded in ancient theological sources rather than secular rules of social and individual congeniality, how do you think they will be able to cut the umbilical cord of the supernatural moral roots from which all humanity sprang? And should they want to?

NE—Even if there were a God, I think it would be intellectually confused to think that morality could depend on him. God (if he exists) wills the good because it is already good—it does not become good by his willing it. This is a truth which is accepted by a good number of both atheists and theists. A supernatural being could of course lay down some rules for humanity, and attach rewards and punishments to them, but that would have nothing to do with morality. (We now think quite rightly that many of the injunctions supposedly issued by God are morally outrageous—"whosoever doeth any work in the Sabbath day, he shall surely be put to death" (Exodus 31:15) is one example among dozens.)

So there is no reason why atheists cannot be "shaped by morality" if that phrase means trying to become a morally decent sort of person, or trying to do the right thing.

LR—As an atheist, how do you face the fact of a definitive, personal, and existential extinction? Facing that prospect, where does a meaning of life stand?

NE—I do not find in death anything that needs "facing," if that means confronting a problem or a challenge, or coming to terms with something disturbing or upsetting. There can indeed be something fearsome about the *process* of dying, because that can be painful and humiliating. It is also true that death can prevent one from witnessing or participating in future events to which one may look forward—an eclipse of the sun, a birth of a grandchild—and that can be a cause of regret. But such regret stems from being unable to witness/participate, not from death. Poverty, for example, might have just the same effect, and give rise to just the same regrets.

As for the "meaning of life," I think that that is constructed by each person for himself or herself, and one does it by valuing a wide variety of items—relationships, activities, causes, objects, and so on.

It is possible that some of this valuing may be erroneous, in that it essentially involves false beliefs. To give a secular example: I may think of myself as the inheritor of a long-established family name and title and estates, and I may give meaning to my life by devoting myself to passing on to future generations what I have myself inherited. And this may be true even if my beliefs about my forebears are quite erroneous. In a similar way, it may be true for theists that their meaning-giving activity essentially involves God. But that simply means that that activity is based on some important falsehoods.

Peter H. Gilmore

Peter H. Gilmore is a US author and administrator of the Church of Satan. He was appointed High Priest of the Church in 2001 by Magistra Blanche Barton. Within the church, he is known as Magus Peter H. Gilmore, High Priest of the Church of Satan. As a representative of the Church of Satan, Gilmore has been interviewed on numerous television and radio programs, including venues such as *The History Channel, BBC, The Syfy Channel, Point of Inquiry,* and *Bob Larson's Christian* radio show. Gilmore was raised in upstate New York. He visited New York City regularly throughout his youth and moved to Hell's Kitchen in 1980. Gilmore read *The Satanic Bible* (1976), by Anton LaVey, at age 13 and has described the Church of Satan as "the motivating philosophical force in my life" ever since. In 1989, he and his wife, Peggy Nadramia, began publishing a Satanic journal, *The Black Flame,* and they continue to publish issues sporadically. In 2005, Gilmore wrote the introduction to a new edition of LaVey's *The Satanic Bible,* and his essay on Satanism was published in the *Encyclopedia of Religion and Nature.*

Luís Rodrigues—In the 19th century, the Positivism movement of August Comte assumed that there was no God; nonetheless, Comte favored a church without the metaphysical component. Aren't you doing the same thing? How meaningful can a church be without a transcendental aspect?

Peter H. Gilmore—Comte saw three different evolutionary stages of humanity, and Satanism certainly agrees that a valuable social evolution occurs with the movement of society away from God beliefs toward the use of science and reason as a basis for understanding existence. However, Comte felt that there were innate human rights, and we Satanists know that rights are simply privileges handed out by governments—in fact, there is nothing innate about them. So, his Positivist approach is ultimately not congruent with Satanism. It should be noted that Anton LaVey did not create Satanism in a vacuum, and was aware of earlier pioneers of free thought. He adopted and adapted elements of many prior philosophies. Satanists deny the existence of any spiritual component to existence and are deeply satisfied to be living without such illusions. So, to the Satanist, no transcendental aspects are required to lead a joyous existence. To us, the indifferent universe serves as a canvas upon which we paint the saga of our exciting lives, and any meaning assigned to the universe comes from our own self-determined hierarchy of values—such is our responsibility since we are each our own highest value, and thus our own gods. Hence, the Satanist moves beyond atheism toward I-Theism, with each individual Satanist as his or her primary value. People of a spiritual bent have a fundamentally different nature from the Satanist and thus would not be able to sustain this perspective. They require authority figures and values imposed on them from outside sources, regardless of whether they claim to be supernatural or societal. They don't have the ego strength to feel fulfilled without trying to find enhancement through the illusion of being embraced by something they consider to be "greater" than themselves. So they bow to authority naturally, and submission is their comfort. We Satanists find such a way of living to be anathema and grotesque. We don't expect spiritual people to grasp our nature, but we generally understand theirs, and it is not to our taste. We have no desire to enforce our perspective on that type of person as it doesn't suit them, and we demand the same respect in allowing us to have our individualist stance.

LR—Anton LaVey founded the Church of Satan. What makes him different from other religious founders? Is he subject to the same kind of criticism that most religions and religious leaders receive from atheists, secularists, and nonbelievers in general?

PHG—The founders of most religions claim that they are transmitting some sort of supernatural mandate from a deity. Anton LaVey founded Satanism as a rational exercise in melding psychology and philosophy, and said as much. He did not claim supernatural authority, simply the authority that comes from rigorously crafting a logical thought structure by his own mental efforts. That approach is radically different from the founders of most religions. Because of this, he is absolved from the secularist critique of spiritual religions that claim that their authority is supernaturally derived. Secularists and Satanists see that approach as a form of madness. Additionally, since Satanism is not meant to be a philosophy intended for all humans—contrary to most religions, which intend that all people should come to their way of belief—this rejection of universality as well as the practice of proselytizing also sets Satanism apart from other spiritual doctrines in a way that secularists often find refreshing.

LR—Although you're not a theist, you hold Satan as an inspirational and fictional figure of opposition to God—like, for example, Milton's Satan in *Paradise Lost*. Why do you need to oppose the concept of God?

PHG—There is no inherent need to oppose the concept of God, and Satan is far more than that simplistic concept of being an anti-god. Personally I don't hold in my consciousness a God versus Satan paradigm, and primarily use that imagery only when explaining things to people saddled with dualist perspectives; nor do I find any pressing need to rely on Satan as an opposer of that mythical tyrant. Satan, for me, serves as a symbolic projection of my abilities raised to their highest level of realization, which serves as an opposing and questioning agent toward *anything* that tries to repress or inhibit my will—not just the nonexisting Yahweh. So my personal imagery is of the sentient individual making his way against the indifference of the universe. Here is self-generated dynamism versus shuffling inertia, without the need to even think of calling that dead weight "god" or anthropomorphizing it in any other way. Being one's own god could be construed as monistic, and even, with tongue in cheek, polytheistic when one realizes that many other Satanists see themselves as their own gods, but it is certainly not dualist.

LR—When you're opposing God, aren't you doing him a big favor by permanently legitimatizing its character? In one of the satanic statements of LaVey, it is said that "Satan has been the best friend the Church has ever had, as He has kept it in business all these years." I always thought that the worst enemies of God are not those who fight him, but those who forget or despise him. So it seems that the Church of Satan is not God's enemy after all, isn't that so?

PHG—The Satanic Bible was written in the context of a society that had long accepted Christian symbols as being a standard means for creating definitions. God is a popular belief and so it must be addressed. We can't forget that many people operate under this delusion. That would be like forgetting that people suffered from leprosy in a leper colony. Far from legitimizing the Judeo-Christian concept of this character, the atheist stance in this book is rhetorically spitting in the eye of a God embraced by many in society, making it as iconoclastic as a few pieces of popular literature have been. The final part of your question reiterates the Ninth Satanic Statement, which suggests that the spiritual churches require an enemy with which to frighten people into accepting their doctrines, because many of these are contrary to natural human behavior. People would never elect to deny their own pleasures and to live for a mythical afterlife without the motivation of fear. Thus, the people of power in a religiously oriented society who want to enforce a belief in God require a Satan to play the "bogey man," herding their cowardly followers into the pews and down upon their knees. Satan is obviously their "best friend," in a de facto manner. Satan as a symbol of pride, liberty, and individualism, however, does not require having God as an adversary. Satan can stand alone as a heroic loner. Additionally, Satan symbolically offers acceptance of human nature realistically and pragmatically, without forcing any idealization on the Satanist whatsoever. Embracing the actual without contrasting it with a false ideal does not require dualist tension. We Satanists are not like most secularists, and that includes Comte, in expecting that all humans will evolve away from God beliefs. Contrarily, we think that only a small percentage of humans have the strength to do that, and we think that the herd will always be sheep in need of a shepherd to comfort them in their fear of existence and lack of self-love and inability to embrace self-deification. Thus we aren't activists fighting to liberate them from their belief in God; we just consider belief in God a characteristic, inherent in the majority of humans, which must be understood to be circumvented on the way toward advancing science, technology, and culture.

LR—The principles of Satanism, as you put them, seem to hold on to consensual moral absolutes with a particular emphasis on personal freedoms—no discriminations about sexual practices and same-sex relations, freedom to use drugs, freedom to wear

strange kind of clothes without social concern, etc. Can we call Satanism a philosophy of egotism?

PHG—Satanism requires responsibility to people who are responsible, most importantly including oneself. It is epicurean, expecting rational enjoyment of the full range of physical and intellectual pleasures, not hedonistic in compulsory slavery to simple physical gratification. Our principles are intended to maximize joy and not to force anyone into situations against their will, unless it is their will to be forcing some behavior on others who do not wish it. We stand counter to such tyrannical behavior. So we prohibit sex with children or animals—they have not the maturity or free will to make informed consent, and we are against drug addiction or dependence upon alcohol or any other substance as a means for anesthetizing one's consciousness and escaping from reality. Being hyperconscious is the Satanist's goal, and that comes from being educated and aware, not from chemical props. Egotism is often seen as having a negative connotation, implying an individual sacrificing all others to his own pursuits. Satanism is instead egoistic, championing a healthy self-love, which then allows for the love and respect of others who have worth based on the individual's personal value system. Satanists understand the social contract which our species requires, and so we know how to deal with the hierarchies of humans we encounter in our daily existence. Always remember that we are pragmatic, not idealistic. We deal with the way our species actually behaves, with no intention of turning it into something else. Life is too short for such windmill tilting.

LR—Isn't Satanism more of an "artistic manifesto" rather then a religious—or irreligious—movement committed to a philosophical or metaphysical system of thought? I mean, when we look at your rituals, your symbolic constructions, aren't you trying to create a kind of "atheist artistic *pathos*"—one that was only achieved by the theist art of Christianity?

PHG—No. Aesthetics can play a large role in Satanism, and each Satanist—depending upon their own talents—will decide just how much of Satanism will be explored through artistic pursuits, whether it be in the creation of any of the arts—visual, musical, literary—or through the employment of the cathartic psychodrama that is the definition and purpose of Satanic ritual. It is important to note that not all Satanists employ the tool of ritual, nor are all Satanists artists. Certain symbols and signs and colors can serve as a theatrical shorthand, and thus we avail ourselves of such effective means for communication. However, it would be a mistake to assume that all Satanists wear black or like music that uses devil-themed lyrics and imagery. Thus anyone who thought that Satanism was primarily an artistic manifesto would be seen to be a shallow poseur and sham by authentic Satanists. The actual foundation of Satanism is a commitment to the rejection of spirituality as a myth and the understanding that all religions are human inventions and thus not in any way sacred. Satanism for all true Satanists is primarily a philosophical system of thought that is antispiritual and thus irreligious. It can also be seen as a source of an adversarial artistic manifesto to those Satanists who consider themselves to be artists, and that can span many schools of expression, but that aspect is only an addition to Satanism being a materialist and misanthropic philosophy.

LR—It seems that Marilyn Manson, one of your members, more than just trying to shock people's moral standards and conventional ideas, is trying to achieve an artistic objective through what we could call an "inverse *pathos*," one that uses the reversed symbolical models of Christianity to obtain the same result: people's awe. Don't you see here the same kind of opportunistic attempt to manipulate the masses—one that he so much criticizes in our contemporary society?

PHG—Brian "Marilyn Manson" Warner is simply using propagandistic and entertainment techniques to make himself a great deal of money based on the forgetfulness of past orthodoxies inherent in the consumers of his products. I frankly don't care what his personal artistic intentions are, since they are his self-expression alone and are not considered to be a representation of Satanism or the Church of Satan. He is free to express himself in whatever way it suits him—he is not speaking for me or Satanism. He appears to use whatever symbols push the masses' buttons, and the result is that he has at times shocked the crowds and ultimately laughed all the way to the bank. His techniques are utterly opportunistic, and why shouldn't they be? He's a successful entertainer, not a prophet, and he sells prepackaged images of rebellion to people who are not authentic rebels. I'm sure he's aware that the masses exist to be manipulated, it has been done by governments and churches throughout all history, and the irony of selling individualist badges to people en masse is a concept beyond most of his listeners, affirming the Satanic disdain for the majority of humans. If a young person wanted to truly rebel, he would listen to something different from what those around him are playing. He wouldn't opt for the music presented by the media as conforming or the music labeled by others as rebellious. He'd listen to music nobody else his age had found, like obscure popular songs from the 1920s through the 1950s, or ancient madrigals, or symphonic compositions by largely unknown composers and other music that would require some searching to obtain. He would not be conforming—he would be exploring realms that are hidden to his peers because of their narrow-cast attention span that absorbs only what is paraded before them.

LR—You appreciate composers like Beethoven or Bruckner; as a Satanist, how do you deal with some of these composers' lyrics? "Te Deum Laudamus" (We praise you God) doesn't seem to me very Satanic.

PHG—Music is emotional, not didactic. Since I'm an atheist, it doesn't matter to me if somebody creates a marvelous structure in either stone and brick or musical tones arranged in complex structures evoking splendid emotions, if these creations were inspired by something I know doesn't exist. Wagner was a collectivist in his anti-Semitism, a position that is utterly un-Satanic, and probably quite an annoying individual to be around, but that doesn't stop me from admiring the great music he wrote. I'm not a small-minded, knee-jerk opponent to anything that uses words that aren't congruent with my values. I don't eat seafood, but if someone painted a brilliant still life of fish in a market, that wouldn't stop me from appreciating the piece. If you've read my writings about the great composers, you'll have noted that I admire the emotional and architectural power in their works. Some composer could write a fabulous cantata about elves or pink elephants. If those images of inspiration brought out that musician's highest achievement, such mythical sources wouldn't sour me on the work's greatness. Music arouses complex emotions as a response to abstract organized sound, so if a composer evokes emotions in me that I treasure—joy, pride, grandeur, nobility, heroism, and so on—and if they are embodied in a tonal architecture that impresses me with its discipline, elaborateness, and brilliance of balanced flux, then it matters not what personal inspiration fueled that creation. Additionally, using sleight of mind, one can always place apparently objectionable lyrics in a different light: If one sees oneself as one's own god, a work singing praises to God can easily be viewed as singing praises to yourself!

LR—You once said that you love cathedrals. Doesn't a cathedral offend you as a form of "Christian propaganda"?

PHG—Not at all. Just as I don't mind the wonderful frescoes and other visual artworks that were used to teach illiterates the tales from that storybook called the Bible. I'm solely offended by the ideals and beliefs of Christianity themselves, since they are not suitable for me and appear to be perversions of human nature, but if they inspire others to create something of grandeur and brilliance, I appreciate and admire the human achievement and disregard the source as irrelevant. Architecture strikes me as music made three dimensional, and so if it is a fine effort, the intended function of the building is not critical, unless there is an additional brilliance in achieving advanced function through original form.

LR—You assume that the Church of Satan is an atheist church. But, by choosing this way to profess your atheism, aren't you opening the Pandora's box for the sprawling of atheistic and theistic Satanic amoral congregations or other dangerous occult societies? Why don't you profess your atheism or indignation about the actual social order without appealing to such a device as Satan?

PHG—We don't "assume that the Church of Satan is an atheist church"; it *is* an atheist church. And Satanism is a moral philosophy, though our values are quite different from those of other churches since they are crafted to promote liberty, responsibility, pride, and individualism. The fear you express of "atheistic and theistic satanic amoral congregations" is opposed by our stance since we are the only legitimate Satanists, and that our philosophy is rational and coherent precludes distortions amongst intelligent individuals. You should be aware that humans have created insane religions throughout history, and they are theistic, and that includes Christianity in all its denominations and Islam as well, and anyone who can read should know from the blood-soaked pages of historical chronicles that no new "satanic amoral congregation" could possibly begin to match the reigns of terror and the millions of victims slaughtered by these currently accepted spiritual religions. Satan is a magnificent device since the symbol energizes and inspires we Satanists. You might be making false assumptions that all Satanists have "indignation about the current social order," which if observed carefully is seen to vary globally. Political issues are decided pragmatically by each Satanist so there is a wide range of viewpoints amongst our membership depending upon nation of residence. So, no, we have not opened Pandora's box—that prison of concepts that might be inimical to establishments was blasted wide millennia ago, hence its enshrinement in that Greek fable. Are any "occult societies" dangerous? Satanism is not occultism. Before any reasonable answer can be given, you need to define your terms as to what sort of society you consider to be "occult" and to who or what they might pose a threat, and just what that threat might be.

LR—I was thinking about something like Freemasonry, Skull and Bones, the Trilateral Commission, the Bilderberg Group, and so on. Can these groups of individuals be identified with Satanism? After all, they pursue their self-interest, the enhancement of their personal power, the "domination of the herd," and so on. Can their agenda also be understood as a threat?

PHG—Satanists always laugh at people who believe in conspiracy theories since such thinking is just plain paranoia. Behaviorally speaking, the impulse to think this way is simply another element of scape goating, wherein powerless individuals who fear that the world is evolving around them in ways they don't understand need to blame somebody, and so they pick acknowledged groups of powerful and wealthy individuals who live on social strata that cannot be entered by these people. Since these "have-nots" are Christian, anyone who is much more successful than they must be seen as being in league with Satan. However, the real truth is that they are not. They aren't Satanists, they aren't occultists. They are just an aristocracy of money and power, and many consider themselves to be Christians. Freemasonry at one time was a society of moneyed intellectuals and freethinkers who enjoyed meeting with other like-minded individuals who had ideas both scientific and governmental, which were not supported by Europe's dominant Christian denominations. Today, Freemasonry is essentially just a networking club for midlevel businessmen. All of their "secret writings and rituals" have long been published. Nothing to fear, and not connected to Satanism. The Skull and Bones Society is a university fraternity that counts as its members the children of wealthy families, and so it is a form of social club that has some spooky theatrical rituals (Satan is not mentioned in them) that make it seem more serious than it is. Christian churches have far more macabre rites and rituals. So this is how some of the wealthy enjoy interacting—it makes them feel powerful, but has nothing to do with Satanism. The Trilateral Commission and the Bilderberg Group are organizations that are global in scope that gather people, again the wealthy corporate magnates, but also others who might be brokers of ideas relating to the globalization of business and the concomitant homogenization of culture that follows when you have a world consuming the produce of a limited group of corporations. People who fear change and who fear cultures outside of their own might not like that the world is becoming a more unified culture that is losing entrenched local uniqueness, but this will eventually lead to less xenophobia and higher standards of living worldwide. Again, Satanism is not involved here, but people who have faith in ancient scriptures and can't deal with the fact that there are many millions of people around the globe who do not share their beliefs might see a diabolical hand threatening the parochialism of their mindsets. There is no danger to their personal beliefs, only to their ability to force them on others, especially their children, who can see that there are alternatives. They fear that their minds might be opened to different points of view, and that is a dangerous position to hold. We Satanists applaud the advance of secularism that comes with rational globalization, but we also are sad to see the oddities of certain cultures vanishing, since many of us are students of the human animal and enjoy the weird and wacky ways of all peoples. Finally, the ultimate truth behind why there are no real conspiracies, Satanic or otherwise, is that people cannot keep secrets and are far too inept to actually make one succeed.

LR—Since they did not worship ancient pagan gods, early Christians were seen as atheists, cannibals, and bloodsuckers (for supposedly eating the flesh and blood of a man called Jesus Christ); isn't it ironic that the Satanists are now dealing with the same levels of incomprehension that once afflicted early Christians?

PHG—It is entirely expected, not ironic. We are not ignorant of history or the human psychology of "scape-goating" behavior. Christians, when empowered as the official religion, did the same thing to the Jews with the very same tales of blood drinking, cannibalism, and atheism. That's why we Satanists enjoy the idea of using the goat head in our Sigil of Baphomet. It reminds us—beyond the celebration of fertility that goats have been historically—that people will always dehumanize their enemies, which then allows for empathy to be abandoned and utmost cruelty to be employed in extermination of what is considered to be alien. Xenophobia is one of our species' less attractive traits, and we do not forget that.

LR—Is part of Satanism's appeal to you based in the idea of being a member of an underground subculture? Have you ever wished for a Satanic state, a Satanic society?

PHG—As a Satanist I participate in whatever parts of human culture interest me, moving freely amongst various strata. Since Satanism is extremely individualist, trying to peg it as a subculture simply saddles it with stereotypical images that are far off the mark. Satanism itself is a tool for achieving the most out of one's existence, and that tool is a pragmatic philosophy. And it is hardly underground—all of our literature and the creative works of our members are readily available to anyone interested. Calling it a subculture makes false assumptions that lead to a misunderstanding of how Satanists actually live and pursue their personal bliss. Satanism is realist, and so all human society is essentially Satanic since it exists as the framework through which we all move in a never-ending struggle for our share in the world's bounties. The few who deeply understand human behavior, the passions and drives of the feral primates who arrogantly call themselves "*Homo sapiens*," can get the most out of whatever situation they find themselves in. They are Satanists in society who live satanically; they are not ghettoized in some caricature-laden "underground subculture." In fact, many people wouldn't even realize that they are dealing with a Satanist unless that Satanist decided to reveal their personal philosophy. There are no required badges, colors, or choices of symbols, music, or clothing styles that would give them away. Satanists are free to enjoy whatever is pleasing to them. A truly Satanic state would not identify itself as such, since that would be counter-productive—frightening the populace. It would be recognizable in its profound support of individual liberty. Many might see the basic concepts that inform the founding documents of the United States to already be quite diabolical in their celebration of meritocracy and rejection of hereditary aristocracy. So if you look carefully, you might see that by some definitions, a Satanic state and Satanic society might already be in place, which may be one reason why repressive spiritual religions could call the United States "The Great Satan." To Satanists, there would be some appropriateness to that moniker.

A. C. Grayling

A. C. Grayling, M.A., D.Phil. (Oxon) is professor of philosophy at Birkbeck College, University of London, and is a supernumerary fellow of Saint Anne's College, Oxford. He has written and edited many books on philosophy and other subjects; among his most recent are a biography of William Hazlitt and a collection of essays. For several years, he wrote the "Last Word" column for the *Guardian* newspaper and is a regular reviewer for the *Literary Review* and the *Financial Times*. He also often writes for the *Observer, Economist, Times Literary Supplement, Independent on Sunday,* and *New Statesman* and is a frequent broadcaster on BBC Radios 4, 3, and the World Service. He is the editor of *Online Review London* and contributing editor of *Prospect* magazine. Grayling is a past chairman of June Fourth, a human rights group concerned with China, and has been involved in UN human rights initiatives. He is also a fellow of the World Economic Forum and a member of its C-100 group on relations between the West and the Islamic world; of the Royal Society of Literature; and also of the Royal Society of Arts, and in 2003, he was a Booker Prize judge.

Luís Rodrigues—When and why did you become an atheist?

A. C. Grayling—I think I was always one; I was not brought up in a religious household, and therefore came into contact with religious beliefs and practices only after going to school—and they seemed to me as alien and surprising as the beliefs of the ancient Zoroastrians would seem to most people today.

LR—Most people tend to see life as the product of a divine will or plan: "nothing happens by chance," they say. If people are

not "condemned to be free" (as Sartre has said), are they condemned to be manipulated?

ACG—Most people are manipulated because they do not think and
choose for themselves, partly because they are never encouraged to and
mainly because they are too reluctant to—thinking and choosing for
oneself is hard. Most people would rather be told what to think than to
have to work it out for themselves.

**LR—If one believes in a personal God (or the idea of the super-
natural) apart from any organized religion, there wouldn't be an
argument to refute such a deity. How can a dialogue be established in a society that more and more tends to profess such a
subjective view of "spirituality"?**

ACG—Personal, cherry-picked, convenient "spiritualities" are increasingly commonplace, because people cling to superstitious beliefs while
not wishing to observe the strict traditional moralities and practices
associated with them. The argument against any supernaturalistic outlook applies here as it does to organized religion. The question of any
given supernaturalistic belief and the question of the role of religious
institutions in society are separate though connected matters. The first
is a question of metaphysics, the second a question of secularism and
politics.

**LR—What are, for you, the most convincing arguments that can
help people conceive of the existence of the universe without
the intervention of a supernatural creator?**

ACG—If you point out to people that believing in the God of Christianity or Islam is the same as believing that there are fairies in your garden, then, from the point of view of tradition, evidence (including
scientific views of nature), and reason, anyone capable of grasping the
point will see that, as it is irrational to include in one's thinking about
the world a commitment to there being fairies in the garden, so it is
irrational to include in one's worldview, still less to base one's worldview on, a belief in the existence of any supernatural entities. And one
can point out that believers in any of the traditional religions' deities
includes atheism about all the others—so, today's Christians do not

believe in the gods of Olympus (Zeus, Hera, Poseidon, and so on) or of the Hindus (Vishnu, Siva, and so on). Why stop at the last one after disbelieving in so many dozens of others? The same reasoning applies to the last one as to the others.

LR—You say that 80 percent of British charities are nonreligious, and nonreligious people give more to charity than self-described adherents to a faith. But what if the contrary happens. In Portugal, for instance, religious charities and organizations have a stronger presence in society. In such conditions, how can atheism be more morally acceptable?

ACG—The fact that most British charities are nonreligious and most charitable giving is by nonreligious people proves that charity does not need religion. The fact that matters are the other way in Portugal is a function of history; Portugal as a Catholic country has had a harder time shaking off the influence of the Church and the associated mindset.

LR—Most believers aren't informed about atheist literature and philosophy—maybe because they think they will be tempted by Satan on every page of such books. (In the case of Nietzsche, for example, just the title "The Antichrist" is enough to scare a lot of Christians.) Can you recommend some atheist books or authors designed to reach the liberal and open-minded believers as well as the most devout ones?

ACG—It is a condemnation of believers that they are not open-minded or secure enough to accept the challenge of reading atheist works. But for the literature that might be more agreeable to sensitive souls on this score, I recommend the great classics of the ancient world, from Plato to Cicero, in which the occasional reference to deities has no connection with the kind of religion that the world has been led to regard as proper religion ever since Christianity and Islam—latecomers on the scene—became dominant.

LR—Most religious people insist that their religion must be respected, even by nonbelievers. How can an atheist respect

something that, from his point of view, constitutes a downgrading of human rationality?

ACG—An atheist cannot respect belief systems that are based on irrationality, the ignorance of the past, and superstition. I certainly do not respect them, and one of the biggest shifts of recent times is that the courtesy paid to people who choose to have a religious faith has begun to evaporate. This is not the same thing as being disrespectful to individual human beings who believe for many reasons in addition to not thinking clearly and honestly about the matter—they might be fearful or lonely and in need of solace (churches prey on such people to recruit new members), or they might have been indoctrinated as children. In the case of Islam, there is a massive social pressure to conform and believe, with death being the punishment for apostasy in some cases.

LR—Eastern European countries were once subjected to atheist materialism. Some of them are now turning to Christianity. As an atheist, how can you explain this "philosophical and intellectual regress"? Doesn't this prove that atheism got something wrong?

ACG—Communism was and is officially atheist, but not only did traditional faith never die out in those societies, it was kept alive by the poverty and hardship from which (as Marx pointed out in his "opium of the people" remark) religion provided a relief of sorts. Active persecution, too, is an excellent way of keeping a religion alive. When Judaism was not so heavily persecuted, it began to fade—see the 19th century in the German-speaking countries—but when it is persecuted it flourishes. If the Communists had really thought properly about liberating minds, they should have allowed religion to die a natural death—by not encouraging religious indoctrination of children, by making life good and satisfying, and by leaving religion otherwise alone. That is, they should have followed the method being applied (unconsciously) in most of Europe, where religious observance is slowly diminishing.

LR—How can atheists use their voice and spread their ideas in conservative societies?

ACG—By continuing the debate, the argument, the information, the discussion, the challenge; by writing, lecturing. By living good and honorable lives on humanist principles. By showing people that there is a rich, deep alternative to superstition and religion, via humanism—and by inviting others to live with a free mind.

LR—How do you think atheism will evolve in Europe?

ACG—Atheism is growing, has grown, is the default of almost all societies now, despite the noisy protestations of the religious lobbies who seem bigger than they are because of the noise they make—but that is characteristic of any movement that is in decline: The more it dies, the louder it shouts.

LR—What is, for you, the meaning of life without a God?

ACG—The meaning of life is the meaning that we give it by our endeavor, our work, our choices, our responsibilities and ambitions. At the heart of all good lives are good relationships; a life is good if it is a welcome, willed striving toward goals that are themselves good—for even if we do not attain them, the effort to attain them is what confers value on a life. There are as many kinds of good lives as there are people to live them, for we all have different talents for making good lives. We must be able to defend our choice of values, must seek never to harm others but to see ourselves in fellowship with them in allowing them or helping them to their own idea of a good life too. And then there can be a chance to flourish and achieve, to grow, to know friendship and affection, and to do something that feels deeply worthwhile, and which might be of value to others too. That is what a good life means, and therefore that is the meaning of life.

Chris Hedges

Chris Hedges is a journalist and author specializing in US and Middle Eastern politics and society. Hedges is currently a senior fellow at *The Nation Institute*, a lecturer in the *Council of the Humanities*, and the Anschutz distinguished fellow at Princeton University. He spent nearly two decades as a foreign correspondent in Central America, the Middle East, Africa, and the Balkans. He has reported from more than 50 countries and has worked for the *Christian Science Monitor, National Public Radio*, the *Dallas Morning News*, and the *New York Times*, where he was a reporter for 15 years. Hedges was part of the *New York Times* team that won the 2002 Pulitzer Prize for coverage of global terrorism. In 2002, he received the Amnesty International Global Award for Human Rights Journalism. Hedges's bestselling *War Is a Force that Gives Us Meaning* (2002) draws on his experiences in various conflicts to describe the patterns and behavior of nations and individuals in wartime. The book was a finalist for the National Book Critics Circle Award for Nonfiction in 2002.

Luís Rodrigues—Can you tell me how and why you became a believer?

Chris Hedges—I grew up in the Church, so it was never a question for me. I learned very early on to distinguish between institutional religion and the religious impulse. My father—although a minister—was often in conflict with the institutional church. But that side of life, that honoring of the nonrational forces of love, beauty, questions of meaning and forgiveness, all the things that we cannot measure empirically, was always part of my life and my education.

LR—You were a foreign correspondent in countries shattered by war. What is the general feeling of the local populations

concerning God? Do they feel abandoned by God? Is their faith reinforced?

CH—In conflict or wars, institutional religion usually is part of the problem rather than the solution in the sense that religious institutions often back or support nationalist causes. One saw that, for example, in the wars in the former Yugoslavia where the Catholic Church in Croatia would back the Croatian cause, the Serbian Orthodox Church in Serbia would back the Serbian nationalist cause, and the mosques in Bosnia would support the Bosnian nationalist cause. So, in all of the conflicts that I covered, institutions used their religious authority to support one faction or another in the war. Now, there were always courageous individuals—people who often came out of those institutions—who defied the message of war, but they were always pushed aside by those institutions. In terms of the actual people who were caught up in the conflict, I would say that the reactions varied: In some cases there was a deep bitterness, a feeling that they had been betrayed by God, while, at the same time, others found sustenance in belief. But I wouldn't say that there was a uniform or a common response; I would say that it varied according to the individual.

LR—Do you remember any story about someone who either found or lost God in that process?

CH—I often ran into people who exhibited great compassion and courage on behalf of another—including a stranger or somebody defined as the enemy. If you look at my book *War Is a Force that Gives Us Meaning*, you can read the story of Fasil Fajdic, a Muslim who saved the life of a small Serbian infant girl. Those kinds of stories, those acts of human compassion and human kindness, I think, sustain the divine spark—which is love. Those figures exist—certainly not a majority by any means—in every conflict I covered, and they cross religious boundaries. But I think that what they do is, at its essence, deeply religious.

LR—Talking about boundaries, do people's feelings change when religion or country changes? I mean, according to religion or nationality, who do you think are the most disappointed and the most optimistic people concerning an intervention of God in their current state of affairs?

CH—The more dangerous your world becomes, the more loss of control that you experience, the more you appeal for divine intervention. I will argue that's probably a form of superstition rather than belief, but it's not something that anyone—including myself—was exempt from. When people are desperately afraid—especially when they believe that they're facing their own mortality—they will instinctively appeal to a higher power, and that is true for people who come out of a religious tradition and people who don't come out of any religious tradition at all.

LR—A title of one of your books tells us that "war is a force that gives us meaning." What about religion? Isn't religion the main force that gives meaning to people in times of distress?

CH—I think many people seek meaning through violence and war, It ultimately betrays them, however; ultimately does not give them meaning. But there is an intoxication with power and a seduction of violence that functions like a malformed theology, a kind of godless religion and has a very enticing appeal to many people. Power and violence are seductive forces, and it's very difficult for authentically religious voices in moments of war to speak out on behalf of compassion, acceptance, tolerance, and dialogue; they became very lonely voices.

LR—How do you define authentic religious voices?

CH—Authentic religious voices are ones that recognize our common humanity; a humanity that crosses ethnic, racial, and gender lines, lines of class, lines of nation; that sees within all human individuals the sanctity of life. That's for me an authentic religious voice.

LR—What if faith, not truth, turns out to be the best tool to provide comfort to humanity? What would you choose: comfort or truth? Why?

CH—Well, I don't think the truth is ever comfortable; I think that many religious figures—for instance, the evangelical or Christian right in the United States—make people feel comfortable, but they do so without engaging in that process of self-criticism or self-reflection; they don't grapple with the nature of their own sin, with their own evil. So, I don't think truth is ever comfortable. I think moral responsibility creates a kind of anxiety—or in Freudian terms, a neurosis—that always makes life difficult, but I think that's what the religious life is. I don't think it is meant to be easy or comfortable.

LR—You've certainly talked to people involved in humanitarian aid. Are religious motives relevant for their commitment to help others?

CH—There is no such thing as a simple motive—that's something that I experienced as a war correspondent. For instance, you can be appalled and angered by the abuse that is being carried out by Bosnian Serb forces against the residents of the city of Sarajevo and you may want to help them genuinely, but you're not free from those adrenaline rushes, from the excitement, from that elevation of yourself as the savior coming from the outside. Motives are always mixed; no act is ever quite as moral in our own eyes as it is in the eyes of our colleagues, and certainly, in the eyes of our foes. I think that's important to remember. I think the motivation for aid workers—like the motivation for war journalists—can sometimes be good and sometimes be dark. Just as people who embrace orthodox religious views can sometimes do so for very dark reasons, reasons that have more to do with self-exultation, for instance. In that sense, I think that there are always many undercurrents that propel people to do things—and even when they're ostensibly doing good things, sometimes their motives are not good.

LR—Do you privilege the process or do you privilege the result?

CH—Well . . . finally, it's the result. There is a huge difference between delivering United Nations' food and gunning people down in the streets; so yes, it's finally the result. But I don't believe in saints. I think that even when we carry out an act that we define as virtuous or good, we have to be honest that there are motives that go into that act that are not healthy. There is a huge difference between affirming life and taking life, and that's the difference between war and everything else. The essence of war is death, it is a kind of worship at the feet of the god of death, it's about the destruction of all systems of life—economic, familial, political, social—and that's the chasm between war and everything else.

LR—You are very skeptical concerning humanity's moral progress. Don't we move forward when we abolish things like slavery or promote things like women's suffrage?

CH—We make advances, certainly, although the sex trade, for example, is alive and well—and it is certainly legitimate to describe it as a form of slavery. Yes, we make moral advances, but then we make moral reverses. The 20th century is marked by industrial warfare, which is primarily about the killing of civilians; by the creation of the atom bomb—probably the ultimate weapon of terror; by technology and industry, which are destroying the very ecosystem that sustains the human species. So, yes, we make moral advances, we make moral reverses. I don't think there's anything in human nature or human history to support the idea that we progress morally. The tools change, but we do not. I think that people who embrace linear concepts of time are self-deluded; often the idea that collective moral progress is possible becomes dangerous when it's wedded to a belief that we can use violence in order to carry out—or eradicate—human impediments to progress. The war in Iraq for instance, is a utopian vision—and I use the word *utopia* the way Thomas More meant it to be used when he coined the word in 1518: "no place"; it doesn't exist, it's not a reality-based vision—and I speak as someone who was a Middle East bureau chief for the *New York Times*, spent seven years in the Middle East, much of that time in Iraq, and is an Arabic speaker. The notion that we would be greeted as liberators—I'm talking about the American occupation forces—and that democracy would be implanted in Baghdad and emanate outward, that the oil revenues would pay for the reconstruction: These are utopian visions, they are not reality based. When you wed utopianism to violence it always descends into criminality and moral depravity—and that is precisely what the war in Iraq is.

LR—Are you against any utopian vision of progress or specific visions of progress?

CH—We have nothing to fear from people who don't believe in God; we have everything to fear from people who don't believe in sin. Every genocide that I ever covered was carried out by idealists. What I'm against is this notion that evil is somehow externalized in other human beings—or other social groups—and that if we could only eradicate this evil, the world would be a better place. Once you employ violence—especially war—you become the demon you set out to fight, even if that violence is justifiable; and so, utopian schemes frighten me. I'm a great believer in what the philosopher Karl Popper called piecemeal engineering: that we best make changes, incrementally, slowly, calculat-edly. The wholesale sweeping away of one order and creating a new order is always disastrous, and I think human history bears me out on that.

LR—But don't you uphold the utopian vision of progress of Martin Luther King when he says "I have a dream"?

CH—Yes, but first of all, he embraced nonviolence—that's not a small difference—and second of all, he spoke very specifically about integra-tion, about the breaking of racial barriers—and that was a reality-based vision, there was a real possibility. Utopian dreamers dream of a society—or a human construct—that is not reality based, and that would be the difference between Dick Cheney, who pushed the war in Iraq, and Martin Luther King. One of the visions was possible, and therefore, *not* utopia. Utopian visions can never be fulfilled; they can't exist—that is the root of the word *utopia*: no place.

LR—Speaking of utopias, Lewis Mumford wrote a very interest-ing book called *The Story of Utopia*. Is there any utopia that appeals to you—for instance, the utopia of Christianopolis?

CH—I haven't read Mumford's book. It may be the way we define the word, but I'm very skeptical of all visions that call for a kind of perfecti-ble human society. I don't think that human society is ever perfectible; I think that we are always going to be captive to our animal instinct and our self-interests. If you look closely at most philosophical and theolog-ical systems, they act as a kind of justification for our own power; so many theological or philosophical systems have been advocated not because they had superior intellectual or moral content but because they were backed by force. That's how Christianity was spread throughout Europe. I have a very dark view of human nature and I don't believe that it's redeemable. I've seen what happens when societies break down; I understand that Hobbesian universe that we all have the capacity to create.

LR—Socrates had a capacity for making questions that we now lack in our contemporary societies and daily lives, isn't that so?

CH—Yes, it's fascinating to me that most of the great moral thinkers excused the written word. Socrates, Francis of Assisi, even Jesus: They never wrote anything down because they were terrified about the codification of belief. That great Wittgenstein line: "Tell me the questions you ask and I will tell you what it is you seek"—I'm very much in agreement with that notion, with that constant process of questioning. Not only ourselves but the world around us leads us to the possibility of a moral life.

LR—You said that worse than not believing in God was not believing in sin. Why do you think theological constructs like the concept of sin are necessary to inform morality? Don't you think it's possible to construct a moral code without reference to religious background?

CH—Yes, of course. There's nothing intrinsically moral about being a believer or a nonbeliever, and many people have led lives of great moral courage and probity without recourse to religious ritual, religious belief, or religious language, just as many people who are ostensibly very religious have used their religious authority to carry out bigotry, intolerance, exclusion, persecution, and violence. I'm very aware of that, not only on a theoretical level but on a personal level in virtue of the wars that I've covered. I used the word *sin* because I think it works; you could use another word. In Freudian terms, it is the fact that we are captive to instincts, or to a subconscious, or to a libido, powerful forces within us that we can't control. I think there is a kind of wisdom to the understanding of Original Sin, but in psychoanalytic terms there are other ways to describe the limitations of being human without using the word *sin*.

LR—When the stoning of women to death in countries like Iran, Pakistan, Afghanistan, Nigeria, and Saudi Arabia is justified by religious law—the Sharia—and when the same source of religious moral code informed Moses to massacre the Levites, how can one see "religious morality"—or the source of morality coming from religion—as something good, as something desirable?

CH—There's a big difference between what's written down in religious texts and the religious impulse. There's no shortage of examples within any scriptural text of the morally indefensible. This is a very imperfect and flawed attempt—I'm talking about the writing of religious texts, the creation of religious dogma—by human beings to acknowledge the power of the transcendent, those forces that do not lend themselves to empirical study: love, beauty, grief, alienation, mortality, our struggle for meaning. These are all real forces in human life, and I think, at its best, religion struggles to do what art does, which is to honor and acknowledge those forces. In many ways, I don't think we can be complete human beings until we are in touch with the rational and the nonrational—that doesn't mean irrational, that means those nonrational forces. In Buddhism, you can memorize as many sutras as you want but it will never make you wise. Wisdom comes from intuition, from an understanding of human nature and the world around you and how it works. There are many routes to that that I would define as religious, but outside the confines of institutional religion. Institutional religion throughout human history has often been part of the problem because institutional religious figures habitually use religion to consolidate their own power and authority and carry out acts that are not morally justifiable. That's sort of the history of religious institutions, but I think we do have to separate those very human institutions. The theologian Paul Tillich said that all institutions—including the church—are inherently demonic because ultimately they are concerned less with morality than with their own self-perpetuation. But that doesn't mitigate or cancel out the religious impulse itself—which I think is real.

LR—Being an envoy to various countries in the world, have you ever noticed relevant differences in commitment between the various strands of, for example, Christianity? Are some "Christianities" better than others, or, because they share the same institutional character, do they have no differences?

CH—I would say all institutional religion is flawed and that people who care about belief should be very wary of institutional authority—no matter where it comes from. That said, there are, of course, differences between fundamentalist movements and more tolerant strains of religious belief. Fundamentalism frightens me and I don't really care whether that comes as Christian, Jewish, Hindu, or Islamic. These fundamentalists have far more in common with each other than they do often with fellow believers in their own religious society. So, yes, fundamentalism as a movement is a very dark and terrifying one which, at its core, is really about self-worship, self-exultation—or in biblical terms, a form of idolatry. There are differences, but I think, for those who have a conscience, they can probably expect to be in defiance of any institution—even one defined as liberal.

LR—How can people understand the frontier of "what is good" if some religious institutions are the only example of goodness that they see around them? For example, Hamas provides health care for a considerable number of people in Gaza. By capturing the hearts of the people, aren't these political/religious institutions projecting an image of goodness and love of themselves?

CH—No, because love is unconditional, so it's not love. In return for that kind of support, women have to wear headscarves, men are expected to pray five times a day in the local mosque, and Hamas expects to get support in return for that assistance. There is a political calculation behind that assistance and the tragedy is that Palestinians have been pushed to such a subsistence level that that's the only alternative they have. I've spent a lot of time with Hamas and they're probably—and ironically—some of most idealistic people I've ever met. They're also some of the most frightening because they believe in their absolute truth—and in their world vision; they believe that they have the right to kill in order to make that vision possible. Revolutionaries, religious fundamentalists, are often very earnest and very idealistic. When you spent time with them—as I have—there is a kind of naïve, childlike belief that they can make a better world. The problem, of course, is that they embrace violence or force to do that.

LR—Do you think they lose the frontiers of good and evil with that idealism?

CH—Well, I think that, again, it gets to that kind of utopianism. Once you marry that utopian belief with violence it becomes an evil in the name of good. Most people kill in the name of virtue and goodness; I mean, we kill in Iraq in the name of democracy, freedom, and liberty.

LR—What do you think are, actually, the worst religious, secularist, or atheist governments in the world?

CH—Any totalitarian government, religious or secular, is the most frightening because it has a complete and utter disregard for the sanctity of human life. I think it's better to define these movements as utopian. Fascism was a utopian movement; Communism was a utopian movement; religious fundamentalism is a utopian movement. These movements all believe they have been anointed—either by God or by history—to eradicate those human beings who stand in the way of their utopia or their perfected idea of society, and those are always the worst kinds of government.

LR—What about atheist governments?

CH—What's Communist China? That's a good example of totalitarian atheism.

LR—You have a book entitled, *I Don't Believe in Atheists*. Can you summarize what and why you don't believe in them? Are you referring to all atheists or some atheists?

CH—I'm referring to the new crop of atheists who use the language of scientific rationalism to promote a kind of secular fundamentalism, a belief that they have a moral superiority over other people. Like any serious student of philosophy and theology, I have a great deal of respect for self-defined atheists—people like Camus, Nietzsche. I fully understand that atheism has an honored and important place in the Western intellectual tradition, that most great religious and philosophical reformers in their day were condemned as atheists and heretics—people like Spinoza and Martin Luther—so, the title is sort of a cue because what I'm really fighting are people who, under the guise of atheism, promote a kind of utopian vision that scares me, a kind of fundamentalist vision in secular clothing that I find frightening—whether that comes from religious believers or atheists.

LR—What do you see as the greatest threat to a religious liberal standing: atheism or postmodern relativism?

CH—Not atheism. No, it's probably postmodern relativism; the fact that they don't know what they stand for—or if they *should* stand for anything, what they should be tolerant of or not tolerant of. There's a terrible kind of flaccid quality to bourgeois liberal belief that makes it frighteningly incapable of taking on these fundamentalist movements.

LR—As a Christian, what are your feelings concerning the Christian right in America?

CH—I think that they are the most dangerous mass movement in American history. I think that's what they are—a mass movement. They seek secular power. Any group that fuses the iconography and language of American nationalism with American Christianity is terrifying and, I think, probably rightly termed fascist—and that's what they are.

LR—Do you believe that the Christian right is subverting the message of the Bible?

CH—Yes, I think they're Christian heretics.

LR—But how can you define what standards must be used to interpret the Bible?

CH—That's the problem with liberals: They don't believe they can define any standards, and therefore they have nothing to say to us. You can't make a moral choice if you don't have standards. The notions that Jesus came to make us all wealthy, that America is somehow blessed over other nations, that Jesus would want us to drop iron fragmentation bombs all over the Muslim world—as somebody who has spent his life reading the Bible, these are forms of heresy. That is a complete corruption of the message of Jesus Christ—who, by the way, was a pacifist. I'm not a pacifist but Jesus was clearly a pacifist.

LR—What has been the role of the media concerning the national and international conflicts between different religious groups? Has it promoted it with a kind of "us and them" rhetoric, or has it diminished it by informing the viewers about the broader social, political, and economical context of those conflicts?

CH—The problem with the media is that it tends to speak in clichés or through stereotypes so that it will define, for instance, the conflict in the former Yugoslavia as a religious conflict. It was not a religious conflict, it was not about ancient ethnic hatreds: It was about the economic collapse of Yugoslavia, the rise of nationalist proto-Fascist movements that set off the personal and economic despair of various groups. It becomes a facile and easy way to describe a conflict without actually investigating its roots or its antecedents.

LR—Aren't the media manipulating the demons inside us by giving people a stereotypical image to hate—or to love?

CH—Stereotypes are dangerous, and I think the media—and this is often true in foreign conflicts, when things are incomprehensible to the media—just certifies them as incomprehensible to everyone else. They blame suicide bombing on the Koran or Islam without understanding that despair and desperation pushes people to turn themselves into human bombs. So, until you do that kind of investigation, you don't truly understand the world around you.

LR—But, for example, the suicide terrorists of 9/11 were literate people with no economic problems. How can their acts be "justified" in that context?

CH—That is true. It's not always the poor—oftentimes isn't the poor—who carry out acts of self-destruction, but they tend to be or feel very disenfranchised, very alienated, very cut off. I think most suicide bombing is a reaction to feelings of collective humiliation—this isn't even my own theory. Most psychiatrists and psychological studies of suicide bombers I think would agree with this (Robert Pape and others)—that there are feelings of a loss of identity. It's no accident that most of the bombers of 9/11 came from Saudi Arabia—a country that many Saudis feel is controlled and occupied by the United States. So, when you peel back the motives, they always go far beyond religion; religion becomes a wonderful way to sanctify what it is they're doing, what brought them to that point. Usually, it has more to do with socioeconomic and historical distortion than it does with religious belief.

LR—In the book *The Shock Doctrine*, Naomi Klein emphasizes the role of crises to implement the agenda of corporate America. Doesn't religion operate in the same manner? With the decrease of social and economic distress, fewer people will tend to rely on religion (in prosperous countries like Sweden, Finland, Norway, Japan, or Australia, religious impulses are decreasing). Don't you think religion fuels itself on the problems of humanity?

CH—I think religious institutions certainly thrive on the problems of humanity. But those who carry out what I would define as religious acts—people like Martin Luther King—not only often have to fight their own institutions, but call on people to stand up at times when they must face the possibility of their own self-destruction. So again, I think we have to distinguish between what it is religious institutions do in a time of crisis—and you're very right, they do do this—but these are human institutions, and they carry with them all the flaws of any other human institution. I just make a distinction between religious belief and these institutions that claim to speak for God.

LR—Can we say then that poor people are more vulnerable to this kind of manipulation because they haven't got the critical tools to evaluate the role of the institutional religion that they're committing themselves to?

CH—I think that's exactly right.

LR—Richard Dawkins holds the view that it is incorrect to label a child according to the religion of their parents—a Muslim child, a Christian child, and so on. Do you think religious identity is an essential and indispensable part of a broader cultural identity?

CH—No, but I think a kind of artistic sensibility and understanding, the ability to acknowledge the power of the transcendent, is vital. But it doesn't have to come through religion, and oftentimes it doesn't come through religion. I think that at its core, what a great artist is attempting to do is much the same as what a great religious person or thinker is attempting to do; I think they're very, very similar endeavors.

LR—What do you think could be the best ways to establish empathy between cultures and people so far apart—religiously, economically, and politically speaking?

CH—Well, the intermingling of cultures. We fear what we don't understand. People fear the Muslim world because they don't understand it. I don't fear it: I lived there, I know it intimately.

LR—But aren't barriers always being created? By isolating people in their own frontiers, some agents of conflict seem to profit and benefit from that lack of contact.

CH—I think people who have a vested interest in control over their own societies and in their own empowerment indeed create barriers. A good example would be in the war in the former Yugoslavia. The first people who died in a village were not the warlords of the opposing ethnic group but those people within your own community who still maintained channels of communication, contact, and friendships with the group that they were supposed to hate. They were the first people to get a bullet through the back of the head—because they shared another way of being, another form of community. So, I think you're very right, and religious authorities throughout history have been guilty of this time after time after time.

LR—If people in a community do not wish to act in accordance with what they see as a bad conduct in that community, they're marginalized—and sometimes, even eliminated. So, back to Hobbes: "Man is the wolf of men."

CH—That's right.

LR—What was the most helpful book that you've read in your worst moments of war coverage?

CH—I would say Shakespeare or Marcel Proust. Any great book—and not always literature—that understands human nature. Joseph Conrad, Primo Levi, I love Elsa Morante. I don't know if there's one, but I think books, as a rule, sustained me; great literature sustained me; great philosophy and theology sustained me; because they understood the reality of a world that is broken down—Primo Levi is a perfect example of that—and even through that reality, called for a kind of adherence or loyalty to the great humanistic values. Those books sort of spoke to me, over and over.

LR—If you had to recommend one book to the president of the United States, what would it be?

CH—In times of accommodation of political theory, a realistic understanding of the world around us: I think Karl Popper's *The Open Society and Its Enemies*.

Shelly Kagan

Shelly Kagan is the Clark Professor of Philosophy at Yale University, where he has taught since 1995. He was an undergraduate at Wesleyan University and received his PhD in philosophy from Princeton University in 1982. Before coming to Yale, Kagan taught at the University of Pittsburgh and at the University of Illinois in Chicago.

Kagan's research focuses on normative ethics, the part of moral philosophy that is particularly concerned with articulating and defending the main principles of morality. Among other topics, he has published articles on the nature of well-being, Kantian ethics, the role of game playing in utopia, and the use of moral intuitions in moral philosophy. His first book, *The Limits of Morality*, was a philosophical attack on two widely held views about the demands of morality, and his textbook, *Normative Ethics*, is a systematic survey of the field. He is currently writing a book on the concept of moral desert.

Professor Kagan is a popular lecturer at Yale, where his two introductory classes, ethics and death, often attract over 200 students (lectures can be viewed online at http://oyc.yale.edu/philosophy/death/).

Luís Rodrigues—Existentialist atheism—and here I'm referring to Sartre and Camus—is very much associated with this idea that life is absurd and meaningless since we're going to die. If one is an atheist, how can we escape this feeling of absurdity and meaninglessness?

Shelly Kagan—There's a common thought that if life comes to an end, then nothing can really have any value, nothing can really have any point, nothing can really have any purpose. No doubt part of the motivation for religious belief—whether belief in a god, or belief in an afterlife, or what have you—is by way of trying to find an answer to that worry. That is, it grants the assumption that, unless there's an afterlife, unless there's a god, then life has no meaning, nothing makes any sense, it's all absurd, it's all pointless, it's all meaningless—but it just goes on to say: "but happily, there is a God, there is an afterlife" and so forth.

Now, I don't myself believe in an afterlife, I don't believe in a supernatural being that has created the universe. So, if I granted the assumption that unless there's a god of that sort, unless there's an afterlife, then nothing has any meaning, then I would have to agree with some of the existentialists—and some of the nihilists—that life has no meaning. But I think it's the assumption itself that needs to be challenged. I don't see any particular reason to agree that, unless something lasts forever—let's say, there's an afterlife—then it's not really valuable.

Actually, I think the points are pretty obvious when you step back from the philosophical conundrum: I mean, suppose you're enjoying a candy bar of chocolate. It's not the most important thing in the world, but you get some pleasure from it. Now does the fact that you'll die in 10 years, or 20 years, somehow show that that pleasure wasn't genuine? It seems to me that there's no reason at all to think it would show that. Does it show that there really isn't any value in eating the candy bar? Why would that follow at all? Does the fact that the pleasure of eating the candy bar doesn't last forever—that it comes to an end in 10 minutes—does that show that it is not a genuine pleasure, or that pleasure isn't really valuable? That strikes me as a rather implausible claim, to think that something has to last forever in order to have any real value. Similarly, a beautiful painting by Rembrandt or Picasso is valuable even if it doesn't last forever. These things may last hundreds of years, but they're not going to last thousands of years, they're not going to last tens of thousands of years. So what? While it existed, it was a valuable thing, and there was value in appreciating it, enjoying it, trying to understand the work and what it communicates to us.

So, the candy bar was a trivial example, the painting is a less trivial example, and I think that same thought carries through much more broadly: That is, most of the things that we find meaning from in our lives aren't intended to last forever; we never expect them to last forever. There's value in having loving relationships with your wife, your children, your friends. Those things are worth doing—trying to be a decent human being, trying to understand the universe—these things are valuable even if, as is indeed the case, you're going to die and you won't continue to exist. To have solved, suppose, some mathematical conundrum. Let's take Fermat's last theorem, the great mathematical conjecture that, for hundreds of years, mathematicians unsuccessfully tried to prove. Everybody believed it was true but nobody could prove it—although many, many mathematicians tried. It's only 10 years ago that Andrew Wiles, a Princeton mathematician, was able to prove it, making one of the greatest mathematical accomplishments in quite some time. That's worth doing, it seems to me—even though Wiles is going to die, the universe is going to explode. I don't see why the value of understanding something deep and profound about the nature of math should depend in any way on the existence of a god.

So, the assumption that, unless there's a god, unless there's an afterlife, everything is empty, everything is meaningless, this is, I think, a kind of childishness. It's a kind of childishness that's attempting to be grown up. This is too crude, but here's the picture I've got in mind. When people are children, there's a kind of childish view which says, "Oh, you know, there's a god up in heaven, smiling down at me"—the big man with the big beard and so forth and so on—"who looks after me, makes everything okay, and makes everything have a point," and so forth and so on. The existentialists come along and they say, "You know, that simplistic religious picture is false. If it were true, it would give everything meaning and value. But it isn't true. We share the simpleminded religious view that, without that—a god in heaven—everything's pointless. And so, everything's pointless."

But I think that this existentialist nihilist conclusion is itself just one more childish view. Real maturity comes in recognizing that things can have value, things can have significance, things can have importance, even if there is no big cosmic daddy, no cosmic parent, supernaturally looking down and smiling upon us.

None of what I'm saying takes a position on whether there is a god. I've said that I don't myself believe in a traditional supernatural deity, but you could certainly believe that there was a god without thinking that for life to have a purpose, a point, or a meaning requires that there be a god.

Indeed, we can also push at the assumption from a slightly different direction: to question the thought that having a god would give life a purpose all by itself or in and of itself. The thought here is typically something along the lines of "God created us, and he created us to do something." Different religions will then fill in the blank differently as to what it is God created us to do—and the thought then is: "Ah! So that shows that human life has a purpose and a meaning; what we're supposed to do, what we're here for, is to do the job that God built us for."

It doesn't take a lot of work to realize that this, by itself, can't suffice to make life meaningful. Suppose that God was some kind of super-cosmically powerful moron who builds us just out of boredom to do something completely stupid—well, that's our purpose and that's our point: to do this stupid task. It would hardly follow that now, suddenly, life has a meaning in any important sense. What we would then say is, "Gosh! Just because God built us for that stupid purpose, doesn't mean that that's really what is worth doing with our life." We want to know what's really worth doing, and it doesn't follow from the fact that there is a God—if there is a God, and that he chose such and such a job for us—that this job is really worth undertaking. That's a further thought, that's a further assumption that has to be made. It's at least a further claim that has to be investigated: Are the things that God has in mind for us, that he created us to do, the jobs he intended us to do, are these jobs worth undertaking?

Now, the answer could well be yes. The given religion might go on to give us more reasons why that is: God might be asking us to fight the good cause on behalf of truth and justice, trying to eliminate suffering; God may be trying to tell us to spread peace, beauty, and knowledge— and all those things are worth doing. Obviously, the mere fact that God told us to do something certainly doesn't prove that there's *no* point in doing it! But pursuing truth, and justice, and beauty and peace, if these things are worth doing—as indeed they are—if these things are worth doing, then they're worth doing. They don't become worth doing sim-ply because God told us to do them. They're worth doing because they're valuable, they're worthwhile undertakings, they're goals worthy of our time, endeavor, and striving. That then remains true whether or not there is a god.

So the nihilist worry that with no god, life is absurd, although it is an understandable thought—a natural thought in the progression from the childish or simplistic religious view to a more mature, sensible outlook—is still a childish view.

I say all this, incidentally, without in any way meaning to impugn re-ligion. One can certainly believe that there is a god, believe that he gives us tasks that are worth undertaking, that the tasks would be valuable even if God didn't give them, but that we now have this extra reason—that God created us to help serve these worthy goals. So I don't in any way mean to be critical of religion per se; I just want to reject the thought shared by some fans of religion and some atheist nihilists that unless there's a god, nothing is worth doing. That, I think, is just mistaken.

LR—Can it be that the despair of those atheist nihilists arrives when they stop living at their temporal and spatial scale, becoming "cosmic megalomaniacs"? I mean, when one starts thinking about the future, the explosion of the sun, the end of life on Earth, the heat death of the universe in billions of years from now, and so on, one starts living and thinking at a despairing cosmic scale, ignoring the pleasurable existence at a human scale.

SK—That's right. There's a perfectly understandable human tendency, when you begin to reflect, to move back from your own situation and look at it in terms of larger and larger points of view, larger and larger scales—as you just said. If you look at things from the standpoint of the universe, you might begin to wonder how could anybody, any individual person's life on Earth, make any kind of difference? After all, it can't possibly alter anything on a cosmic scale.

Well, that's true, but then I just have to ask: What of it? Who said that the cosmic scale is the only relevant scale? I don't know how big you are, Luís, but let me imagine that you're a big man. I am, in fact, a slight man; I'm not very tall. Now, suppose somebody said to you, "Shelly doesn't matter morally as much as Luís because Luís is so much bigger than Shelly, and size is the measure of moral significance." We would laugh if somebody said that; that's absurd. Being big, being small, having more or less kilograms, is irrelevant to the question of who's doing something worthwhile or who matters morally.

Now just as it would be silly to think that somebody who is five feet is more or less important than somebody who is seven feet, it's silly to think that the only thing that matters is what affects the universe as a whole. So although one can certainly feel the pull toward thinking that, I think, again, it's just a mistake. It's a prejudice, an illusion, to think that only something that registers on a cosmic scale deserves importance. Value is not a function of size or time.

LR—Some say that the belief in God is a delusion, a wishful thinking. If the belief in a higher being can fill one's life with happiness, why shouldn't one prefer the "sweet delusion" over the "miserable truth"? How can we philosophically justify the preference of "knowledge" over "feeling"?

SK—Well, that's a great question, and to really do justice to it you would want to step back from the particular focus on God—which may or may not be an illusion—to the larger question of what is the nature of human well-being or individual flourishing. That is to say, the thought behind the question you just raised was, "Couldn't you be better off to be deceived but happy, than to be knowing the truth and unhappy?"

Now there are at least two things we would want to get clear about in asking that question. We want to know about the nature of happiness, and we want to know about the nature of being "better off."

We can evaluate lives or people as being better or worse off (philosophers often use the term "well-being" for this, we talk about how "well off" somebody is). So, what we really need is a theory of well-being—what makes somebody better off or worse off—and we want to know how important happiness is as a component of that. Furthermore, there's an additional assumption in the question, which is that happiness—as you were just using it—is a synonym for something like "being in a pleasant mental state."

Really, then, what you're asking was something like this: "If belief in God gives you nice mental states, warm feelings about your place in the universe and so forth, then are those pleasant feelings all you could want out of life?" In ordinary circumstances, we might think truth is useful, knowledge is useful as a way of getting those good feelings, but they're not the payoff in itself: The good feelings are what's really worth wanting for its own sake.

So, this question raises large questions about the nature of individual well-being, flourishing, value, intrinsic value, and the like. Unsurprisingly, this is a philosophical question that people have been arguing about for thousands of years. Certainly from the Western philosophical tradition this question goes back to the very beginning—Socrates, Plato, Aristotle—and there's no agreement about it.

In very broad strokes, the question you posed presupposes the truth of a particular view about the nature of well-being, a view that's called hedonism: The claim that well-being in and of itself is a matter of having pleasant experiences and avoiding painful experiences. Now, hedonism has a very long and distinguished history, and there are certainly many philosophers nowadays who still embrace it, but there are also many philosophers who have challenged it. Again, right from the beginning, Plato raised very serious worries about hedonism, as did Aristotle.

Let me mention an example, a thought experiment, that was raised by a contemporary moral philosopher named Robert Nozick—he taught for many years at Harvard University and died a couple of years ago. He asks us to imagine something he called "the experience machine." We're supposed to imagine that scientists have made big breakthroughs in figuring out how to directly stimulate the brain. We can, of course, do this in a very crude way right now, but he asks us to imagine being able to do this perfectly, so that by electronically stimulating the brain in the right way, we can create whatever experiences you'd like, identical ("on the inside") to the ones you would have if you were really doing the thing. So you put on this helmet, let's say, and you're just sitting in the chair or floating in the tank in the psychologist's lab while the tape is playing—that's what he mentioned, a tape, nowadays we could talk about the CD or the program playing—anyway, you feel like you are having whatever experience is relevant. Fill in the blank: climbing Mount Everest, writing a great novel, painting a great work of art, or whatever.

LR—Something like a "brain in a vat" experience.

SK—Something like that. Of course, you're not a brain in a vat in this example, you are an entire body, not just a brain. At any rate, the idea is this: You think you're climbing Mount Everest, say, when you're not. It's like a perfect virtual reality machine—so perfect that you don't even remember that you are on this machine; you think you're actually having this experience.

All right, so now, we ask ourselves: Imagine somebody who's on the experience machine and plug in whatever you think would be the best kinds of feelings, the best kinds of pleasant experiences. You know, is it finding the cure for cancer? Is it getting elected president of the United States? Is it marrying some wonderful movie star? Put whatever mixture of all those things you might think would be the best, most pleasant wonderful experiences, put all of those into the tape. What you're feeling is exactly what it would feel like if you were really climbing Mount Everest. You feel the cold of the wind, you think, "Here I am on Mount Everest! If that rope snaps, I'm going to fall down!" It's identical on the *inside*, but in reality, of course, you're just floating in the psychologist tank.

What Nozick asks us is this: "Do you want to spend your life on that machine?" If when your child was born the fairy godmother came along and said, "Good news! There's a free experience machine opening. I'm going to put your newborn child on it and he will spend his entire life having all these wonderful experiences," would you pick that for your child? Would you pick it for yourself? Would you pick it for other people? The answer most people give when they think about this case is: "No, I don't want that for myself; there's something missing from a life spent on the experience machine."

I've been teaching moral philosophy for many years and I usually find that there's always a group of students who do vote to go on the machine; they think that it really does have everything worth having in life. Maybe 15 or 20 percent of the students think that. But most students—three-fourths of the students or more—think, "No, no, there's something missing." That's certainly how I myself vote when I think about that case. I don't think, "Oh, there's a perfect life!" I think that such a life is missing something.

Now the point of the story is that, if hedonism were true, then there would be *nothing* missing from that life—because, by hypothesis, that machine is giving you all the best, wonderful, pleasant experiences on the inside. If, however, you think that there *is* something missing, what that shows is that you think there's more to life, there's more to individual well-being than just getting nice, pleasant insides. We think there's something more to life than that.

At this point, of course, you will have philosophers disagreeing about what that "something else" is, what that "more" is. One very plausible thought to have at this point is that you're mistaken in the experience machine; you don't really have knowledge of the world. You think you're on Mount Everest, but you're not: You're floating in the lab.

LR—But consider this question: When religion offers the prospect of an eternal, blissful existence in "paradise" or "heaven" (after one's death), isn't it offering the same hedonistic experience

that the machine does? I mean, isn't the idea of paradise (or life after death) something like living in the experience machine perpetually?

SK—Okay, let me just finish off the first thought and I will come back to your question about heaven. One thing to keep in mind is that the point of the experience machine example is not supposed to be "so feelings don't matter, so mental states don't matter, so experiences don't matter." Of course they matter, but the point of the thought experiment is to show that they're not the only things that matter.

Now if you thought that one of the missing ingredients was knowledge of reality—actually having a correct connection to the world, knowing how things really are—then what you're saying is that if you make a complete theory of human well-being, feelings won't be the only thing on the list. Knowledge of reality belongs on the list, too. That's what allows us to answer the second question that you posed (about how to justify the preference for knowledge over feelings): I can say to you that I believe that, on a correct theory of well-being, knowledge is valuable in itself. You are better off for having knowledge; feelings aren't the only thing that matters.

Of course, even if we agree with that, there's still a further question. Suppose you have a tradeoff? We now have at least two things on our list: knowledge, on the one hand, and good feelings, on the other. Ideally the best kind of life would have both of them. That's going to be the key for when we come back to the question about heaven in a minute—but suppose you couldn't have both? Suppose we agree that good feelings and knowledge are both worth having, they're both elements in the best human life, but you can't have both. Which would you trade off? It's probably not going to be all of one versus all of the other, but at least we open the door to the possibility that there might be some cases where one could correctly say, "I'm better off being less happy, having less pleasant feelings, because despite all of that I've got more knowledge about the nature of reality. I'm better off when you count both of these goods, taking them both in consideration. The hedonist made the mistake of thinking that the only good was pleasure, when there are really two kinds of good." If that's true—and I am inclined to think that it is true—then it could turn out that, even when recognizing the lack of god, even if that made us less happy, we might still be better off, because we would have more knowledge of the truth.

Now, I'm not actually agreeing with you that it will make us less happy. No doubt it would make some people less happy, but I think it makes other people more happy, to realize that they're not under some constant surveillance, the big cosmic father who's going to scold you and send you to hell for enjoying sex or whatever it is. I saw in the paper just the other day that there was an ad, a bus campaign in London, where they're running this ad saying "There's probably no God, so enjoy your life." Right? So for a lot of people atheism isn't some unhappiness-making discovery, it's a happiness-making discovery. Still, the point that I was just pushing a couple of minutes ago was this: Even if it was an unhappiness-making discovery, it still might leave you better off.

Getting back to that question about heaven, let's suppose we've got two things leading toward a good life—good feelings and knowledge. Notice that it's not very likely that all kinds of knowledge are equally valuable: After all, knowing how much it rained in Bangkok in 1998 in February, that's not going to be as valuable as knowing "Am I really on an experience machine or am I really teaching at Yale University? Am I really on Mount Everest or am I really floating in a lab?" So, some kinds of knowledge are more valuable than others.

Among the kinds of knowledge that probably would be very, very valuable—if there is such knowledge—is this: Suppose there is a god. And suppose God has a plan for us and that's why he created the universe—and his plan is a valuable, worthy one, worth our allegiance. Well, knowing all those things would be knowing some of the most important truths about the universe!

So when you say, "Isn't heaven just life on the experience machine?" I want to say no, no, not at all. The point about the experience machine was that you had all these pleasant experiences but they were based on mistakes; they weren't based on real knowledge of reality. In contrast, a traditional religious view might hold that in heaven we might have what traditional theology sometimes calls "the beatific vision," a kind of direct knowledge and experience of God, both grasping whatever of his intentions humans are capable of grasping, and having this be an extremely pleasant experience. So that would be a kind of life that combined both of the goods that I was just talking about. You'd have pleasant experiences, but, unlike the experience machine—where they're based on illusion—here you'd have the pleasant experiences based on knowledge of some of the most important truths in the world. So you'd have good experiences and knowledge.

Now, whether or not we could continue to fill that story in with all the other goods that might emerge from our theory of well-being is a complicated question. But I myself would not want to dismiss heaven as no better than an experience machine—as long as, of course, what's going on in heaven is comprehension of the ultimate nature of reality. I myself regret that I don't believe there will be an afterlife in which I could have that kind of experience.

So, even though I said some rather harsh things about religion earlier, I don't at all mean to be claiming that all religious views are infantile. That's not at all the case. Many religious views are extremely admirable. I similarly would not want to equate religion per se—or being religious, or being involved with religion—with accepting theism, the traditional Western view that there is a supernatural being and so on. I think religion is not the same thing as theism; many religions take a theistic form, but not all religions do. I'm no foe of religious belief as long as it is done in a sufficiently mature fashion.

LR—You talked about the beatific vision. As I understand it, beatific vision does not presuppose either a complete knowledge and total apprehension of reality or the accomplishment of all our desires. If that were so, we would ultimately be gods ourselves. So, even contemplating God, there will always be something missing that only God himself possesses.

SK—I certainly think on a traditional view—and here I'm just conjecturing, these are not religious beliefs that I share myself—the beatific vision does not give us complete understanding because to have complete understanding we would need to be omniscient; we would need to know everything that God knows—and that's presumably beyond human capacity. On the other hand, you also said that we surely can't have a satisfaction of all human desires. I think that's less straightforward; it depends what we want, it depends what the genuine desires are, the satisfaction of which would truly lead to human well-being. Could it be the case that there's some state of being—whether heavenly or earthly—in which people have wonderful lives, lives so good that you can honestly and correctly say with regard to them, "I don't need anything else; I'm as happy, I am as complete, I am as well off as I could be"? I believe that's a perfectly coherent notion—but I don't in any way want to suggest it's simple to spell what that life would look like; that's a very deep and difficult question. So, I think the idea of working to make people perfectly happy, completely well off, is an intelligible goal. Whether or not it's within our grasp as humans is another matter.

Now, I certainly recognize that there's an element of striving that figures importantly in a lot of what people value. If we've got everything, then we won't have anything to strive for, but if we don't have anything to strive for, then that will leave us unhappy. So isn't there something paradoxical about the notion of heaven, on the one hand, or utopia, on the other? I think there is something troubling and difficult about that notion, which is why, a moment ago, I said I don't think this concept is simple or easy to articulate. In life as we live it, as incomplete and far from perfect as it is, it's clear that striving is an important part of the human condition. But I don't myself believe that striving is an essential part of the best human life. So, I think the notion of a satisfying heaven—or for that matter, a satisfying utopian life on Earth, a perfect society—it's a coherent ideal.

However, in my lectures at Yale, I also talk about whether immortality would be a good thing. I am inclined to believe that, in fact, it would not be. When I imagine heaven, I don't really want it to be something going on eternally. I think, eventually, it will grow horribly tedious and boring. So I don't think immortality is truly a desirable state of affairs for human beings.

LR—Is it because, just like the myth of Sisyphus, one is condemned to do the same things over and over again?

SK—The reason that Camus and others have turned to Sisyphus as an image of the human condition is this: What he does has no purpose, has no point, has no meaning. The human task, they think, is to somehow find it satisfying to do it anyway. As you know, however, based on what on I said at the outset, I don't belief that assumption. I don't think that we are limited to pointless, empty, meaningless tasks like Sisyphus.

LR—So, the problem wouldn't be the circular recurrence, but the linear infinity?

SK—Yes, I think that's right. There are plenty of goods in life, far more goods than I will ever be able to come close to experiencing—and even the goods that I can experience, I won't come close to having as much of them as is worth having. But saying all of that is not remotely close to saying that an infinite amount of this stuff would be good forever. I think that's wrong.

To use a trivial example, let's say I love chocolate. The first piece of chocolate is wonderful, the second piece of chocolate is wonderful, the third piece of chocolate is still very, very good, the fourth piece of chocolate is still very, very good, but after a while, you get tired of eating chocolate. Of course if you take a break, then you kind of forget and the pleasure of eating chocolate is renewed again. The challenge, the question when thinking about immortality, is this: Can we even imagine a life that is so rich, so varied, that you would never get tired of it even if you had to do it forever? No question in philosophy has an obvious answer, but I think the answer to this one is "no." Eventually, no matter what life was like, it would grow horribly tedious and excruciatingly boring.

LR—Talking now about morality, there seem to be two different poles in which an action can be morally thought of: the consequentialist position and the deontological position. Can you explain them both in brief words?

SK—I actually have an entire textbook called *Normative Ethics*, which is devoted to laying out the basic ideas of contemporary moral philosophy, and a lot of the book is devoted to exploring that distinction, but let me try to be very quick about it: Consequentialist moral views say that the rightness or wrongness of an action is ultimately a function of, a matter of, what the results are, what ends up happening, what the world ends up being like. You'll need a yardstick of course, you need a way to evaluate better or worse outcomes, and so different versions of consequentialism disagree about what the best yardstick is. The most famous consequentialist theory is utilitarianism—associated with the great English philosopher John Stuart Mill—and that's a hedonist version of consequentialism that says that good and bad results are a matter of good and bad experiences—pleasure and pain—but counting everybody (because we're talking about a moral theory, not just a theory of individual well-being, but everybody's well-being). So utilitarianism says right and wrong is a matter of producing as much happiness as possible and eliminating as much pain as possible, counting everybody's pleasure and pain equally and taking everybody into account. That's one kind of consequentialist theory; there are other kinds of consequentialist theories that use other yardsticks.

Now how they all differ from deontology is this: Deontology says that there are certain features that our actions can have that are relevant to their moral standing—whether they're good actions, bad actions, right actions, wrong actions—that don't reduce to the consequences or the outcome. So there are cases where some action might be wrong, morally forbidden, even though the results would be good. Why is it wrong? Maybe because, although you're bringing about good results, you're bringing them about in a morally unacceptable way.

To give you a very quick and intuitive example, suppose the only way to bring about a great, wonderful result was to harm some innocent person who's not going to benefit from the good results. Even if, when we add up everybody's happiness we say, "Ah! There's more happiness in the long run, so the results are better," it still could be, claims the deontologist, that it's wrong to harm the innocent person—even though the results are good. Consequentialists say, "No! If the results really are good, then this is the right thing to do. It's permissible; it's the right way to go."

A very famous example of this deontological outlook in literature comes up in Dostoyevsky's "The Grand Inquisitor" scene in *The Brothers Karamazov*, where one of the brothers poses to another one of the brothers: "If you could bring about peace on earth, solve war, poverty, and hunger, by killing some innocent child and making him suffer, would you do it?" And the other brother says, "No, of course I wouldn't do it." Well, that's the way that the world looks to a deontologist. There are some things that are wrong, even if the results would be wonderful. A consequentialist hears that and says, "My god! If you don't do it, all these other kids are going to die in poverty, hunger, and suffering. It's worth hurting one innocent child if that saves many, many more innocent children."

LR—Can we say that an atheist is more willing to follow consequentialism and a theist to follow deontology? Is there any identifiable pattern for theists and atheists in that regard?

SK—No. As an empirical matter, for all I know there could be correlations, but as a philosophical matter, there is no connection whatsoever.

Many theists have been consequentialists, many theists have been deontologists, many atheists have been consequentialists, and many atheists have been deontologists. You have both kinds on both sides.

LR—The foundations for any "God-based morality" rely on the authority that self-appointed interpreters of such morality make of it (here I mean: religions, gurus, saints, prophets, imams, etc.). Why do you think that, for most people, morality appears as something transcendent or divinely given?

SK—Most people get taught, they're brought up to think, that certain ways to behave are appropriate ways to behave and others ways to behave are inappropriate ways to behave. We learn how to talk well before we learn English grammar—we just learn how to talk. We learn the fundamentals of arithmetic well before we learn that part of mathematics which proves the fundamental truths of arithmetic. Indeed, most of us never learn the part of mathematics called "the foundations of mathematics" or "the foundations of arithmetic." We never know why it's true that $1 + 1 = 2$. We've just had it taught to us so thoroughly from infancy that we just take it for granted.

Here's an example I like to use: America has 50 states. You're taught the state capitals as a school child in the United States. Nobody actually proves to themselves that the state capitals really are what they're told, they just take it on authority. Almost everything that most people believe, they take on authority. Now, as we grow up, sometimes for certain little areas we become authorities in our own right, we become experts: You become a chemist and suddenly you don't just have to take it on authority that the laws of chemistry work the way they are said to work—you can see that for yourself. You become a mathematician, you become a historian, you learn something about the Civil War and now you become yourself an authority. Most of us eventually learn to question some of the authorities we accepted as children. You say, "Well, my dad was wrong about this, he was wrong about that, maybe he was wrong about some third thing that he taught me."

However, very, very few of us ever then go on to learn anything about the ultimate basis of morality, so this is an area where very few of us go on to question the moral authorities of our childhood. We simply go on believing what we were taught. As you grow older, you find yourself in moral conundrums, and you may begin to wonder whether some of the things that you were taught about morality were really true. But you don't have the tools to think about this, because most people are not taught the tools, not given the tools to think about how you might go about arguing for a better moral view. So we say, "The view I was taught may not be perfect, but I don't really see what the alternative is; I don't see how to have a better view." And so we stick with what we were taught since a young age.

LR—Do you think that humanity should adopt a universal code of ethics (some kind of "monistic ethics"), or would that lead toward some kind of totalitarian society?

SK—Let's start by thinking about a simpler case: Should humanity adopt a single view about the nature of physics? Well, I suppose one can deny this, but I believe that there's probably a single set of true views about physics. Physicists still debate a lot of this, they haven't come to any complete agreement, but I assume that there is a true view of physics. So, in some sense, humanity should believe the truth about physics once we figure it out, because it's better to believe the truth. I believe in knowing the truth—that's a very valuable thing to do, it's an important part of human well-being. I believe in the value of learning the truth about physics and so, yes, it would be better if we all believed the truth about physics. I similarly believe there's a truth about ethics. And so I believe it would be better in the long run if everybody believed the truth about ethics.

Nonetheless, that doesn't mean that it would be better for society to impose a particular worldview on everybody. What experience shows us is that societies are very, very bad at figuring out the truth about things that matter deeply. So many societies will think they've got the truth and be mistaken about that; if the society then imposes their views on everybody—instead of letting people figure it out for themselves—in the long run, the results are probably going to be worse.

So there's a consequentialist argument against society imposing what it takes to be the true view on the members of society. Should society force us all to believe the single true moral view? Probably not, because the results of doing that would be very, very bad.

There's also a deontological argument to the same conclusion, to the effect that one of the things that's important is human autonomy—and that's important not only in the practical sphere, but also in the intellectual sphere. It's important, it's valuable, it's right, for people to be able to think for themselves. What that means is that even if the consequentialist story I just gave is wrong, and even if the results would turn out to be better if society imposed the truth, brainwashed everybody into believing it, the deontologist could say, "Look, that might be another case where we got a good result from a bad method, a morally unacceptable method. Violating people's autonomy is immoral even if the results would be better. It's morally important for people to be free to come to their own conclusions." So both consequentialists and deontologists are likely to agree for the most part about many of these cases and say, "No, what we really need is moral education, not moral indoctrination."

LR—How do you see some secular positions that regard religion as some kind of collective poison of the mind, leading to intolerance, violence, and irrationality?

SK—It's an empirical question isn't it? If we pose the question "Over the course of human history, has religion done some good?" clearly the answer is that it has. "Has religion done some bad?" Clearly the answer is, it has. And indeed, no doubt different religions have different scores, different track records—we would give them different grades in terms of how much good they did and how much bad they did. On balance, has religion done more good than bad? That's a very, very complicated question and I'm not at all confident what the answer is.

I certainly do think that many, many people have a kind of childish, unreflective view about the nature of reality that would not hold up if you started investigating what were the reasons for thinking that. And many people have detrimental religious views. Does that mean that, on balance, it would be better if there was no religion? I understand and respect the claims of people like Richard Dawkins and others that that might be the case. But one of the reasons I've said I'm not myself any foe of religion is that I don't think we can simple mindedly put all religions in the same group, all religious views in the same group. To talk about whether religion is good or bad is as silly as asking whether politics is good or bad. Some states do good things, some states do bad things, some states have mixed records, some states are better or worse than others.

I several times skirted around saying this, but I guess I haven't explicitly said it: I myself am a religious Jew. So I'm not going to join the forces of those people who say religion is horrible and must be eradicated. I have a great deal of respect for atheists; I often have more respect for atheists than I do for the kind of unreflective religiosity that a lot of people have. But a knee-jerk, simple-minded atheist is still knee-jerk and simple-minded—and what's wrong is being simple-minded!

If, after adequate internal reflection and humility about our ability to get at the truth, one ends up having a religious faith, indeed even for that matter a theistic faith—which I don't myself share—I have complete respect for that person, intellectually. The big divide for me isn't really "Atheists, yay! Theists, boo!" or the reverse, "Theists, yay! Atheists, boo!" It's "Do you think hard about your views and what reasons there are to believe them versus what reasons there might be to have other views instead? Or do you not think hard about these important questions?" My heroes and the people I most admire and respect are those who subject their views to this kind of careful, rigorous self-scrutiny—and that's more important to me at the end of the day than whether they end up sharing theological views with me or disagreeing with me theologically.

LR—If you had to recommend four books—two for an atheist and two for a theist—what books would they be?

SK—That's a great question! I'm not quite sure what the answer to that should be. I know that there's a book on religion which I love. It was a book by one of my teachers. His name was Walter Kaufmann. Actually there are two books. He was a great student and admirer of religion—though he was not a religious man nor any kind of religious believer—and he wrote two books which I guess I would be happy to recommend.

One is called *Religion in Four Dimensions*. This book is a comparative religion book. One of the funny things about religion and its place—at least in American society—is that people sometimes act as if all religions say the same thing. (Of course that's just stupid; that shows a kind of ignorance of what their own religion and other religions say.) Walter Kaufmann was a great student of religion, and the book compares and contrasts the outlooks of different religions—not just on theological matters, but on moral issues and what kind of vision they had of how people should be living. So I think that's a wonderful book, and I've often recommended it to people who want to know about different religions and how they compare.

Another book of his that I think extremely well of is called *The Faith of a Heretic*. Maybe the title says it all: He himself was not a believer, and he lays out in that book, in a series of connected essays, his own alternative worldview and why he doesn't himself accept a religious outlook. He also describes the virtues of living what you might call an "atheistic life." His point of calling himself a heretic was really just emphasizing the importance of thinking for yourself, not just believing what everybody else believes. So those are two books that I think I would recommend to any number of people. It's not four, but I will stick with these two.

Paul Kurtz

Paul Kurtz is professor emeritus of philosophy at the State University of New York at Buffalo, chairman of the Committee for Skeptical Inquiry (CSI), the Council for Secular Humanism, and Prometheus Books, and editor-in-chief of *Free Inquiry Magazine.* He is also founder and chairman of the Center for Inquiry, Transnational. He is a former co-president of the International Humanist and Ethical Union (IHEU). With degrees from New York University and Columbia University, he is a Fellow of the American Association for the Advancement of Science and humanist laureate and president of the International Academy of Humanism. He is the author or editor of 48 books and over 850 articles and reviews. He has appeared on many major television and radio networks and programs in North America and worldwide, including National Public Radio, HBO, CNN, Fox, ABC, CBS, NBC, *The Today Show,* and *Good Morning America.* He lectures widely in North America and throughout the world.

Luís Rodrigues—As a secular humanist, you advocate life as a process of creative joy. Cunning and warmongering are some of the ways human creativity reveals itself—and great names in history have made use of it: Napoleon, Hannibal, Alexander, and many more. Doesn't this intrinsic and perverse "will to power"—as Nietzsche once said—refute the idea that human beings are able—and willing—to develop a project of harmonious coexistence?

Paul Kurtz—In my view, human beings are neither good nor evil but can become either or both, depending on social and environmental conditions and how the person reacts to them. I consider humans to be potentially capable of either moral virtue or evil conduct. I submit that human beings are capable of developing a moral sense. I agree with Darwin that social groups develop moral conduct and transmit them to their offspring. However, some men and women may be selfish, interested in their own advantage or the will to power. Nietzsche has been misinterpreted on this. I agree with Walter Kaufmann, who gives a positive humanistic flavor. The will to power is the drive to achieve, to realize your talents, to leap over the abyss. It defines us as creative beings capable of great things in our own lives. We all have some measure of self-interest and need it to live (sex, food, love, economic security, etc.). It can be enlightened and include some measure of altruism and a genuine feeling of empathy for others. We can learn to live with others in a spirit of competition and harmony at the same time. We should be interested in fulfilling our talents and attaining new heights of discovery and excellence. Plato's Thrasymachus in the *Republic* need not be the barbarian but can become civilized, interested in his own fulfillment, but also be genuinely concerned with the good of others. Alexander and Napoleon can be admired for their sheer audacity, and that is a mark of humans who break new frontiers. They were destructive, yet contributed to culture—the Hellenization of the East and the Napoleonic code. We need both audacious adventure and discovery and some moral concern for others. I try to embody both in my own life. I am overwhelmed by the desire to advance the cause of humanity, but I also have great love for every person that I encounter and I try to find some good in each individual. No one is perfect, we are all too human.

LR—As far as I know, you tend to privilege a life of action (a life of "becoming"), over a life of reflection (a life of "being"). Does this active attitude prevent us from thinking about life in an anguished, existentialist way—as something finite, absurd, and intrinsically meaningless? Isn't this "to do" an escape from the perception of our pointless and frail human condition?

PK—I cherish the life of reason, and, like Kierkegaard, am reflective from beginning to end. So we need to develop our rational capacities. On the other hand, what defines humans is the fact that they are doers, and that they enter into the world to understand it, yet to bend it to their own purpose. We are not cows chewing our cuds in quiet contemplation (though that has a place, we need to engage in thinking). Humans are defined by their activities, they enter into the world to change it as well as enjoy it. We are the builders of culture; that defines us. We are explorers, adventurers, voyagers, both as men and women of action, but as seeking mightily to understand the world (science, philosophy, etc.). Does life have meaning per se? No, it presents us with opportunities and we invest our lives with meaning. A male ejaculates billions of sperm into the vagina each time and of the 500 or more eggs that a female produces in her lifetime, only one or two or three or a few more make it and become a human person. Similarly for the acorns, seeds, and spores ejected in the life world, a bountiful plenitude, very few make it. It depends on chance and contingency. Given this, life is a wonder to behold, not a gift but something that every being seizes and fulfills. Life is intrinsically good in its own terms. There are so many opportunities to find joy and exuberance, so why moan about existential angst? Live life fully. The great "sin" is to sin against life, by mortifying the flesh, repressing our natural inclinations (within reason). Among the great crimes against humanity are celibacy, repression, denial. We should live life fully, not evaporate into our own islands of despair.

LR—There's a notion that atheism is a philosophical option that should be available only to the "elites"—because atheist "masses" would turn out immoral and anarchical. What do you think of this? Even if atheism is true—as you think it is—should the truth be available to everyone (and with no "disclaimers")?

PK—Is atheism only for "elites"? No. The great problem that we face today is the fact that we are the generation that knows not simply that each of us will die, but that the human species most likely will become extinct some day, as all other species. Similarly, if we studied Toynbee we should know that our civilization, like all others of the past, will decline. But more so, we now know that our sun will most likely cool off and all life on the nearby planets will die (we have several billion years for that—though Woody Allen tells us that he cannot sleep at night worrying about that!). Is atheism too bitter a pill to swallow for the masses? I think not, for virtually everyone I know is an atheist (or agnostic) and they can handle that with no problem. This applies to my colleagues but also to the many students that I have had in the past. It is also true of my friends and relatives, my children as well. They all seem to be able to handle that without any difficulty. Death is a fact of life, and we have no illusions about immortality, we have no need for a crutch. My wife is French and practically everyone in her family is an atheist. The up-kick to that is that if God is dead, we are alive. We killed him, but She (she's Chinese, you know) never really lived. She is a myth invented by human fantasy to soothe the aching heart. But virtually everyone I know goes through life without the need for God, and indeed there has been a good deal of research that freethinkers have less fear of death than believers, who worry about sin. Why not tell the truth that revelation has not been corroborated; moreover, death is better than holding hands and singing hymns throughout eternity. The God story has been told to weak-minded persons who lack the courage to become. Without God, one can live life fully, without fear or guilt. Our option is to improve life for ourselves and our sister human beings. What joy in living without illusions.

LR—Philosophy, history, art, mathematics, theology: If you had to rate the importance of these five disciplines in the education of the youngster, which would you classify the most and the least important? Why?

PK—How would I rate five disciplines? Please add a sixth, science, which I would put at the top of the list; second would be history, third philosophy, fourth art, fifth mathematics (or put it up with science). The very last would be theology.

LR—Most people tend to see knowledge as a burden; more knowledge brings sadness and disappointment—"happy are the fools," some say. In your case, wisdom and knowledge seem to bring more optimism. How do you explain this "Kurtz's paradox"?

PK—Is knowledge a burden? Luís, are you serious? I find it a great joy. Curiosity is one of the great sources of human inspiration and achievement. The right to know is a human right. It, along with praxis, defines who and what we are. We are rational animals, said the Greeks, yes indeed, but that is not the be all and end all of life, for we are pulsating, throbbing doers and actors on the stage of life. Not to realize our cognitive capacities is to be less than human, much like the cow in the field.

I do not know why knowledge brings sadness and disappointment. To my mind it brings us opportunities and new powers, because only in the light of our knowledge of the causes and consequences of our actions can we control our futures. I ask you this question: If you have an illness and visit specialists, would you want a diagnosis so that you can use the best methods of therapy? Or do you wish to remain in ignorance? "Ye shall know the truth (scientific and philosophical) and the truth shall make ye free!" I do not see where ignorance is bliss. Of course, what I am recommending makes most sense in an open, free, and pluralistic society, where we have options. I know of no alternative to optimism (realistic of course); it is crucial to the life well lived. We need some measure of hope that if we do our best all will turn out in the end. But if it does not, then some stoicism is essential. If we fail, we go on to the next challenge. Is that a naïve American attitude based on a frontier society? Perhaps. But it is in my mind essential to live a full life. It is not a paradox. Some knowledge of what is and is not within our power is essential. (Please see my books *Exuberance* and also the *Courage to Become* where I spell this out.) The person who is incapable of the zest for living—if exacerbated—is suffering from depression. If this is not extreme it is due to what I call need fulfillment, including the satisfaction of our basic biogenic and sociogenic needs. In my book *Embracing the Power of Humanism*, I include in this health, exercise, the need for love, especially orgasm, the need to love and be loved by other persons, belonging to some community, the need for self-respect, rationality, high motivation, and the expressing of a person's creativity. I would also add Abraham Maslow's peak experiences.

LR—Concerning the "burden of knowledge" issue, I'm just playing the devil's advocate of those who think in the manner of the book of Ecclesiastes 1:18: "Because in much wisdom there is much grief, and increasing knowledge results in increasing pain." I perfectly agree with you that knowledge is what makes life more vivid and enjoyable—and the great pleasure with which I'm making this set of interviews is an indicator of that! But do you think that's what most people think—or want to think? Rather, don't they want to stay quiet and remain protected under the shell of the great and compassionate heavenly father who punishes them if they want to start building a

Tower of Babel—in other words, a Tower of Knowledge and, as you often say, a "marketplace of ideas"?

PK—The Old Testament was written at a time when science had not been developed and the world was engulfed in mystery and fear. Jehovah expels Adam and Eve from the Garden of Eden because they ate of the fruit of the tree of knowledge of good and evil. I disagree with the idea that wisdom is a source of grief. On the contrary, in my book *Eupraxsophy: Living Without Religion*, I argue that wisdom is the source of the good life. Surely the Greek philosophers, from Socrates to Plato and Aristotle, extolled the life of wisdom as the source of well-being. The ancient priests wished to keep mankind obedient and ignorant. True human liberation occurs when we can develop our cognitive skills and understand how and why things happen the way they do—and how to live a satisfying life in the light of this knowledge. (I might add that some Portuguese Port and Madeira wines, sardines, cheese, and olive oil will contribute enormously to the good life!)

LR—I think ethics has a problem that I call a problem of generalization. At a general level, everyone agrees with the broader issues of ethics: don't kill, don't steal, don't lie, etc., but when the scale tightens, that consensus starts to fade away. In some countries you are allowed to kill others in the name of Allah, you are allowed to kill your wife because she betrayed you, in the age of the Crusades and the Inquisition you were allowed to kill in the name of Jesus, in most democratic societies you are allowed to kill in self-defense, you can kill animals to eat, etc. Since ethics is a function of a specific culture in time and space, how can a "planetary ethics"—as you define it—be possible?

PK—I have spent the lion's share of my professional life as a philosopher, teaching courses on ethics and value theory. I found the theories of the great philosophers out of touch with the life of moral choices. Ethics should descend to the blood and guts of lived experience. General (or universal) ethical principles do not help us to deal with concrete moral situations, of either the individual or the society. That is one reason why in 1991 I retired from university to devote my time to building centers for inquiry which dealt with questions of value.

Nonetheless, I have worked out what I consider (following W. D. Ross) the prima facie general principles that can guide us in some sense. I call these on one level "the common moral decencies." I spell these out in my just reissued *Forbidden Fruit*. They include integrity, trustworthiness, benevolence, and fairness. Under these come kindness, sincerity, honesty, fidelity, goodwill, nonmalfeasance, sexual consent, beneficence, gratitude, accountability, justice, tolerance, and cooperation. In traveling to all parts of the planet (some 60 countries), I find them widely practiced, especially on a person-to-person basis, though some societies are less developed in their appreciation. There is some empirical basis for these. Other general (or universal) doctrines are human rights (now widely respected), though some still need to be fought for, such as the right of privacy, rights for women, gays and lesbians, the rights of children, etc. So, new ethical principles emerge that gain acceptance. There is a constant need to reconstruct morality; this is part of the moral revolution of our time, and it is humanist in character, focusing on human interests and needs, not independent absolutes and commandments.

There is of course cultural relativity in some moral practices. However, the present time is a world-historical time of change. Former social and cultural barriers are breaking down. Many processes contribute to this: trade and commerce, travel, tourism, immigration and emigration, intermarriage, etc. This is especially the case with the emergence of new means of communication, the Internet, movies, radio and television, and also a common literature for all to share. There is an urgent need to develop a curriculum of education, recognizing that every child and adult has a right to know and to be informed about the findings of the sciences. There are also common problems that we share, and these can only be solved by developing solutions in cooperation. Today a new planetary civilization is emerging. The great need is to develop planetary ethics, or planetary humanism.

The first principle is that every person on the planet Earth—no matter the national, racial, ethnic, or religious background—needs to be considered as equal in dignity and value. That is a new universal principle. And second, of course, is the recognition that we share the same habitat, namely the planet, and this means that we need to respect the environment, and other species on it, and treat it with loving care. The justification for that is both utilitarian and deontological.

LR—The title of a book by the American philosopher Richard Rorty is very suggestive of his way of thinking: *Take Care of Freedom and Truth Will Take Care of Itself.* Knowing his skepticism—to say the least—about the possibility of achieving "the truth," Rorty denies religion/theology as a mechanism of coercion, but doesn't seem to bother to put it in the same grounds of other epistemic disciplines (history, physics, sociology, etc.) since they're all fallible and reflect "a truth"—not "the truth." What do you think about this view regarding religion, God, and human knowledge?

PK—I knew Rorty and knew his work. He is responsible for the revival of John Dewey in the United States in recent decades, though I feel that he misinterpreted Dewey, for he abandoned Dewey's emphasis on objective methods. Rorty reduces philosophy to metaphor. I think that there are reliable standards for testing truth claims, and they are the methods of the sciences. Concerning theology, which is the study of God, I believe that the proper subject matter of theology is not God (since there is no evidence that God exists) but human psychology; that is, the predisposition of many humans to postulate such a being to rescue humans from existential angst. This is something akin to the "transcendental temptation," though it is absent in the secular societies of post-Christian Europe and parts of Asia.

LR—Secular humanism seems to defend that a worthy life is a life well lived. Is this utilitarian view about life correct? Some great lives and great deeds for humanity were obtained through the pain and misery of those whose lives might not be classified as "well lived" by our hedonistic standards: Van Gogh, Giordano Bruno, Thomas More, and even Jesus are some of those examples. As strange as it seems, some lives demand high degrees of pain to fulfill themselves. How does a secular humanist perspective and its hedonistic project deal with that?

PK—Interesting that wherever Roman Catholicism is strong there is an emphasis on this being a vale of tears. This was true for the human condition before the advent of modern science, agriculture, medicine, and affluence. I find the cup of life running over, not half empty. Clearly there are tragedies, failures, defeats in life. Van Gogh, Bruno (burned by the Church), Jesus, and so forth, experienced pain, but that is only part of life. The fullness of life allows for satisfaction and achievement, as well as sorrow. Secular humanism focuses on improving this life here and now, and it is possible to live a life full of enrichment. Incidentally, although hedonism is surely part of the good life, it is more than that, since it involves the realization of our goals and plans, and it involves creative joys. Why emphasize the negative?

LR—In a recent Vatican survey conducted by Wojciech Giertych, the seven deadly sins are committed differently according to gender. The main sin for men is lust, followed by gluttony, sloth, anger, pride, envy, and greed. For women, the first is pride, followed by envy, anger, lust, gluttony, greed, and sloth. For a secular humanist, how do you see the concept of sin? Do these results say anything about human nature?

PK—As a secular humanist I am not overwhelmed by sin or vice but rather with actualization, exuberance, shared values, cooperation, progress, health, vitality—all positive virtues and excellences. Indeed, I have written about excelsior, the life of excellence. I do not accept the doctrine of original sin but of the capacity for improvement. The seven deadly sins are not the full catalog of sins. There is gullibility, submission, obedience, repression, censorship, dishonesty, self-delusion, defeatism, cowardice, ignorance, failure of nerve . . . and so on.

LR—According to statistical polls, 85 percent of the scientists in the National Academy of Sciences—which represents the top elite scientists in the United States—are atheists. Why is there such a disparity between what a broad spectrum of society believes and what their main thinkers believe? Are these thinkers unable to convey a materialistic and scientific message to the society? In your opinion, should they want to?

PK—Actually, 60 percent of scientists in the United States are atheists or agnostics, as are 93 percent of the members of the National Academy of Science. If you examine polls on the lack of religious belief in Europe, it is growing, so that it includes a very large minority, in France, Germany, Scandinavia—30, 40, 50 percent. So unbelief is growing as Europe secularizes. If you look at the category of "the nonreligious" it is a large majority, in Denmark, Sweden, Britain, Netherlands, France, even Italy. Only a small percentage practice religion. Yes, secular and scientific thinking is growing worldwide. When I was in Spain and Ireland about 15 years ago, attempting to set up secular humanist groups, the residue of religious belief was evident. Today it is diminishing rapidly, especially among the young. The same thing is happening in the United States and Canada, particularly among people under 30 (an estimated 25 percent), though on a lesser scale.

LR—Do you recognize any advancement to human progress made by theologians or "saints"? If so, is it possible that supernaturalist motivations can have positive effects on society?

PK—I think that orthodox and fundamentalist religions have often been negative, destructive, and repressive. They have condemned women to a lesser role and have repressed homosexuals, freethinkers, many of the heroes of modern culture. They have censored truth, often blocked progress in science—such as stem cell research—or the use of contraceptives in India and the third world where populations are growing. But surely I do recognize that religions have also had positive effects: They have contributed to charity, relieved suffering, maintained hospitals, and so on.

LR—What do you think are the prospects for secular humanism in the 21st century?

PK—I am not a prophet and surely cannot say that some new religious madness will not overtake the world in the future. Who could have predicted in the sixth century that Islam would grow so rapidly from the Atlantic to the Pacific in a couple of centuries? Or indeed that Marxism would sweep a significant sector of humanity in the 19th and 20th centuries and then begin to collapse? Or that fascism would capture some of the countries of Europe, as it did?

What are the prospects for secularism and humanism? They are in one sense equivalent to modernism; that is, committed to the proposition that knowledge and science, democracy and human rights would advance human progress, decrease poverty and disease, advance literacy and education, ameliorate the conditions of life even for the poorest sectors of the world. In that sense—unless there is some disaster that overtakes humankind, such as a financial collapse, collision with an asteroid, global warming, a global plague, environmental degradation—I think that humankind can very well continue to progress, maximize freedom, democracy, and improve the prospects for a better life. But if this is to happen we need to use reason, science, and education, cultivate humanist values of goodwill, and distribute the fruits of the good life, including the arts as well as the sciences, as widely as possible. The world can become more peaceful and prosperous. But this takes great effort. We should not place our faith in salvation by an unseen deity, but rather in our powers and capacities as fallible human beings to ameliorate human life on the planet Earth. This will occur, I believe, if we develop a new planetary consciousness that focuses on planetary ethics in which we consider every person on the planet Earth as equal in dignity and value as part of a planetary community, and if we develop a cooperative effort to improve the human condition. Humanist Manifesto 2000 presented a new set of ethical guidelines for the future: these are naturalistic, secular, and humanistic. Perhaps they are overly optimistic. But our future depends on our forging new ideals for humanity and in resolving to bring them into reality. It depends on our inspiring an awareness of our responsibilities to our planetary habitat.

Gerd Lüdemann

Gerd Lüdemann was born in Germany in 1946. He completed his doctoral and postdoctoral work at Göttingen and at Duke University. He has lectured in Georg-August-University Göttingen, McMaster University, and Vanderbilt Divinity School, and has authored dozens of scientific papers and books including *Jesus after 2000 Years* (2001); *The Acts of the Apostles, What Really Happened in the Earliest Days of the Church* (2005); and *Paul, The Founder of Christianity* (2002);

Luís Rodrigues—What are the main differences you encounter today in the studies of Jesus and the New Testament in Europe and in the United States of America?

Gerd Lüdemann—In order to understand the situation in Europe, you must know that all the professors of New Testament have ties with the churches, so they're very much influenced—consciously or subconsciously—by what the churches proclaim. In the United States, you have evangelicals, you have fundamentalists, you have radicals, you find all sorts of things—anything goes—and so, I wouldn't dare describe the situation in the United States since there are so many different people.

LR—But Germany, for example, has a very rich tradition in the field of religious studies: I'm thinking of names like Reimarus, Albert Schweitzer, F. C. Baur, D. F. Strauss, and many others.

GL—Yes, but as you also know, Friedrich Strauss was fired, he never occupied the chair of New Testament studies. Regarding F. C. Baur, he became professor of dogmatics at a very early time, but, if he had written then what he later wrote, he would have never been appointed to a chair. His students—for example, Edward Zeller—had to leave the theological faculty and taught classical philology. So, the German tradition is very rich, but many of those people who wrote interesting books and had a great influence in New Testament scholarship did not become professors of New Testament. Another example in the 20th century is Albert Schweitzer, who's still read and quoted by everybody, but he was never a professor of New Testament. The 19th and 20th centuries are very different, but the current situation in Germany is very much stamped and influenced by the confessional theology—Catholic and Protestant.

LR—Do you think that happens only in Germany or in other countries in Europe?

GL—Well, Finland is different—but there, the churches are not as strong. France has very few faculties—one Protestant faculty in Strasbourg. I would also make a distinction between Catholic and Protestant faculties: The Catholic faculties are more under the influence of Rome. Concerning Germany, I would want to make this point: If you count the number of chairs in New Testament studies in comparison with other European countries, you'll be amazed how many New Testament chairs there are and how much money is spent on the studies of the New Testament in Germany, yet so little is coming out of that. I would say that some chairs with less money produce more productive stuff than many German chairs with a lot of money.

LR—In your opinion, is it impossible for New Testament scholarship to develop something like the Jesus Seminar in Europe?

GL—Yes, because who would pay for that? Who would be interested in having that? In Germany, the chairs of every New Testament professor have money. If you ask me about the possibility of a Jesus Seminar in Germany, you would have to talk about the money—who's funding it? So the question would be: Would it be possible to raise enough money for the establishment of a seminar? And I would say "no." We wouldn't find the people's response to it, again because confessional theologians would devaluate it. They wouldn't want it.

LR—What about the book publishing business? Wouldn't there be a market for that kind of investigation—independently of any religious agenda?

GL—It's an interesting question. I was just thinking, who would be interested in that? Some books from the United States have been translated into German and are doing fairly well, such as the book by Crossan and also the books by Elaine Pagels. But these are projects of one or two books. When we talk about the Jesus Seminar, we would have to talk about sponsoring our lectures, etc. Again, I doubt we would find the money because the people who would be asked about it would be the New Testament professors who are not impressed or not inclined to support that sort of thing.

LR—Concerning the studies about the historical Jesus, according to the deliberations of the Jesus Seminar, 82 percent of the words assigned to Jesus seem to be fictitious or unreliable. Do you rely on these numbers?

GL—No, I'm relying on my own studies. First of all, I'm a fellow of the Jesus Seminar and I published one book with them, a critique of Pope Benedict XVI's book on Jesus, called *Eyes that See Not: The Pope Looks at Jesus*. But back to your question, no, I'm relying on my own studies, but, when I became familiar with the Jesus Seminar, I liked their approach. It's the approach to distinguish between the redacted tradition and the historical kernel, which is in the best tradition of German scholarship of Rudolf Bultmann and David Friedrich Strauss, and I still like that approach. As you may know, they work with colors—each color assigning a degree of authenticity to each individual statement made by Jesus. I didn't do it, but I did my own study. I looked at the same texts and arrived at similar results. The book has been published and it's called *Jesus After 2000 Years: What He Really Said and Did*. So, I was surprised and glad to find these people in the United States having a similar agenda.

LR—So you conducted an independent investigation and the results were similar?

GL—Well, quite similar. The big difference is that the Jesus Seminar—or more correctly, the majority of the Jesus Seminar, that is to say 85 percent of fellows—thinks that Jesus was not an apocalyptic prophet. So, Jesus did not predict the end of the world to be imminent. That, I think, belongs to Jesus. So I'm not in agreement with the main point of the Jesus Seminar, but I'm in agreement with the approach—namely, the way of looking at the material and also the skepticism concerning the reliability of the Gospels.

LR—After surveying all documentary evidence, what do you think most resembles the true message of Jesus?

GL—First, he talked in parables. He had a tendency toward the poor. He was an immoral hero. He surrounded himself with quite immoral people. Cynic-like Jewish teacher that he was, he thought, with his teaching of repentance, that the end was imminent—which it wasn't. It didn't come.

LR—What are, in your opinion, the novelties brought by Pope Benedict XVI in his biography of Jesus? What do you think are its main flaws?

GL—I think that his main flaw is that he does not think it necessary to take into account the basic research of the last 200 years. So, if I may compare with the scientists, he's a scientist who still presupposes that the Earth is in the middle of the universe.

LR—Do you think that any factual account of what happened or didn't happen with Jesus can change the strength of people's faith in Christianity? If not, isn't the "historical Jesus quest" an inconsequential project—mainly for the believers?

GL—Well, I think—and it's quite radical what I'm saying—that believers deceive themselves at this point. They think they have to do historical research and that's very good. But for me—and I'm not a believer—historical research is the death of faith. Whoever does historical research—that's my experience—will have to say, "I no longer believe." To give an example: Historical researchers work on God and they discover that God is a projection; they work on Jesus and discover that Jesus didn't say most of things that the Bible claims he said. And so, they take one stone after another from the house called "the church." By doing this they seem not to realize that they have done away with the house. To say it again, I think that historical research and modern studies destroy religion. If I may say one more thing, liberals are deceiving themselves to a degree that they seem not to realize. Although, at the same time, I support the liberals. I think it's the only way to approach religion—by studying it historically—but I'm sorry to say that this research, as such, destroys religion.

LR—Do you think that religion, reflecting a good or bad projection about God—as respectively Feuerbach and Freud have proposed—is then, nothing but a human pathology?

GL—Well, I'm an exegete. I'm talking to you about an experience. I have no theory of religion. But what it comes down to is this: When studying the Bible, we discover nothing but opinions of people about God—which they ascribed to God or whoever they want to. We never come across God or the holy. We just come across the opinions of people. Then we tie them to the situation of their time and look at them from a new vantage point. We try to determine their agenda, what they wanted to do or what they wished had happened—it's wishful thinking. By arriving at these results, we deprive religion of its threat, of its capacity to destroy people. It's the language of people from the past, not the present, and thereby, our research is a critique of ideology. That, I think, is very important. As such, historical scholarship is destroying religion. Having read the Bible historically and critically, you can no longer read it piously, because you know if you do, you deceive yourself.

LR—But aren't there also exegetes who are pious?

GL—Of course there are.

LR—And how do you think they cope with the situation?

GL—Well, in my opinion—and I've written a book on the Resurrection as a self-deception, a pious self-deception, but still a deception—the pious exegetes wouldn't need their historical study to believe what they believe. I'm respectful of these colleagues, but I think they deceive themselves.

LR—What are your main contentions concerning the "Resurrection of Jesus hypothesis"?

GL—It didn't happen. The Resurrection didn't take place and it's rooted as a reflex of the various experiences of people. Analytical research of the sources has shown—and it's generally accepted—that at the beginning of the Resurrection tradition, there was this experience, that people saw something, and they concluded from their vision that something happened. So, that's the sequence. That's my main argument against the historicity of the Resurrection.

LR—So, you seem to believe that the disciples had hallucinations when they report sightings of Jesus. But in a culture overcrowded by prophets and reports of wondrous deeds—like those in the Old Testament—is the "hallucination hypothesis" really necessary to justify the beliefs of Christians?

GL—Well, I'm reading the stories, the texts about the Resurrection we have in the New Testament, and I see that they are contradictory. On the one hand they describe the visionary experience—Paul says, "I saw, I saw, I saw, something appeared to me"—and this visionary experience then is connected in the Gospels with the discovery of an empty tomb. Thus, the historical character of the Resurrection is defended, and that's a contradiction. I had to explain to myself how the rise in the Resurrection belief came into existence and my answer was, to begin with, hallucination. Well, I now avoid hallucination. I describe it as a vision, a visionary experience. From that visionary experience, the disciples concluded that the Resurrection had happened.

LR—How do you characterize the apparitions testified to in places like Fátima in Portugal or Lourdes in France? Also visionary experiences?

GL—Yes, is an analogy. Fátima, Medjugorje, and all these visions of Mary are analogous to the experiences of the first-century Christians, and they show how powerful such visions can be. They show how much our own mind has this visionary side. We dream at night and that's also a kind of visionary experience. It's a little bit suppressed by technology but it will always be there. The people in the first century had more access to it. But let me remind you that the critique of visions as reflecting reality was already conducted in antiquity.

LR—But religion is not only grounded in visions: We also have the stories of wondrous deeds. The deeds of Jesus are very similar to those made by "prophet-type" figures—like Elijah or

Ezekiel. Why are Jesus' deeds more distinctive? Why has he achieved a superlative status?

GL—He would not have this status if Paul hadn't planned, hadn't changed Christianity. I think that without Paul the message of Jesus would not have gone out. So, Christianity reached the gentiles through Paul, the message was spread, and Jesus became such an important figure in our culture.

LR—So you emphasize the role of Paul in the spread of Christianity.

GL—Of course. Jesus had no message for the gentiles, and as we all know, Jewish Christianity—that is, the people who followed Jesus such as the Ebionites in the second century—were made heretics. So the expansion of Christianity is due to Paul and his followers. Without Paul, we would not know anything about Jesus.

LR—Some scholars say that, rather than Paul, the Hellenistic Jewish communities in the Diaspora were the "Horse of Troy" that allowed Christianity to enter the pagan world. What is your response to that theory?

GL—Well, let's be precise with that point. I'm just working on an article about the first years of Christianity. Paul persecuted Christians in Damascus who had already opened up to the gentiles and had already made no difference between Jews and gentiles, slaves and freemen, males and females. So there was this radical breach in Christianity at the very beginning, but not in Jerusalem. These Christians whom Paul persecuted knew very little about Jesus, and Paul himself knew very little about Jesus—he quoted words of Jesus in only two places. So that's Hellenistic Christianity, and Paul gave that Hellenistic Greek-speaking Christianity a twist and a direction. He was the one who organized it. He was the one who then connected it with the disciples in Jerusalem.

LR—Why has Paul talked so little about his personal experiences? We have a few accounts of his persecutions, his conversion in the road to Damascus, and so on.

GL—We have only seven authentic letters and we have them by accident, but he may have written other letters. He talks a lot about

persecutions in Galatians, and in Galatians chapter 1 he already presupposes that people were talking about him, that the communities he had
persecuted were already thanking God that the one who had persecuted
them is now preaching the gospel that he tried to destroy. So the
legends and stories about Paul were already spreading, and he talks
about that. He also talks about his call at more than one place. I don't
see that he doesn't speak about it much. He leaves enough information
to be quite precise about what happened.

**LR—Jesus seems a more pacifist prophet than the prophets of
the Old Testament. At least he doesn't kill anyone, for example,
like Elijah did in 1 Kings 18:40. Why does he become—or why
is he interpreted as—a more peaceful character than the prophets of the Old Testament? Were his followers the ones who
made him so?**

GL—As far as Jesus is concerned, he was a radical. The impression that
he was peaceful is going back to the interpreters. It has nothing to do
with Jesus. Number one, he left his family. He should have helped his
mother. He left his family and his family tried to get him back and
declared him to be out of his mind. He was radical. He himself said—
and that's an authentic saying—"I'm not here to bring the peace;
I bring the sword." He was, I almost say, hallucinating about his role
at the end of world when the 12 tribes of Israel would be there and his
12 disciples would sit on the thrones and then judge the 12 tribes of
Israel—and he probably had a special role in there. So somebody who
is predicting that the end of the world is not peaceful knows that peace
is brought through power. I cannot disagree more with you when you
say that Jesus was peaceful. He was not peaceful. That's wishful
thinking.

**LR—So you see Jesus as someone who has more affinity to
aggressive groups like the zealots?**

GL—Yes. He was not a zealot, but he was a zealot type of guy. Someone
who had cut the ties with his family . . .

**LR—In that context, is the Jesus that some portray as belonging
to an Essenic tradition of misanthropy pure fiction?**

GL—Yes, Jesus was not an Essene. When you lift what is reliable, one of the most reliable items is that he was baptized by John the Baptist. So he made his way from there to Galilee, was part of that apocalyptic movement in Judaism, and he knew exactly what God's will was. So he felt himself inspired by God to tell the people what they should hear.

LR—What was the role of John the Baptist in the transformation of Jesus?

GL—Some of the disciples of John the Baptist must have joined the Jesus movement, but some of them remained disciples of John. So, they were rivals. What John the Baptist did not get was a Paul. He didn't have a Paul, which Jesus got. He lacked an interpreter of his message; therefore, he was not as influential as Jesus.

LR—Influence is often grounded on tradition. The place that is now known as the Holy Sepulchre—supposedly, the burial place of Jesus—was only chosen at the time of Constantine by his mother. Also, bodily remains that the Church claims to be those of Peter—although Pope Pius XII stated that no one can be sure about that—are now in display at St. Peter's Basilica. A few centuries from now, nobody will remember the origins and the uncertainty in which these assertions were grounded. Doesn't tradition help to obliterate what is history and what is true?

GL—Well, tradition is important because tradition goes back to somebody's invention or somebody's opinion. The historian's job is to compare the traditions with one another to arrive at a judgment. So, I work on any tradition that is there because it helps me to find out what really happened.

LR—Yes, of course, but what I meant was the following: When the tradition becomes the transmission of something false, doesn't that undermine historical research?

GL—No, it doesn't undermine it, because historical research, I hope, will remain free and independent. It's only historical research under the influence of the church and bound by the church that is dangerous.

LR—What about the transmission of historical facts filtered by the religious traditions? Can the historical research be transformed—or even distorted—to serve the purposes of the religious tradition? How does the historian deal with that fact?

GL—He or she just tries to convince people that it's untrue. Then the question of power comes in—and education also—and whether the countries have the luxury to pay for theological faculties where these traditions are critically looked at. I think our Western society will always support institutions that, at least, make it possible for people who want to be educated to come closer to what really happened and emancipate them from these traditions.

LR—How do you see the role of television and the mass media in general concerning the transmission of the most accurate historical messages?

GL—Well, I would say I cannot give a general opinion. But my own experience in Germany tells me that churches are very influential and try to control programs. By law they have representatives in the various TV and radio stations that are funded by the state. I will give one example: A colleague of mine, James Robinson, was approached to participate in a TV special on Pope Benedict's book about Jesus. He sent an e-mail to the producer in which he said he was willing to participate, but that his German colleague—me, Gerd Lüdemann, who had just written a book critical of the pope—should also participate. They didn't give me the chance to become part of that program. They tried to keep me out and they were partly successful. But I'm optimistic. I share the vision of the Enlightenment that the truth will come out after all. If I'm not on the program, somebody else will tell them, will give them the information that they need.

LR—Do you have personal accounts of incidents with the church?

GL—Oh yes! I have incidents. In one incident, I was invited to be on a public TV program in Germany and somebody reported about my views. The Evangelical Institute heard about that and they complained to the president of the TV station and the producer had to change things and take me out. I have had lots of incidents, and that includes radio and TV. Concerning newspapers, there was a time when people wrote about me. I was very generous in giving information but then, some journalists—mostly sons of pastors—took revenge and wrote nasty things about me. Since then, I prefer to write essays—where nobody can misquote me—and send them to the newspapers. So I have a long history.

LR—Do you still maintain hope and believe that through scholarly work you can transmit your message?

GL—Yes, and I basically believe that reason is stronger than faith. Reason is stronger than faith and we have to follow reason, and by education, by educating people, we will get rid of religion.

LR—But religion can transform itself in more appealing New Age Spirituality movements. Don't these movements undermine reason also?

GL—I think that New Age Spirituality is almighty. Just like Jesus they know everything. They have access to the whole and, as far as I'm concerned, they're not humble enough.

LR—Do you see more danger in their message or in the traditional message of the church?

GL—Both. There's danger in all people who think that they know the whole universe—and New Age makes that claim. I think Ken Wilber, for example, talks like that. Christians also talk like that—like they know exactly what God wants. I think they are overrating themselves and they are not humble enough. So I'm reluctant to follow them.

LR—But do you think people, when listening to them, expect to find someone humble?

GL—Yes, I know, they are looking for power. They want to be almighty like Christianity promises. Well, I read these things, and since I myself studied Christianity so intensely, I have a tendency to be attracted by these promises which overcome death and everything. So, I've learned my lesson and have taken a down-to-Earth approach. I'm delighted about the exercise of reason with which I can read things and liberate myself from any religious claims that cannot be substantiated. So, that's my approach.

LR—Can rhetoric defeat reason?

GL—Oh, beware of rhetoric. I think we should stick to what we know. I'm grateful for what I have, for the years that I lived, and I'm grateful for the insight of knowledge that I have, and people before me had. That's my philosophy. I had given up on eternity and all the things religions promise.

LR—Don't you feel sad about that? I mean, one moment believing that eternity is achievable and, in a glimpse, it all comes down to the conclusion that existence is finite and comprised to a few years of life.

GL—It's a projection. It's wishful thinking. It's false. We should go to what's true and stay away from falseness once we know about it. And I'm not sad now. I'm full. I'm full and I'm glad that I'm here on this Earth and hope that many, many people will have the same experience and enjoy life.

Michael Martin

Michael Martin (born 1932) is an analytic philosopher and professor emeritus at Boston University. He completed his PhD at Harvard University and has concerned himself largely with philosophy of religion—though the philosophies of science, law, and sport have not escaped his attention. On the former, he has published a number of books and articles defending atheism and various arguments against the existence of God in exhaustive detail (among them, the transcendental argument for the nonexistence of God). In his *Atheism, A Philosophical Justification* (1990), Martin cites the general absence of an atheistic response to contemporary work in philosophy of religion and accepts the responsibility of a rigorous defense of nonbelief as, jestingly, his "cross to bear."

Luís Rodrigues—Religious people say that without God, there would be no moral values: God is what makes the recognition of morality possible. Why and how has morality been hijacked by religions (namely, the "revealed" religions) to justify God?

Michael Martin—I answer these questions at great length in my book *Atheism, Morality, and Meaning*. Here are the main points: (a) God cannot be the basis of morality since God either (1) commands what we ought to do because it is moral (prior to his command) or (2) what we ought to do is moral because God commands it; that is, his command makes it moral. But if (1), then morality is independent of God. However, if (2), then morality is arbitrary. For example, if God commands us to kill all infants, then we ought to. (b) Religious moral ideals such as Jesus are flawed. See my book *Case Against Christianity*, chapter six. (c) Viable nonreligious foundations for morality are possible. For example, in *Atheism, Morality, and Meaning*, I develop and defend the

Ideal Observer Theory, which has nothing to do with religion. (d) Morality has been hijacked by religions because the above points are not understood.

LR—One of the most used arguments to prove the existence of God refers to the origin of the universe (the Big Bang), asserting that "our moment in time" could not be possible in an infinite line of progress or regress; that what exists must have an uncaused cause—the Kalam cosmological argument. What are the problems with this argument?

MM—I have answered this in detail in my book *Atheism: A Philosophical Justification*. The main points are these: (a) No one has shown the impossibility of an infinite regress of causes. So there might not be a first cause of the universe. (b) The universe might not have a cause; that is, it may be uncaused. (c) Even if the universe has a cause, the cause may not be the theistic god. Other possibilities are finite gods and an impersonal force. (d) According to the Big Bang theory, time came into existence with the Big Bang. A cause comes before its effect in time. For God to be the cause of the universe, God would have to exist in time before the universe. But this is impossible since there was no time before the universe.

LR—Theists also say that only God could "fine-tune the universe" for human existence. What are the problems with this argument?

MM—The argument for this is based on the Anthropic Principle (see *Atheism: A Philosophical Justification*, pages 132–134) according to which seemingly arbitrary and unrelated constants in physics have one strange thing in common—they are precisely the values you need if you want to have a universe with life. Even the slightest deviation from these constants would make life impossible. Accordingly, this principle provides a teleological explanation of these constants and is an embarrassment to the prevailing mechanistic view of science. There are two questions to ask about this use of recent evidence and thinking in astrophysics: Does the use of the anthropic principle commit one to some cosmic purpose? Does the existence of a narrow range of physical constants that are compatible with life show that human life would be extremely improbable without a cosmic purpose? If the answer to the second question is yes, is there any reason to suppose that this cosmic purpose is connected with God? Are there any nonteleological explanations that are as good as or better than an explanation in terms of purpose? Regarding the first question, it can be admitted that some scientists use the anthropic principle in an explicitly teleological way; for example, they argue that the universe has certain properties in order to produce intelligent human life. However, this kind of reasoning does not necessarily entail a commitment to some cosmic conscious purpose. Thus, for example, the statement that the heart beats in order to circulate the blood does not necessarily imply a conscious purpose; it can merely mean that the function of the heart is to circulate the blood. Similarly, statements in astrophysics of the form "X is Y in order for W" can be understood functionally. In addition, it is possible to use the anthropic principle in a purely methodological way. For example, the statement, "The universe is isotropic in order to produce intelligent life" can simply mean "The universe's being isotropic is a necessary condition for intelligent life." Although here there is not even the suggestion of a functional analysis, there is an obvious anthropomorphism in the sense that the focus of attention is on human life. However, this anthropomorphism entails nothing about the metaphysical makeup of the universe and seems to be justified on purely heuristic grounds. With respect to the second question, although the argument is not clear, a plausible reconstruction of it is this:

1. There is an extremely large number of possible values for the physical constants in the universe.
2. Only a very narrow range of possible values is compatible with human life.
3. All of these possible values are equally probable.
4. Hence, it is extremely improbable that human life occurred by chance.

It is important to note that although this argument requires premise 3, no evidence is provided for 3 and it is difficult to see what support could be given it. Of course, one might attempt to justify 3 a priori via the principle of indifference (PI): Assume all possibilities are equally probable unless there is reason to suppose otherwise. But although theists may tacitly assume PI, there is no reason to embrace this principle. One could instead attempt to justify 3 empirically in terms of the frequency interpretation of probability. On this construal the claim that life in the universe is improbable would amount to saying that the relative frequency of universes with human life relative to the class of all universes is low. Since, however, we have only knowledge of one universe—this one—the frequency theory is not applicable. In short, the rationale for supposing that life is extremely improbable without a cosmic purpose fails. It must be realized that judgments of probability are possible only when we have certain kinds of information. This information is lacking in the present case. However, let us suppose premise 3 in my reconstruction of the argument is true and that the conclusion follows. This brings us to the third question. Theists assume that recent cosmological evidence and reasoning establish the existence of God, but how does one derive the existence of God from 4? They seem to be tacitly assuming a further argument that can be formulated as follows:

4. It is extremely improbable that human life occurred by chance.
5. If it is extremely improbable that human life occurred by chance, then the best explanation of human life is that it was created by God.
6. Hence, the best explanation of human life is that it was created by God.

But why should one accept premise 5? God, as usually understood, is by definition a being that is all-good, all-knowing, and all-powerful. Nonetheless, human life could have been created by many gods or by an evil being or by a finite god or by an impersonal creative force. Why is God in the traditional sense a better explanation than these alternative accounts?

LR—Jesus, Muhammad, Abraham, Buddha—supposedly historical figures around whom have developed mythological and dogmatic narratives. In the debate between religious dogma and philosophical skepticism, why hasn't the critical thinking of philosophy won?

MM—Surely it *has* won in the sense of presenting the stronger argument. Any objective impartial judge would vote for critical thinking. Of course, it has not "won" in the sense of converting believers to nonbelievers. But conversion is not the goal of a debate and debates are not scored in these terms. If the question is why believers have not been converted, then psychologists and other social scientists, not philosophers, should be consulted. The answer may be complex, involving innate human needs, how most people are raised, and the religious culture in which we live. It is a task for social science to explain why. But the causes may have little to do with the use of critical thinking and more with economic and social factors. It is worth mentioning that in some societies nonbelievers are in the majority—for example, Norway—which suggests that in these societies nonbelief is "winning" (see *The Cambridge Companion to Atheism*, chapter three).

LR—Paradoxes, contradictions, and parables are fundamental parts of the Bible, and theologians often use them according to their convenience. Is it possible to use the rules of logical reasoning in debating religion when all logic breaks down due to the symbolic, metaphorical, metaphysical, poetic, and emotional nature of the arguments used by the religious interlocutor?

MM—Yes, it is. I do this in my *Case Against Christianity*, chapter eight. A Christian might maintain that the arguments and evidence presented in my book do undermine Christianity if one takes its doctrines literally, but that they should not be so understood; these doctrines need to be reinterpreted in a way that brings out their deeper meaning. This strategy is typical of many sophisticated contemporary believers. Unwilling to accept traditional Christianity and yet reluctant to abandon it completely, they attempt to reinterpret its doctrines in such a way that they can accept them without being irrational. Given this reinterpretation, they maintain, one can be a Christian and a person committed to reason, the truths of history, and scientific inquiry. However, logical reasoning shows that there are several problems with this approach. It is not clear what counts as a legitimate reinterpretation. How can one tell whether some particular reinterpretation really does get at some deeper meaning? Why is one interpretation correct and another is not? Nor is it clear what is left of Christianity that is recognizably Christian after the reinterpretation. In addition, it may be the case that after such a reinterpretation of Christianity the basic doctrines are still unjustified. Do the reinterpreted doctrines also need to be based on faith? I examined in *Case Against Christianity* three representative attempts to reinterpret Christianity: Boslooper's interpretation of the virgin birth, Bultman's demythologizing of Christianity, and Braithwaite's noncognitive interpretation of Christianity. I showed that they do not stand up to philosophical criticism.

LR—Is there a reason for theology to exist as an epistemological discipline?

MM—"Theology" means either: (1) the study of religion, especially the Christian faith and God's relation to the world; or (2) a religious theory, school of thought, or system of belief; or (3) a course of specialized religious training, especially one intended to lead students to a vocation in the Christian church. But in none of these definitions can theology be an epistemological discipline, that is, a field of study for achieving knowledge. Necessary conditions for knowing a proposition are that belief that the proposition is true is justified and that the proposition is true. So for theology to be an epistemological discipline religious propositions must be justified and true. But in part I of my *Atheism: A Philosophical Justification*, I showed that religious belief is unjustified and in part II that it is false.

LR—In an article written in *The Cambridge Companion to Atheism*, you mention some religions (or sects of a religion) that are atheistic. What is the logic behind an "atheist religion"?

MM—Some belief systems have many properties of Western religions but no belief in God. It is illuminating to think of them as religions. In my essay on "Atheism and Religion" in *The Cambridge Companion to Atheism*, two definitions are considered which allow atheistic religions and indicate what it is about them that allows them to be so classified. Such usage is in accord with scholarly practice, which classifies certain belief systems as religions that have no belief in God.

LR—With the spreading of the "New Atheism" movement (Hitchens, Harris, Dawkins, Dennett, etc.), isn't atheism as a "philosophy" becoming more "politicized" and "scientificized," losing its real meaning?

MM—Perhaps. But the only thing I see happening so far is that logical and analytic standards have been lowered or have become nonexistent in the New Atheism writing. Harris does not seem to see the need to argue, Dawkins argues superficially, and Dennett wrongly rejects strong atheist arguments without argument (see *The Open Society*, vol. 80, no. 4, Summer 2007, pg. 16). So the New Atheism writing may be easy to read but it is thin philosophically. Moreover, this writing shows no knowledge of atheistic literature of the past or present.

LR—How do you envision atheism in the world in the near future?

MM—In the near future in the United States, I would predict, although atheism may become a little more popular, in general not much will change. For example, there will be few atheists in the United States (less than 10 percent) and no avowed atheists will be elected to high public office. On the other hand, in countries such as Sweden, New Zealand, and Japan there is a relatively large proportion of atheists and atheists do hold high public office. This is likely to continue. Loss of belief in God occurred over the course of the 20th century in Canada, Australia, and various European countries, including Germany, the United Kingdom, the Netherlands, and Scandinavia. However, secularization is limited to specific advanced industrialized nations and has not occurred throughout much of the rest of the world. It is likely that this trend will continue. The United States is an anomaly in that it has a low percentage of atheists and is an advanced industrialized nation (see Phil Zuckerman's "Contemporary Numbers and Patterns" in *The Cambridge Companion to Atheism*).

LR—How does an atheist like you face death?

MM—Facing death as an atheist is much easier than facing death as a believer, for example as a Christian. As an atheist I know that I will not exist after death. I will not have a strange new existence. I will not have an uncertain future, since I will be no more. I will have no existence strange or otherwise and no future uncertain or otherwise. But a Christian will not know what his future will be or what his existence will be. Christian doctrine is unclear what the afterlife is like and how one is saved in order to get there (see *Atheism, Morality, and Meaning*, chapter 17). The questions that are usually asked are, if I will no longer exist after death, what was the point of living? Is life meaningless or absurd without life after death? However, life after death does not necessarily give your existence meaning. What if it were life like the life of Sisyphus, who performed the same act over and other for eternity? Moreover, not having a life after death does not mean one's life is meaningless or absurd. Surely, Martin Luther King's life was meaningful even if he did not survive after death. We give meaning to our lives through our work, our accomplishments, and our relations with others (see *Atheism, Morality, and Meaning*, part IV).

Alister McGrath

Alister McGrath was born in Belfast, Northern Ireland in 1953. He studied chemistry at Wadham College, Oxford University, and later did research in molecular biophysics in the Oxford University Department of Biochemistry. In December 1977, he was awarded an Oxford D.Phil. for his research in the natural sciences, and he gained first-class honors in theology in June 1978. The interaction of Christian theology and the natural sciences has subsequently been a major theme of his research work and is best seen in the three volumes of his *Scientific Theology* (2001–2003). In 1999, he was awarded a personal chair in theology at Oxford University as professor of historical theology. He earned an Oxford doctorate of divinity in 2001 for his research on historical and systematic theology. As a former atheist, McGrath is respectful yet critical of the movement, and in recent years, he has been especially interested in the emergence of "scientific atheism." His main research interest at present is the area of thought traditionally known as natural theology, which is experiencing significant renewal and revitalization at the moment. His 2008 book *The Open Secret: A New Vision for Natural Theology* engages this theme in more detail.

Luís Rodrigues—As far as I know, in your youth you were an atheist. What made you change your mind to embrace God, and namely, the Church of England?

Alister McGrath—When I was an atheist, I had not really understood exactly what Christianity was and, in many ways, I think my atheism was based on a series of misunderstandings and misrepresentations. When I went up to Oxford University, I had an opportunity to rethink things and began to realize that I had rejected Christianity without really understanding what it was. So, I began to study Christian theology, to start going to church, and I became involved with the Church of England mainly because it was the most numerous church in Oxford and so, it was the one I naturally got involved with.

LR—Of these five areas of knowledge, which ones do you think have the strongest and the weakest arguments for the defense of the existence of God: ontology, cosmology, biology, teleology, or morality?

AM—Well, I think you can make a case for all of these, and in many ways, the order in which you rank them will depend on how you access some evidence. I personally would say that arguments from morality and cosmology are actually very strong arguments and particularly in recent years, as we have begun to understand more about the way in which the fundamental constants of nature seem to be fine-tuned for the existence of life, the traditional cosmological arguments become much more important. But I would still say that the argument from morality—as you find it in writers like C. S. Lewis—is actually a very significant argument today.

LR—But why does Christianity emphasize the regular laws that permeate reality—like the cosmological constant, for example—to justify an omnipotent creator God, but neglects the irregular or random aspects of that same reality? I'm thinking about chaos theory.

AM—Of course, and I think one of the things that chaos theory tells us is that chaos is actually, paradoxically, the basis of order. What I think you are doing is, you're emphasizing that there appears to be something very ordered or organized about the universe which permits the existence of life to take place, even though some of the processes that lead to this emergence do seem—I emphasize the word *seem*—to be random in character. In other words, an apparently random process can nevertheless navigate its way toward a very limited number of outcomes.

LR—In your opinion, chaos, as a manifestation of randomness, of irregularity, is something that does not exist?

AM—Well, chaos is reasonably well defined. It's not about nonexistence: It's about seemingly unpredictable events taking place within the natural world. That certainly does not have negative implications for the existence of God because unpredictability is actually a reference to the capacity of the human mind to predict what is going to happen. It doesn't have ontological implications.

LR—How do you see the relationship between religion and science?

AM—I think the relation between religion and science has real potential for a very significant dialogue. Of course there are those who would argue that there is a tension—or even a warfare—between science and religion—and I think of writers like Richard Dawkins who take that position. As a historian, I would want to say that the relationship between science and religion has varied over history; it's never been one of constant antagonism. There have certainly been tensions, but there has also been some very important collaboration. So, I would want to say that I believe there is some very significant possibility for collaboration and dialogue while at the same time recognizing that science and religion are quite distinct disciplines, each with their own identity and their own distinct way of working.

LR—Having been a renowned scientist, and now, a renowned theologian, do you think that you can obtain more knowledge useful to your life from religion, rather than from science?

AM—I think that science is very helpful in understanding how the world works, how natural processes take place, and, in many ways, much of the technology that we take for granted is dependent upon scientific principles. But I do want to make the point that for most people, the really important questions have to do with meaning: Why are we here? What is the meaning of life? Natural sciences cannot really answer those questions. I think one of the most interesting things is that natural sciences raise questions which they themselves cannot answer. I want to argue that religion begins to engage the great existential questions of life, which deal with meaning. These are questions that religion definitely engages. I can see science and religion genuinely having a dialogue in that they are actually approaching questions at different levels.

LR—Although science cannot yet answer all the questions about reality, why do you think religion can fill that gap left

open by scientific inquiry? Can't we find a meaning for life without relying on religious answers?

AM—Certainly we can invent meaning; we can say that "I choose that this world will mean this." I am determining for myself what its meaning shall be. For me, I was more concerned about discovering what the meaning of the world is; in other words, not about "inventing" but trying to find if there is something already there which I'm able to discover. A religion like Christianity would say that there are meanings to be found; they are made known, for example, through the Christian tradition. I would then say that while everyone is concerned about meaning, there is a question about the reliability of the meanings that people are able to discover.

LR—If that's so, why then do you think that Christianity represents the most universal and accurate vision of meaning and truth? Why not, let's say, Judaism, Islam, Deism, or even Paganism?

AM—That's a very relevant question, and for me, there are several answers I would want to give to that question. One is that I believe Christianity is the most intellectually robust and satisfactory of all the religions I've examined. I want to go further than that and say that, in many ways, we can see Christianity as the fulfillment of the human quest for wisdom—and I would certainly include Judaism and other religious faiths in this quest for wisdom. Christianity does not in any way denigrate these other faith systems but rather argues that it represents their culmination. So, for me, one of the great effects of Christianity is its capacity to make sense of the world, its capacity to disclose existential meaning and also the fact that it seems to rest upon such good foundations.

LR—But that existential meaning can be jeopardized by the ever-changing conditions of human existence itself. Let's say that science discovers a way to prolong the human lifespan indefinitely. Would you still see a purpose for being a Christian and believe in an afterlife?

AM—Well, I think that there's no doubt that human beings are living for longer and longer. In the United Kingdom in the year 1908 I think there were a hundred people who lived to the age of 100 and today, there are 6,000. You can see there's a very significant expansion of human existence taking place even now. I would want to argue that the longer we live, the more important these questions about the meaning of life become for us. We are always going to die, there's no doubt about that; therefore, the full significance of human existence does become increasingly important. So, I don't myself feel that the growing human lifespan is in any way moving us away from the great existential questions of what the meaning of life is.

LR—Theology is supposed to be the study and understanding of God. How can that study be reliable—or even achievable—if there's no particular object to grasp? Isn't theology, then, the history of what some thinkers thought about the idea of God rather than the study of God itself?

AM—I think that is a fair point, and certainly most Christian writers would say that theology is not so much about the direct study of God, but rather about the way in which the Christian faith has understood God. Therefore, it's very much trying to understand the intellectual foundations of Christianity, the development of its idea. And certainly, if we were to define theology as the study of God, that would be very difficult because obviously we know about God, for example, through texts and human experiencing and so on, and this raises a huge range of questions about the reliability of those sources. For me, Christian theology is about the way in which Christians have made sense of God. I think you can make a very good case for saying that you can achieve increasing precision about what Christians believe to be the case, without necessarily proving that that is actually what God is like.

LR—But granting that there are different ideas about God, isn't theology then a subset of epistemological fields of social studies—ethics, history, philosophy, and so on—applied to different religious doctrines? If that's so, theology can't make a universal claim of knowledge as, for instance, mathematics and physics do.

AM—Yes, mathematics is a very interesting example in that it does depend upon a very tightly defined set of axioms and principles; in the case of theology, it's much broader than that. You're right to make the point that the way we think about God is influenced by, for example, our cultural environment and a range of social factors along those lines, but that doesn't stop us from asking: Is there any way in which we can recognize the influence of these social factors and take them into account? So we're able to rise above the impact of, for example, our social situation in terms of the way we think about God. Most social psychologists, for example, would recognize the importance of our intellectual and cultural environment in shaping the way we think, but would nevertheless say that we ought to be able to rise above those specific ideas and achieve a better understanding of the way things really are.

LR—What is your opinion about scholarly investigation— namely the Jesus Seminar and the Copenhagen School of Biblical Studies—that denies some of the historicity of the Bible, the Gospels, and the life of Jesus?

AM—I've read certainly much from the Jesus Seminar and I'm slightly puzzled about their historical method, which seems to imply that 20th- and 21st-century scholars are able to understand the first century better than those closer to the time. So, I'm skeptical about how much these methods can achieve. I think, in many ways, we have to recognize that New Testament documents and others from the same age actually may well reflect a greater knowledge of the situation than what we ourselves have. Therefore, I am suspicious about attempts to reconstruct the past—for the very simple reason that when we reconstruct the past, it very often looks like what we experience at present.

LR—But isn't that "reconstruction of the past" also a modus operandi of the Christian faith? I'm remembering for example, about the Donation of Constantine—a document forged (probably in the eighth century) in the name of the emperor Constantine by Christians with the aim to empower the papacy. It seems that the lack of reliability falls both ways, isn't that so?

AM—That's a very important point to make. Certainly, the example you give is a good one: The Donation of Constantine was, I think, very clearly a forgery and could be shown to be so by both historical analysis and textual analysis. And those two techniques, of course, have been used to look at New Testament documents. I would say that they have helped us to understand why these documents are so distinct, and also give us a much better understanding of the environment that gave rise to them. But I don't see those techniques as, in any way, calling into question the authenticity of these documents. Certainly there are some documents from the first few centuries of Christianity that clearly are of very dubious origins. For example, the Gospel of Judas—about which there has been a lot of excitement recently—is clearly a late writing which reflects the marginalized views of a very small sect. But I don't think these questions are raised for the New Testament documents themselves. I think it helps us to understand, in many ways, why they are so distinct.

LR—You also have the forged correspondence between Paul and Seneca . . .

AM—Oh yes, that was a forgery; and indeed you may know that in the Middle Ages, a so-called Letter of Paul to the Laodiceans was circulating. Again, that was a forgery. There's a real need for vigilance, to ensure that documents of questionable authenticity are identified and challenged. It seems to me that rigorous historical analysis can be very important there.

LR—Given the uncertainty posed by things like these documents, isn't religion a question of "fear and trembling"—as Kierkegaard once said?

AM—I don't think Kierkegaard referred "fear and trembling" to the documents; I think it was much more to do with our understanding of what the faith was. But certainly I would want to say that there are undoubtedly some questions about the documents of the New Testament that need to be raised—as indeed they can be raised about every historical document we possess from any significant length of time ago—precisely because we cannot have the full knowledge of what happened back in those times.

LR—There are many interpreters and interpretations of the Bible. Some see it as a manual for a life of peace, love, and tolerance; some see it as an indictment of war and intolerance. If the Bible is nothing more than a patchwork of divergent texts—each of which by itself can support varying interpretations—why would

an all-mighty God use such an archaic and blurry way to spread his message?

AM—I think the first thing to say is that the text may indeed seem to us to be archaic, but it is the medium that really most people used until very, very recently. I think the point you're making is that there is a fundamental question about how texts are to be interpreted. That's very true; it's certainly true of the Koran in Islam, it's true of the Hebrew Law, it's true of the Christian Bible, it's also true, as you will know, for example, of the Justinian Codex and various other legal documents from the Classical Era. And that's why I think there's a real need to have a very clear understanding of how these texts are to be interpreted. Certainly within Christianity, you find in Catholicism an emphasis on the importance of the Church as the agent of the interpretation of the Bible. In Protestantism you find an emphasis on the natural sense of scripture, and you can certainly interpret the Bible in a way that makes it seem to be a very violent document, but that's not how most Christians would read it at all. I think the mainstream approach within Christianity is to say that Christ is the keystone to the interpretation of scripture; therefore, his nonviolence is actually extremely important in understanding the right way to interpret some of these texts. So, it's a very significant debate, but one which I think certainly we can understand from the context of the Christian community being the interpreter of the Bible.

LR—In some passages of the New Testament, Jesus does not present himself as a very mild character (for example, when he gets angry with the Pharisees and Peter). Is the image of a "loving Christ" a construction of how we wish to characterize Jesus—but maybe he isn't so?

AM—I think there is a case to be made for saying that some Christian interpretations of Jesus present him as being almost serenely disengaged from people, and they neglect the fact that Jesus clearly got angry at times: He's angry about the abuse of power, he's angry about a whole range of things. But I think we need to be clear that anger is not the same as violence. Anger is a realization that a situation is unjust and that something should be done about it. Certainly I would be very happy to talk about Christ being angered by the situation he sees in the world, but that anger doesn't lead him into violence; it leads him to want to transform things.

LR—But don't we see different versions of Christ even in the Gospels? For example, from Mark to John, we see Jesus becoming more transcendent, more detached from the world, more philosophical, and more serene. Isn't it difficult to choose the best and most reliable version of Christ even if we rely solely on the Gospels?

AM—There's no doubt, I think, that each of the Gospels offers us a distinctive portrait of Christ, each one often emphasizing features that its distinct audience might find to be important. Most New Testament scholars would say that each New Testament document in fact does reflect an individual evaluation of the identity of Christ. But that's actually the way in which human beings work; the psychology of perception teaches us that people try to identify what is significant from their perspective about a person or an event, and in many ways, you could see the New Testament as multiple attempts to establish the significance of Jesus. This doesn't mean that they are divergent, doesn't mean that they are contradictory; it does mean however, they place the emphasis in different questions, and sometimes the New Testament writers find different images helpful in conveying the significance of Christ. I think the comparison, for example, between John's Gospel and Mark's Gospel is very interesting there.

LR—Coming back to contemporary age, how do you see this "New Atheism" movement, or "Brights," as they like to be called?

AM—Well, I think the choice of the word "Brights" was very, very unwise—as you know, that began in 2003—and the reason I say it's very unwise is that one of the fundamental criticisms Brights make of Christianity is that it encourages the appearance of in-groups and out-groups. And of course, the use of the label Brights implies that there are those who are bright and those who are dim. The real difficulty is that they are causing the same polarization that they accuse Christianity of causing. This New Atheism actually is not new, there are no new arguments; what I think is new is the aggressiveness of rhetoric with which they are pursued. That seems to me to be the essence of what is new;

the arguments that would have been stated much more graciously and cautiously in the past are now being stated very aggressively indeed—and that to me is not a welcome development.

LR—What do you think are the new intellectual challenges—if any—posed by the New Atheists that were not addressed by the classics of atheist philosophy—for instance, Nietzsche, Feuerbach, Camus, Freud, Sartre, and others?

AM—That is a fair question. I think that many of the questions are recycled—for example, the link between religion and violence. What I think we do find emerging in Daniel Dennett and Richard Dawkins is the argument that recent scientific advances have in some way undermined the credibility of religion. Now, I have to say that I don't actually see that being well defended or justified in those books, but certainly the increased emphasis on the role of science does help us distinguish the newer atheism from an older atheism.

LR—In your book *The Dawkins Delusion?* you say that Richard Dawkins's "hysterical and dogmatic insistence on the atheist implications of Darwinism is alienating many potential supporters of the theory of evolution" into intelligent design and creationism. Can you develop this line of argument?

AM—Yes. It's very strange but there's lots of evidence that this is happening. For example, in the United States of America—where most people are very religious—if you say that the theory of evolution is atheist, a lot of Americans are going to say, "Well, I'm not an atheist and that's why I do not accept evolution." I think that a lot of natural scientists in North America are very alarmed with this insistence that Darwin's theory of evolution is atheist. Certainly Darwin himself did not think so; Darwin, as you know, ends *The Origin of Species* by saying that his theory of evolution bears witness to the creator. So, I think we need to be clear that this is a gross overstatement of what the theory of evolution is implying. There's no doubt that Dawkins believes this is true but I think it's very important to say that he does not speak as the majority voice of the scientific establishment in saying that.

LR—Dawkins seems to be the most recognizable and one of the most important voices of atheism today. Do you think that the

questions he raises are the ones that most represent atheism? If not, what are the interesting ones that need to be posed?

AM—I think you are right to say that Dawkins is the most influential atheist today. I think that's absolutely right. He does represent a departure from older atheist writings—for example, from before the Second World War. My own feeling is that some of the older atheists—for example, Marxist atheists like Theodor Adorno and others—raise much more interesting questions about, for example, the social origins of religion, the possibility that God is the intellectual superstructure on a social-economic substructure; I think those are interesting questions that atheists should be looking at. But I think you're right to suggest that, at the moment, the agenda is being set by Richard Dawkins—and that means moving in a very different direction.

LR—Do you think that the questions that Richard Dawkins and some of the New Atheists pose are successful because they have a higher degree of popular appeal?

AM—I think that Dawkins is writing at a very popular level. He's using very popular ways of expressing himself and there's no doubt that what he's saying is something that a lot of people would like to be true—for example: Religion is evil, religion is delusion, religion leads to violence. There are many religiously alienated people who like to hear that sort of thing. Certainly, that is what a lot of people would like to hear at the moment.

LR—If it were not for antagonists like Richard Dawkins, do you think that theologians would have ever felt the need to reflect more intensely about nature, science, humanity, and God? Nowadays, we see a proliferation of books, radio, and television programs concerned with religious questions—namely, about the rising issue of Islamic fundamentalism and its consequences. Do you think Dawkins and others have caught the wave of indignation brought about by Islamic fundamentalism, for example?

AM—I think that one of the things Dawkins is right to raise is the significance of Islamic fundamentalism—with its new development in the West. Although many of the points Dawkins makes are simply wrong, I think he's right to raise that as a very significant culture issue for our times. Certainly one doesn't need to be an atheist to say that this is an important question to talk about.

LR—In today's world, we see the rising of syncretism: Many spiritual thinkers and spiritual schools accept Jesus, Buddha, Muhammad, UFOs, pagan gods, and all sorts of different super-natural claims in the same frame of inclusiveness (and very often, incoherence). How can Christianity deal with this approach to reality and spirituality?

AM—The development you've described does makes us realize that for many people, you can simply pick and mix your worldview. In other words, you choose what you want to be true, whether you're reaching into, for example, Buddhism or paganism. For me, the challenge to the Christian church is to show, first of all, that its vision of reality is better than anyone else's; and secondly, to show that it has such coherence that this pick and mix attitude simply isn't going to work. I think that is a very big challenge: the reassertion of the unitary truth of Christianity today.

LR—By praising more libertarian forms of living, don't you think that these spiritual movements have the potential to be more appealing to people, overcoming older forms of religions— many of which do prescribe oppressive and dogmatic advice on how one should live his or her own life?

AM—That is a fair point; culturally, people value something that seems to be liberating, nondogmatic, and nonoppressive. The difficulty is that, for some Christian writers, Christian orthodoxy is very often presented in our secular media as being authoritarian, intrusive, oppressive, and in some way, not helping people achieve individual fulfillment. Again, I think there is a need for Christian churches to be able to show this is not true, to bring out the fact that, for example, Christianity brings personal liberation. I think this theme needs to be emphasized and demonstrated in our contemporary culture.

LR—But how can that message pass when, for example, we often listen to some bigoted discourses proclaimed from the pulpit by ministers and priests? Concerning sexual issues, these discourses are not unusual.

AM—I think there's a danger that Christian priests and church officials present Christianity simply in terms of "things that are not permissible" rather than looking at the real change that Christianity can make to people's lives. I think there's a need to try to rebalance this whole issue by emphasizing the positive aspects of faith rather than simply condemning actions or attitudes which some Christians find difficult.

LR—For the theist, the improbability of human existence—an existence packed with the extraordinary features of rationality and emotionality—in such a vast and hostile universe, only seems possible due to the will of a supernatural creator. Even if that's so, why is it necessary to explain that creative process with strange and bizarre mechanisms such as the Atonement of Christ?

AM—The question of the Atonement is very often presented in a way which does seem rather strange. One of the points I'd want to make is that if you go back to earlier forms of Christianity—as for example, in the patristic period—they often define the Atonement as an act of divine love, an action of sense making, of imposing order within disorder. So, I think that if you want to emphasize the scientific background against which I'm thinking the Atonement takes place, there is a need to begin to look again at some traditional ways of thinking about the Atonement.

LR—When we talk about religion, the tendency is to look back in time, trying to justify the historicity of the main religious characters and the truth of their message. What if those justifications are nothing more than a means to deal with the unavoidable finitude of human existence that lies ahead? For example, what do you expect to do for eternity?

AM—That's a very good question. [Laughs.] For me, eternity is not an infinite extension of time: It's actually being outside time. That really means that this question of "what am I going to do with my time in eternity" isn't actually particularly meaningful—if that's what eternity is. Anyway, whatever eternity is, I'm looking forward to being there and maybe we can have a further conversation about this when that happens.

Robert L. Park

Robert L. Park has been a professor of physics of the University of Maryland for 37 years. An Eagle Scout, he volunteered for the Korean War, serving as first lieutenant in the US Air Force. After the war, he returned to the University of Texas, graduating Phi Beta Kappa with high honors. The Edgar Lewis Marston Fellow in Physics at Brown University, he earned his PhD in 1964. In 1982, he founded the Washington office of the American Physical Society and served for 25 years as the Washington "voice of physics." He continues to post his weekly Internet column on science and society at www.bobpark.org. A prolific author and frequent guest on television and radio news, he is a fellow of the American Physical Society, the American Association for the Advancement of Science, and the Committee for Scientific Inquiry. He received the 1995 Joseph Burton Award of the American Physical Society for "Informing the Public on Issues of Science and Society," and the 2008 Philip J. Klass Award of the National Capital Area Skeptics. He authored *Voodoo Science: The Road from Foolishness to Fraud* (2000) and *Superstition: Belief in the Age of Science* (2008).

Luís Rodrigues—What led you to write about "false science"?

Robert L. Park—I'm a professor at the University of Maryland—which is just outside Washington, DC—and on my sabbatical year, I agreed to open a Washington office for the American Physical Society, so I sort of became the spokesman for physics in Washington, DC. When I got there and started dealing with Congress, I discovered how much misunderstanding there was about science and how much really foolish kinds of things are widely believed. I got involved and find it an interesting subject. I don't understand it; I don't know why people believe these things, but they certainly do.

LR—Working in Washington, did you feel that there are some politicians promoting that lack of knowledge?

RLP—Oh, my goodness! Yes, yes.

LR—Why do you think they're doing this?

RLP—Well, some of them because they're foolish, and others because they think the public is foolish. These ideas are popular with some people and if they feel that they have a lot of people like that in their area, they may choose to appeal to those, to gain votes. But some of them are just quite foolish themselves.

LR—What do you think about atheism and politics in America? It's very difficult for an atheist politician to make a stand in the American political arena. Why's that?

RLP—Yes, it would be almost impossible, and I'm not sure why this is so. It's obviously a cultural phenomena that has existed for a very long time. I puzzle over this and envy my European colleagues who live in a more enlightened society. It would be virtually impossible to be elected to public office in the United States if you were an outspoken atheist.

LR—There are many scientists who are committed to a religious worldview. With all these plural theistic visions about science, aren't postmodernists right when they say that scientific discourse is just another form of cultural discourse—like poetry, music, and literature—and therefore, one can use it to justify any sort of theistic claim?

RLP—I'm not sure it's quite that simple. The people I know, the scientists I know who are theistic, they partition their lives. They're theistic because they grew up in a theistic culture. They were indoctrinated with it when they were children, and we're never completely free of what we learn as children. It lasts all our lives. Sometimes we can overcome it, and some of these people simply can't. So, they partition their lives and on one side of this partition they're logical and rational, and on the other side they choose to set that stuff aside and believe in religion.

I don't know exactly how they can do this; I have good friends that do that, and yet I never quite understand them. They live in two worlds and move from one to the other and put the other behind them.

LR—What are the reactions of your colleagues in science regarding your enterprise?

RLP—All of my scientific colleagues applaud what I do. I have no problem; only rarely is there a scientist who objects to my outspoken views. Many are reluctant to speak out themselves but they certainly don't mind me doing it.

LR—Do you think they're afraid to lose their jobs if they do so?

RLP—I don't think so. It's more often within family and community than with other scientists. Certainly almost all scientists in the United States are atheistic; it's overwhelming, but they realize that very few people outside the scientific community are atheistic, and so they're a little cautious.

LR—Who do you consider the most dangerous voices for irrationality nowadays: Priests? Gurus? Pseudoscientists? Religious celebrities?

RLP—Good question. I can think of examples in all of those of course, but I think—at least in the United States—celebrities tend to have a huge impact, and that's unfortunate.

LR—It is a fact that scientific knowledge is not eternal: New things are constantly being discovered and new theories disprove old ones. In such a context, how can a scientist assert that his theory is more correct than any other theory proposed by another scientist, or even someone outside science—like a theologian?

RLP—The only test is experiment; it's what best explains the information. If you do that of course, it rules out theistic opinions completely. Experimental testing is the only way to distinguish.

LR—But there are areas of science more prone to metaphysical speculation than others. Quantum physicists and string theoreticians can surely make a more convincing argument about the

existence of God than a geologist or a biologist. Given that, how to engage a scientific debate when the types of arguments and jargon used by some scientists are as mystical as those used by theology?

RLP—Yes they are, but the point is that in string theory, for example, there is no experimental support at all. There is no experimental evidence for string theory and the greatest problem for string theory is to try to devise an experimental test.

LR—When Einstein exposed his general theory of relativity, there was no evidence backing it up, and the theory surely seemed strange—as did Copernicus's heliocentric view of the cosmos. In these examples, the bizarre claims of the individual genius seem to surpass verifiability and the conventional conceptions made by the collective of fellow scientists. That being said, do you concede that even the most bizarre claim may have at least a small chance of merit?

RLP—Again, the only test there is, is experiment; Einstein's theories have—for the most part—been confirmed experimentally.

LR—We also have Stephen Hawking's examples—theories concerning black holes, time travel, and so on. What do you think of these scientific proposals with—apparently and for the time being—no experimental support? Do you think they are necessary?

RLP—I suppose they provoke some interest, but when these speculations are made, the first thing one has to do is to sit down and see if it's possible to devise an experiment. Whether we can do the experiment is not the question, but it's whether such an experiment is conceivable. If you speculated about what the moon was made of in the 1940s, there would be no test for that. But a test was conceivable: You could imagine sending a spacecraft to the moon and finding out. Well, now we've done that. As long as it's at least plausible to devise an experiment, then it's serious science; but if not, then it has nothing to do with science.

LR—Do you think that science must have a component of imagination?

RLP—Of course, that's why we can speculate, that's where the imagination comes in. But we have to speculate about whether it is conceivable to test the theory. I can give you a good example, the best example I can think of: What happened before the Big Bang? What was the universe like before the Big Bang? What caused the Big Bang? Well, these are things we can't test—and presumably, never will be able to. This erased all the information of whatever happened and there's no way we can go back and look at that. We can get closer and closer—and that's what we're doing today with the Large Hadron Collider and the other big experiments; we're trying to go back farther. But we can't get beyond the Big Bang. To speculate about what happened before the Big Bang is interesting—and it's good philosophy—and may lead scientists on, but we have to accept that it's simply not testable, and presumably never will be. There are a few people who are beginning to talk about possibilities of testing some ideas about what was in existence before the Big Bang, but these are pretty far out speculations at this point.

LR—Some say that one of the strongest arguments for the existence of God comes from the Big Bang (the universe had a cause and presumably, that cause was God). According to your point of view, what other theories are most suited to explain the surge of the universe out of nothing without relying on theistic explanations?

RLP—Well, again I would be speculating as they are—and I find it a sort of pointless exercise. But if you want my "theological" explanation, it would be that the universe is cyclic, that the universe expands; eventually, it will reach a limit at which it will begin to collapse back on itself, and when it collapses all the way back in, it will set off another Big Bang. So, in this case, the universe has no beginning: It's always been doing this.

LR—What do you think about the "multiple universes" hypothesis?

RLP—It's a possibility. This is one of the ideas that people want to test. There are some far out speculations about things we might do that test the multiple universes hypothesis, to see if there are shadows of those other universes on our own. Once again, these would be extremely difficult to experiment; if ever to be done, it will be done far in the future. It's not totally implausible, so it's a valid thing to discuss.

LR—In your opinion, what best explains the recent attraction of a considerable number of Americans toward intelligent design theory?

RLP—It's a cultural phenomena. You notice that it is strongest in the less-educated areas of the United States—areas of the far West and the South—in which the educational standards are not as high. I don't know if it's simply a matter of poor education, but again, there are cultural differences; we simply are never quite able to overcome the culture in which we spent our first years. You speak excellent English, for example, but very few people are ever able to think in another language; they always wind up thinking in the language that they learned in those first years of life—their first language—and the things we learn in those first years of life occupy a different structure within our brain. At birth, our brain has left a lot of connections unmade, and those connections are hardwired in those first few years of life, specifically for learning languages, but it happens that anything that we are indoctrinated in, in those first few years, like language, is very difficult to ever change. So, although some people learn many languages and are fluent in all of them, most will still think in their first language.

LR—What is your opinion about some claims made by the New Age Spirituality movement—namely, those concerned with the law of attraction?

RLP—You're talking about the book *The Secret*? It's just terrible! I can't see how anybody can read that book and take it seriously. It stuns me that it should be such a big seller.

LR—But do you think people are looking for something serious and true? Maybe they're just looking for something that gives them hope.

RLP—Oh sure, they're looking for comfort.

LR—And the ways of achieving ultimate goals . . .

RLP—Yes, but it doesn't involve working for it. Somehow you're just supposed to think the right thoughts and it will happen. I don't understand this. Concerning the law of attraction, I don't even know what it means; I read the words but they make no sense to me at all. I should think about things and they will happen? That's just preposterous!

LR—The tremendous influence of the media reflects itself in the people. When celebrities like Oprah endorse books like *The Secret*, surely a great number of her audiences will take its spiritual and scientific contents for granted.

RLP—Yes, and I wish that she would recommend my book [laughs].

LR—What is your opinion about this phenomenon of spirituality endorsement made by the media? Why do you think media mythmakers try to publicize these kinds of books?

RLP—Oprah is certainly not the only one; there have been others in the past and, in fact, *The Secret* is really about the power of positive thinking. There was a book written on exactly that subject and a great deal of *The Secret* is really taken from this and it's never mentioned: *The Power of Positive Thinking* by Norman Vincent Peale was a bestselling book back in the 1950s. I don't believe that Norman Vincent Peale is ever mentioned in *The Secret*, and yet the power of positive thinking is exactly what he was pushing—and it made no more sense then than it does now.

LR—I think that *The Secret* also comprises the "spiritually updated version" of the content of some self-help books written back in the time you've mentioned: Napoleon Hill's *Think and Grow Rich*, Dale Carnegie's *How to Win Friends and Influence People*, and so on. These were more "materialistic" if we may say so. Now, it's not just about getting rich: it's about getting rich and getting in touch with the universe, with people, with God, etc. Can it be that this "soul-searching" literature is just a reflex of something that is missing in American society?

RLP—Are there such books in other languages? I don't know. I know the books in English but I don't know books in Portuguese or Spanish or other languages that might be like that—but don't you have similar problems?

LR—We have the Catholic versions of it: Some celebrities claiming that they talk to saints, to Jesus, to our Lady of Fatima, and so on. Now, concerning another question: Today's gurus seem to be a mix of scientists and mystics, using the titles "Dr." and "PhD" to achieve credibility. How can people be provided with the critical tools that allow them to detect credibility in an argument about which they have no previous knowledge?

RLP—My advice always to students is that they must think everything in terms "What is the experimental evidence?" There is no other way to know. There is only one way to know and that is: to use our senses and see what's happening. Basically, every time we use our senses, we're doing an experiment, we're making a measurement; maybe crudely, maybe it should be done better, but those experiments, the collection of information in our senses—and making sure that it's consistent—is all there is. So, there is no other way to know.

LR—But we are talking about a small niche of people—like your students. What about the majority of religious people? What is your "strategy of seduction" to help them examine the reliability or unreliability of their beliefs?

RLP—The only strategy that I have—and if you can't get through with that, there's not much hope—is to say, "Just simply use your own common sense and then look to see if there's evidence that supports what you're saying, and if there's not, maybe you ought to rethink it." Some people won't, but again, this is instilled in them as children. Now, why can some of us throw off all of this? I grew up in a family that was nominally religious; many atheistic scientists that I know were as well. What allowed us to throw it off and not others? I don't know.

LR—Some believers ground their faith on miracles. How do you explain "miraculous" events that some people claim to have witnessed?

RLP—The comparison that I always use with people is to point to a stage magician, someone who performs magic tricks on a stage. They can fool just about anybody—including scientists—but the scientist knows that it's a trick. The fact that we can't see through the trick doesn't mean it's not a trick. Frequently, in these discussions, I will perform a few simple magic tricks and ask them if they know how I did that—and of course they don't; sometimes it is just a sleight of hand, nothing very complicated, just a simple trick. They're always stunned when they find out how easy it is to do—sometimes I even teach them to do a trick. I find that comparison with a stage magician to be pretty effective.

LR—Maybe people prefer magic to reality.

RLP—Oh! Definitely they do prefer magic to reality, and they're sort of disappointed that science doesn't have magic in it. In fact, tonight on television, there is an entertainment program called *Fringe* and I've been asked by a popular science magazine to listen to the program and to comment on it. In my view, it's a terrible program because the science there is fictional. Now, like many scientists, I read science fiction when I was young—but *Fringe* is all pseudoscience; they try to pretend that it really is science and that it is pseudoscientists who get it right. When you create science fiction, you have to create an atmosphere of plausibility—and that's not easy to do.

LR—So, can it be that the most effective religions are those that create a better atmosphere of plausibility?

RLP—To some extent, and magic has been widely used in religion forever. There has always been a strong element of magic about religion.

LR—What are your feelings concerning the question of death? Do you wish that a God could grant you eternal life?

RLP—Of course. I have many friends who say, "No, no, no. It is much better to have a single life; it would get boring if it went on forever." Well, I don't know about that. If I could live longer I would, and I'm getting to the point in life when death is not that far away. I'm 77 years old; I can understand the statistics quite well and the odds against my living another 10 years are very high. The odds of my living another 10 years beyond that are almost zero; the odds of another 10 years beyond that are zero. So, I can understand those odds and I wish I had a little more time. I enjoy life, I enjoy every bit of it; I have a wonderful family, but it's true, I also have some physical ailments now. A few years ago I had an accident: I was a marathoner—an aging marathoner, but I still run marathons—and I was just about to turn 70 and was out for a practice run, running on a trail through the woods, and a tree fell on me. Now, I have some religious friends who suspect they know why that tree fell [laughs]. Whatever the reason, it certainly left me with a good deal of pain—which I still suffer. So, the end of life is not quite as unpleasant as it sounded before, and certainly lying in a hospital bed for many weeks after that accident . . . at night I would sometimes curse fate for not taking me. I had always thought that the best way to go was to be hit from behind crossing the street because you wouldn't anticipate it. The lack of anticipation, I almost had that; if that tree had been an inch more in another direction, it might have ended my life without my thinking about it. The anticipation of death is the worst part.

LR—I'm glad you didn't suffer that fate or else I wouldn't have the pleasure of this conversation.

RLP—That's very nice of you to say, but there are others I'm sure—some of the pseudoscience people (because I'm not fondly thought of in that community)—who wouldn't agree. When the police were investigating the accident, my son suggested they dust the tree for fingerprints [laughs].

LR—Ah, a pseudoscientists' conspiracy! [Laughs.]

RLP—Yes, that would be quite a conspiracy theory [laughs].

Alvin Plantinga

Alvin Carl Plantinga (born 1932) is a contemporary US philosopher known for his work in epistemology, metaphysics, and the philosophy of religion. In 1980, Plantinga was described by *Time* magazine as "America's leading orthodox Protestant philosopher of God." He was portrayed in that same article as a central figure in a "quiet revolution" regarding the respectability of belief in God among academic philosophers. Plantinga is currently the John A. O'Brien Professor of Philosophy at the University of Notre Dame. Plantinga refers to his Christian religious epistemology as "reformed epistemology," in which belief in God can be rational and justified even without arguments or evidence for the existence of God. He is a contributor to *The Religion and Science Debate, Why Does It Continue?* (2009) and author or coauthor of several other books, including *Knowledge of God* (2008), *Essays in the Metaphysics of Modality* (2003), and *Warranted Christian Belief* (2000).

Luís Rodrigues—Let's start with a blunt question: Why do you believe in God?

Alvin Plantinga—Well, it seems to me that I have experience of God's presence. Sometimes it seems to me that I experience God's being with me or letting me see something of his glory and beauty. I would say that's a matter of experience.

LR—Is it like experiencing a natural landscape, sensing that something's beyond it?

AP—It's a bit like that—observing the landscape, seeing glorious mountains and the like can put you in mind of God. The idea that there is someone who made this, who must be great and so on, that can just come to one's mind; that's a kind of experience too, but slightly of a different kind from the one I was thinking of.

LR—Being part of a religious tradition, do you think others should also believe in God?

AP—I think there is such a person as God, so, I think others should believe in God too. I think everybody ought to believe whatever is true, I would say so, yes.

LR—Suppose human beings were immortal: Do you think humanity would need religion? Isn't religion a comfort in the face of the prospect of death?

AP—It probably is a comfort for that, but that's nothing against it. I mean, that might be God's way of getting us to know about him, by creating us in such a way that we have a desire to survive death and that thought put us in mind of God. So, maybe it is a comfort, but that doesn't mean it isn't true.

LR—Have you reached Christianity by philosophical inquiry or, rather, do you use philosophical thinking to defend something that has grown in you by faith?

AP—I think it's the latter. I've not reached Christian belief—or even belief in God—by virtue of philosophical reflection at all; but finding myself a Christian, then I think about philosophical questions and problems from that perspective. I think the same way about other minds, the past, the external world. I don't come to those beliefs on the basis of philosophical reflection, I come to them in some other way and then I do philosophy on the basis of holding beliefs about those things.

LR—What do you think are the best and the worst arguments for the existence and the nonexistence of God? Who do you think are—or were—their best defenders?

AP—Well, arguments . . . I myself don't think belief in God requires arguments in order to be sensible or rational anymore than belief in other minds, or the past, or an external world require arguments. But there are some pretty good arguments and I think among the best ones are the versions of the argument from design that Richard Swinburne proposes. As for arguments against the existence of God, I don't think there are any good arguments of that sort, although one perplexity—or problem—for believers in God would be the problem of evil. But I don't think that offers the means of a successful or plausible argument against the existence of God.

LR—Concerning the problem of evil, bad things happen to good people in a universe created by a supposedly all-loving God. Can you summarize your "free will defense" argument that tries to justify this apparent paradox?

AP—The "free will defense" is really an argument for the conclusion that there isn't any contradiction in the idea that there is such a person as God who is all-good and all-powerful on the one hand, and that evil exists on the other hand. There isn't any contradiction: It's possible for both of these to be true. But I think maybe a more interesting—or better way—to approach this question is to ask about what reasons God might possibly have for permitting evil, and there I would think about it like this: Imagine God before creation. God wants to create a good world. There are all these different possible worlds that he could create or cause to be actual. Then you might ask yourself: "What is it that would make one world a better world than another? What would be a good essential property in these possible worlds?" Well, when I think about it, it seems to me that the best property one can think of would be the property of Incarnation and Atonement. According to the Christian story, human beings rebelled against God, turned their backs on God. The first being of the universe was willing to undergo suffering, appalling suffering and death, in order to enable human beings to be in a good relationship with him again. That fact, the fact that in our world the first being of the universe was willing to do that for the benefit of creatures who had rejected him, that seems to me to make our world a truly great world—or that seems to me to make any world in which that happens a truly great world. So, my idea is that the best possible world contains Atonement on the part of Jesus Christ—or maybe in some other way. But all worlds that contain atonement contain sin and suffering; so, why is there sin and suffering? Well, all best possible worlds contain sin and suffering.

LR—How do you see then Voltaire's work *Candide*, where he parodies the argument of "a best possible world" with a continuous flow of disasters?

AP—Well, I don't know . . . I mean, in *Candide*, Dr. Pangloss goes around making silly statements, silly claims. But, I think as a matter of fact, the best worlds do contain sin and evil, since the only way a world can contain incarnation and atonement is by also containing evil. If it doesn't contain sin, there is nothing to be atoned for. So, I don't think there is any such thing as "the" best of all possible worlds, but I think all of the really good worlds do contain those things.

LR—What about natural evil? Tsunami and earthquakes happen indifferently to people's moral behavior.

AP—Yes. My idea is that there are many more kinds of rational creatures and creatures with free will than just human beings. I think there are also angels, Satan with his minions, and others. C. S. Lewis suggested that our world, our planet in particular, is a place where Satan and his minions act, and I'm inclined to think that's a real possibility. I don't know whether or not this is true, but it's a real possibility. So, it might be that natural evil is really a special case of moral evil, but not moral evil on the part of human creatures.

LR—But in order to solve that problem you have to say that God makes miracles and Satan makes natural disasters. Since miracles are rare—some people even doubt that they occur—and natural disasters are frequent, what prevents us from saying that Satan has more power than God?

AP—Satan can cause very bad things but God created the whole world—in fact, created Satan—so, from that point of view, Satan would certainly be inferior.

LR—What's the logic of equating the intervention of Satan and God in the world? In natural disasters, good and bad people die. In the logical sense, isn't Satan helping God providing him with "good souls"?

AP—Good people die in natural disasters but I'm not quite sure I get the question. Satan has a role to play in God's total economy—just as bad people do. So, from that point of view, I wouldn't say they help God but they do play a role; his whole plan includes them and includes their behavior.

LR—But imagine that Satan provokes a natural disaster that kills 900 "good souls" and 100 "bad souls." With fewer souls for him in hell, doesn't Satan seem to lose with the disaster that he himself provokes?

AP—What Satan does is he frustrates God's plans—or tries to. He promotes all sorts of things God is against: he promotes hatred, he promotes suffering, he promotes pain and death, and the like of that. So, these are things that God finds the opposite of valuable; Satan's whole project is to promote these kinds of things. In Milton's great poem *Paradise Lost*, Satan says, "Evil! Be thou my good!" That's what he does. In the long run he loses, but I don't think there's any sense in which you might say he wins. You might say he wins temporary victories of some sort, but in the long run, he doesn't.

LR—Suppose one does not even want to live eternally (some suicides don't). Why then is every human being condemned to live forever, whether with the divine Trinity or Satan? In that line of argument, humanity's free will is only a myth.

AP—You mean that it's not up to us whether or not we live forever?

LR—Yes.

AP—Well, that may very well be true; maybe we're not free to decide not to live forever, but I'm not convinced of that. Who knows what heaven is like? Maybe if somebody really wants to be expunged, to be reduced to nothing, maybe God accommodates them. I just don't know about that, one way or the other.

LR—But why should one desire to live in heaven if one does not know what it is like? Is he or she obliged to embark on a trip without even knowing the destination and not having the free will to choose the hotel? Can you conceive a Muslim expecting virgins after death and then becoming disappointed by coming face to face with Jesus?

AP—I think maybe the Muslim expectation of virgins is a sort of popular Muslim idea, but I don't think that's what most Muslim thinkers think at all. If one did, though, think about what heaven would actually be like, it would be far beyond one's expectations. So, as a matter of fact you're right: One wouldn't know exactly what heaven would be like. One knows it would be a very good thing, but one doesn't know what specific form it would take. But I don't see that that's a problem for the idea at all.

LR—I'm just emphasizing that people from different religious traditions could be disappointed for facing an after-death scenario that wouldn't correspond with the expectations and norms proposed by their specific religious doctrine.

AP—Well, it could be; that's why religion it's a matter of—as Kierkegaard said—"fear and trembling." One could be wrong, and that's a frightening prospect. Just as if you're not religious: You could be wrong, and that's a frightening prospect too.

LR—Why do you recognize the authority of the Bible concerning a personal faith in God?

AP—It seems to me the way this works is, for Christianity—Christians have always talked about it and the Bible speaks of this too—the internal testimony of the Holy Spirit (or internal witness of the Holy Spirit); the fact is, when Christians read the Bible, it seems correct, it seems true. That's the role that the Bible plays. It proposes these beliefs, which are then ratified by the internal testimony of the Holy Spirit. That's one way to think about it, at least. That's how I would think about it.

LR—But if you ground your faith in the Bible, aren't you contradicting the answer you gave in the first place? I mean, you don't seem to find an inner religiosity in you, but rather, a specific religious thinking that is supported by a source that was produced "outside" and independently of yourself—namely, the Bible.

AP—What I was saying was, one reads in the Bible great things such as the Gospels, and what grounds one's belief there is just that upon reading these things, they seem correct, they seem true. Just as I look at a hand, I have a certain kind of experience and I form a belief that there's a hand there. So, the basis of the belief is that experience.

LR—What are the tools that you use to confirm the trueness of the object you're experiencing?

AP—I don't think of it like that. You might also ask me, "What tools are used to analyze whatever it is that's involved in my coming to see a hand in front of me?" It's not like that. Rather, I have a certain kind of experience, and that experience causes me to form the belief that there is a hand in front of me; it's an occasion of the arising of that belief. I think of the presentation of the gospel in the same way: It's not by analysis or argument that one comes to believe in Christian truth or in the existence of God. It is, as I say, a matter of experience.

LR—The Bible says that God rested on the seventh day after all the works he had made. Suppose God is tired "playing God" and wants to rest forever: Is God obligated to exist for all eternity? If God is forever bound to the duty of "being," isn't he a slave of his own mission?

AP—You're a slave in a case in which you want to do something but you can't—because you are prevented by your master—and that certainly isn't how one would think about God. It's not that he might very well get tired of being God and decide "Well, I'd rather not" after a while, but then he couldn't stop being God. There's no reason at all to think anything like that holds for God. Rather, what Christians and theists generally think is that God does exist necessarily, but he is also essentially loving and essentially good; this means that as part of God's very essence, he's perfectly satisfied in playing the role of God.

LR—Is the bulk of Anselm's ontological argument for the existence of God still valid? I mean, if God is a superlative—that "which nothing greater can be thought"—isn't "thought" itself, human thought, the a priori condition for equating the "greatness" of God? In that case, isn't Protagoras right when defining men as the measure of all things—even God—by creating him in their own minds?

AP—I can't see how . . . I'm not following your logic there. You're saying that human thought somehow determines what greatness is or what is great?

LR—Yes.

AP—But why think that? Maybe human thought can recognize what is great but doesn't determine it. In the same way, human thought can recognize mountains but that doesn't mean that human thought determines mountains.

LR—What I mean is that we make the concepts a priori and then fill them with abstract ideas that we call "God," the "divine," the "transcendent," and so on.

AP—I would put it rather that we have a vaster apprehension of the divine. It's not that we somehow just make it up or anything like that, or determine that it would have to be that way. I'd say that's no more the case there than it is the case with respect to mountains, or with respect to numbers, or with respect to the existence of the past. We've got the idea that there's been a past but that doesn't mean that somehow it's by virtue of our having that idea that there is a past; rather, there's a past and we are so constructed that we can grasp that idea and know something about it.

LR—Why are you a "substance dualist"? Aren't these Cartesian dichotomies (material/spiritual, body/soul, etc.) rather unsuitable for a contemporary world ruled by quantum physics and general relativity?

AP—I don't really see that quantum mechanics or general relativity have any bearing on the question of substance dualism. The basic claim of substance dualism is that a human person, I myself, am neither my body nor any part of my body. With respect to that idea, I don't see that quantum mechanics really has any relevance; also don't see that relativity does either.

LR—I was just focusing on the speciousness of tracing boundaries between what is the material and what could be the spiritual.

AP—Right. So, maybe quantum mechanics makes it harder to say what matter is. But the way I was defining substance dualism—it doesn't involve a definition of what matter is; it's just the claim that I'm not my body nor any part of my body.

LR—But we have all these "New Age" and "New Spirituality" movements claiming for themselves a very broad definition of what is "the spiritual" and what is "the body"; some of them even appropriate scientific concepts and mix them with spiritual jargon to create composite concepts like "quantum healing" or "spiritual energy," for example. Philosophically speaking, aren't these religious and philosophical movements updating what is the "old-time religion"?

AP—I don't think so. In fact, I think most of them are only dubiously coherent. It's really hard to make sense of their claims and really hard to make sense of what they think is the connection between quantum mechanics and these claims. It seems to me that what you called "old-time religion"—classical Christianity, Islam, Judaism—these are much clearer and much more intellectually respectable than some of the New Age things you're talking about.

LR—If these New Spirituality movements had some kind of scripture, do you think their respectability could grow?

AP—Well, I don't know. I think a chief problem with them is that they are not coherent; you can't really tell what they amount to. Now, you can probably write them down in some way, but they would still be incoherent. I'm not sure that having something like the Bible or some canonical expression would help.

LR—When theists say what God "is or is not," why must their subjective judgments about God prevail as valid definitions of God's own existence?

AP—Theists say they believe in God. Then you say, "Well, what is that? What do you mean when you believe in God?" And then they just tell you what they mean. They mean: "Well, I believe that there exists a being that's all-powerful, all-knowing, perfectly good, and created the universe." What they're really doing is saying what they mean; that seems perfectly sensible.

LR—But even in the same religious family, let's say Christianity, there are branches—Catholic, Protestant, Orthodox—who disagree about what is God and how God behaves. There are also the subjective judgments about God produced everyday by different religious leaders and denominations.

AP—I think Protestants, Catholics, and Orthodox would all say the same thing about what God is like. They would differ on other points but not on the nature of God.

LR—Do you think that religious education is necessary for the development of a moral society?

AP—I'm inclined to think so. That's a sort of sociological question—and I'm not a sociologist—but my guess is, yes it is. Let me put it like this: I think that morality itself depends on religion. There isn't any way in which naturalism or atheism can really accommodate morality. To the extent that that's true, it seems at least natural to think that morality and religion fit together in such a way that education in the one would promote the other.

LR—What about the ethical thinking present in some writings of ancient Greek philosophers such as Plato? Is it possible for morality to exist outside religion?

AP—It certainly is possible for there to be morality outside religion, just as it is possible for there to be education outside universities. Still, universities are very important educational institutions. The Christian idea here is that God created human beings in such a way that they have a grasp of morality. He created us so that we can see that some things are right and some things are wrong. This is the case whether or not one is a Christian—or even a believer in God. Even if I'm not a believer in God, I'm still created by God in such a way that I can have some valid opinions about right and wrong.

LR—What or who poses for you the greatest danger to religious thinking in general—and Christian thinking in particular?

AP—I think the idea that would have the worst effect would be something like postmodern ideas to the effect that there really isn't any such thing as truth—or what they like to call "absolute truth." Something like that would be a serious problem for Christian belief in the sense that, if lots and lots of people started thinking that way, the whole idea of Christianity—which is dependent essentially on the notion of there really being truth—that whole idea would become inaccessible. But I don't know how much of a danger this actually is. I don't think some of the claims of the so-called New Atheists—Dawkins, Hitchens, and the rest—I don't think those really present much of a problem because they don't amount to much from a philosophical perspective at all.

LR—So, you see the danger coming more from postmodernism rather than atheism?

AP—I'm inclined to think so. I think atheism is, in certain respects, closer to Christian belief than postmodern antirealism—antirealism with respect to truth.

LR—In that postmodern thinking, who do you think best represents that danger?

AP—Perhaps the most plausible or persuasive postmodern writer I've read would be, I think, Richard Rorty. Some other postmoderns seem so extreme that it's really hard to take them seriously; but Rorty, I think, does a pretty good job—although I don't find him at all persuasive myself.

LR—Why do you think these postmodern authors capture the attention of the general public?

AP—I don't know. The general public really likes things like sports, movie stars—why do these postmodern things capture their attention? I wouldn't really know; that's kind of a sociological question again. But partly it is just because they say something that's kind of outrageous; it's fun to think about things that are outrageous.

LR—But on the other side of the fence, we have books like *The Secret*, by Rhonda Byrne which don't walk on the "outrageous" line of thought but have a little of that postmodern attitude.

AP—Yes, maybe so. But when you ask me why postmodernist ideas attract people, that's a hard kind of question to answer. I really don't know the answer to that.

LR—Would you like to live in a country ruled by a theocracy?

AP—I don't think I would. A really good feature of the whole American experiment has been in that particular way the separation of church and state, so that the state doesn't enforce or guarantee or support one particular kind of religion as opposed to other religions—or maybe no religions at all. That seems to me to be the just and fair way for a country to be; so, I'm not enthusiastic about theocracies.

LR—What about the religious feeling in America? Isn't it pointing that way?

AP—No, I don't think so. There certainly are some people who would like a theocracy, but the vast majority of Americans I don't think would like that at all.

LR—Can you conceive a meaning for life without God? Hypothetically speaking, if you knew from a reliable source that God didn't exist, how would you deal with the fact?

AP—Well, that's very hard for me to say. God's presence in the world is such a deep part of my way of thinking that I can't imagine what I would be like or what I would think of if I became convinced that was all wrong. So, I don't really know. I suppose I would go on doing many of the things I do—eating, drinking, visiting people, and the like of that—but as to what this would actually be like, I can't say; it's just too different from the way I actually see the world.

LR—So, you don't conceive ever becoming yourself an atheist.

AP—No, I don't.

LR—What do think about the New Atheism movement? Do you think they make some points right or they are getting it all wrong?

AP—I think, for example, that Richard Dawkins, in his book *The God Delusion*, does get just about everything wrong. This book is, from my point of view, really poor philosophy; and it is philosophy, it's not science. There's almost no science in it—it's mainly philosophy with some kind of sociology thrown in. The philosophy part of it seems to me appallingly bad. His arguments are for the most part, I would say, sophomoric. If they were offered in a college classroom, they would probably receive a failing grade. So, I'm not at all impressed.

LR—What about other authors like Daniel Dennett and Christopher Hitchens?

AP—Christopher Hitchens is a very good writer but I don't think he really offers arguments; he sort of attempts to persuade by virtue of rhetoric. He is a good writer and a good rhetorician, but I don't think he has any substantive arguments against Christianity or any good reasons for anybody to give up Christianity or not to be attracted by it.

LR—Hitchens relies mainly on history, portraying some atrocities committed in the name of religion.

AP—There have been atrocities perpetrated in the name of religion, but not nearly to the extent of atrocities perpetrated in the name of secular ideologies like nazism and communism. I mean, there are just orders of magnitude difference there; I don't know how many millions of people were killed in the 20th century by virtue of communism and nazism, but it would probably be in the neighborhood of a hundred million or something like that. All the religious atrocities put together throughout the whole history of the world don't come anywhere near that. Sure religious people have done terrible things in the name of religion—and that is very unfortunate and unhappy—but of course, that doesn't show that religion is false.

LR—Others, however, like Richard Dawkins, say that those atrocities, though committed by atheists, were not committed in the name of atheism: They were perpetrated in the name of totalitarian utopian principles like the state, the fuhrer, the duce, and so on.

AP—Those are atheistic ideologies; the state is all important, or maybe humanity is all important, the future of humanity and something like that. But those are all atheistic ideologies.

LR—In the same way, you consider Comtian positivism an atheistic ideology too, correct?

AP—Yes, that would be another example of an atheistic ideology. The same would go for nazism, the same would go for communism; I think it's important to see that the atrocities perpetrated in the name of these atheistic ideologies far exceed those perpetrated in the name of religion throughout the whole history of the world.

LR—Since we talked about the 19th-century positivism, could you tell us a little about the role played by the later 20th-century logical positivism concerning the question of God?

AP—The logical positivists said that propositions or sentences allegedly about God, like "God created us" and "God created the world" don't really make any sense, that they're literately senseless; they might be a kind of music or something like that but they don't have any cognitive significance at all. Positivism was very popular for a while, but it turned out that nobody could really state the verifiability criterion; nobody could state that in such a way that it excluded just the things they wanted to exclude and included the things that they wanted to include. Furthermore, the statement itself seemed to be self-referentially incoherent. It cut against itself: It said that a sentence is meaningful if and only if it's empirically verifiable, but that sentence itself isn't empirically verifiable. So now, it's kind of disappeared.

LR—Do you see a future for logic in Christian apologetics?

AP—For logic certainly, but logic and logical positivism have very little to do with each other. Christians of course endorse the use of logic like everybody else, but endorsing logic doesn't at all lead to logical positivism; these are just totally different things.

Robert M. Price

Born in Jackson, Mississippi, in 1954, Robert M. Price moved to New Jersey with his family in 1965. Shortly afterward, he became involved in a fundamentalist Baptist church and youth ministry, then went on to major in religion and in American history at Montclair State College (BA, 1976), where he became president of the campus chapter of Inter-Varsity Christian Fellowship. At Gordon-Conwell Theological Seminary he took an MTS degree in New Testament (1978), then a PhD in systematic theology at Drew University (1981). The same year he met his wife-to-be, Carol Selby, and joined a liberal Baptist congregation where Harry Emerson Fosdick had once been pastor. Bob and Carol married in 1984 on the eve of their move to North Carolina. There he became professor of religion at Mount Olive College. Five years and one baby later, they returned to New Jersey to pastor their old church. A church split came five years after that, once Bob had earned a second PhD, this time in New Testament, at Drew (1993), and announced himself a religious humanist.

In the meantime he had founded (and continues to edit) the *Journal of Higher Criticism*. He taught philosophy and religion for a few years at Bergen Community College, then New Testament interpretation at Drew for a couple more. In 1999, he came on board with the Council for Secular Humanism and founded the North Jersey Center for Inquiry. He and his family, now including two daughters, Victoria and Veronica, returned to North Carolina in 2001, where he continues to teach, write, and edit. His books include *Beyond Born Again* (2008), *The Widow Traditions in Luke-Acts* (1997), *Deconstructing Jesus* (2000), *The Incredible Shrinking Son of Man* (2003), *The Da Vinci Fraud* (2005), *The Reason-Driven Life* (2006), and *The Pre-Nicene New Testament* (2006). He is a fellow of the Jesus Seminar and of the Committee for the Scientific Examination of Religion. He attends Saint Stephen's Episcopal Church in Goldsboro, North Carolina.

Luís Rodrigues—Could you tell us a little about your religious background and how that affected your scholarly quest in biblical studies?

Robert M. Price—Well, I grew up from the first few years as a Southern Baptist in Mississippi and only attended Sunday school, and that didn't make a whole lot of impression on me, although I did believe in God and Jesus, whatever that meant. Then I moved to New Jersey with my family when I was 10 years old and began going to a Conservative Baptist Association church; there, they pour on the brimstone and I accepted Jesus as my personal savior and all of that sort of thing and became very zealous on through junior high school and high school, and in college I switched around to a couple of other evangelical churches, but it was pretty much the same sort of thing. Then, I got interested in Christian apologetics and defending the faith, especially by trying to pretty much prove that the Gospels were reliable, that Jesus did what it said he did, he said what the Gospels report him saying, and he rose from the dead, etc., etc. I was much into that in 1974, 1975.

About two years later, I found myself at Gordon-Conwell Theological Seminary, not preparing for the ministry but just taking a whole lot of New Testament courses, a master's degree program, and during the course of that, mainly through my own reading, I began to find that the arguments for biblical accuracy, the Resurrection, etc., just did not hold water. It seemed to me the Bible was so filled with anachronism and contradiction and so on, that there was just no way to make it a believable authority for today, and beside that, I realized that it was very arbitrary to say that Jesus had risen from the dead, etc. The arguments were really no good; there was no way to show it wasn't a legend like all these other legends. And so I then began to study more theology to see if there were other viable approaches to Christianity, or maybe other religions, and I finally ended up going to the Episcopal church and taking a lot of what I had believed symbolically. For instance, I didn't really believe in historical miracles, but I did believe in God and so forth. And then I became a pastor of a very liberal Baptist church, and a few years down the line I went back to Drew University for a second doctorate—I had one in theology already. This time it was New Testament, and

I understood just how superficially I had studied it, and realized that maybe Jesus hadn't even existed, maybe Paul didn't write any of the Epistles attributed to him. So I left the ministry, I just felt like I didn't really have any more to say. I just have a lot more to learn and I've been writing books based on what I've come up with ever since.

LR—Concerning the atheism issue now: Christianity comes from a Judaic context. In this context, was atheism possible in Palestine at the time of Jesus? Or, was Palestine a country where institutionalized Judaism and apocalyptic prophets coexisted in turmoil against the Romans?

RMP—Well, it seems very diverse. You had what we would call "fanatics"—whoever they were—who wrote the Dead Sea Scrolls. They might have been Essenes, or a type of early Christian, or who knows what. But you had, on the other hand, Sadducees, who were Jewish traditionalists, but for all we know may have taken the traditional faith somewhat lightly. One reason for thinking that is that the rabbis later used to describe them as "Epicureans"—by that they meant pretty much heretics. The Sadducees didn't believe in life after death, they didn't believe in divine predestination, they didn't accept a number of the books that became part of the Bible. So, the Pharisees and the rabbis tended to think of the Sadducees just as philosophers and Epicureans. That would not make them "atheists," but it would make them a little closer to "free-thinkers." The Bible itself argues against people that rejected theism way back in the time of the psalms, when it says: "The fool has said in his heart there is no God." Which implies: "The fool better not say it publicly!" But they knew there were people who, privately, just didn't buy it—which is kind of remarkable. So, there probably was no public atheism to speak of, and if there was a historical Jesus, I can't imagine he would have been an atheist.

LR—Probably Jesus was in the radical fringe of the believers, no?

RMP—Yes, the best argument I have read for a plausible historical Jesus is that of S. G. F. Brandon in his books, such as *Jesus and the Zealots* (he did about three or four books about this), and he makes a very good case that in the Gospel of Mark—and the book of Acts, especially—it looks like early Christians are trying to get out from under the perception that they are anti-Roman revolutionists and that

Jesus was also. Jesus is depicted as being crucified as a rebel king by Rome. You can argue: "Well, it was just a mistaken perception" or that "Jesus was a prophet and the Romans didn't really care what kind, they were just executing him as a rabble-rouser anyway." But why do that? Brandon has a point, for instance, in the cleansing of the temple story: If that happened at all, it must have been an armed assault on the temple in a huge area with posted armed guards all over it. The Gospels don't tell you that. They give you the idea that Jesus is just sort of overturning a bunch of card tables in the basement of a church for their rummage sale and he doesn't like it for some reason; but you had a huge area and Jesus—Mark says—would not let anyone bring the sacrificial vessels back through the temple. Now, he couldn't have done that if he hadn't brought in armed men to occupy it. So, Brandon says (and I'm paraphrasing), now, this story may be fiction, but if it's not, then this is definitive evidence that Jesus was some sort of an armed revolutionist like Simon Bar Giora, or John of Giscala, or Menahem, or various other Jewish kings of the time.

LR—But how can a Jesus like that be harmonized with the Jesus of the Sermon on the Mount? Is the Jesus of the Sermon a fictional Jesus?

RMP—It could be because anyway you look at it, it appears that a lot of Jewish, cynic, stoic, and other moralities have been attributed to Jesus, and that would fit Brandon's theory in that you could say that part of the idea of rehabilitating Jesus in the eyes of the Romans would be to domesticate him, to make him sound like nothing but a safe promoter of platitudes. Not that the two were irreconcilable—you know, when Jesus says "turn the other cheek," he may be speaking of solidarity among Jews, not necessarily among Jews and Romans. But it's hard to say. Jesus is made to sound very gentile friendly, and, as Robert Eisenman says, well, what would you expect in Greek Gospels written for gentiles? Maybe that is all part of the redesigned fictionalized Jesus; and when I say that I mean, fictionalized vis-à-vis Jesus having been a revolutionary or vis-à-vis there having been no Jesus at all. One reason I tend to lean toward no Jesus at all is that though the revolutionary Jesus seems to me the most plausible sketch of a historical Jesus, it looks too much like the stories of John of Giscala, Simon Bar Giora, and other messiahs. It looks like it was borrowed from them.

LR—What about Jesus as an "apocalyptic messiah," as portrayed by scholars like Bart Ehrman? Do you think it is reliable to think of Jesus as one more failed prophet, like John the Baptist?

RMP—Yes, that's possible, though in my opinion, Bart is a little too optimistic about our data. I am less certain than he that Jesus said a number of those things, but assuming he did, that really is no alternative to the notion of Jesus as a revolutionary because he presumably wouldn't have been an idiot who thought a fairly small number of people could beat the Roman Empire. He probably would have thought, like the Dead Sea Scrolls people did, that God would send angels down as he says in Matthew, "Don't you think even now I can call on my Father and He will send me 12 legions of angels?" Well, maybe that was the original idea, and so Jesus as a failed apocalyptic prophet and Jesus as a failed messianic king are hardly different from one another.

LR—Talking about Jesus, people try to emphasize his moral character. Do you think Jesus, as portrayed in the Gospels, really looks like a perfect moral character according to our contemporary standards? I mean, isn't there a flavor of unnecessary harshness? For example, in Mark 3:32, we read: "And the multitude sat about him, and they said unto him, 'Behold, thy mother and thy brethren without seek for thee.' And he answered them, saying, 'Who is my mother, or my brethren?'" Well, I would see a "more perfect" Jesus saying, "Oh! Hello dear mother and brethren! Come and sit with us!"

RMP—I think that story is a rewriting of an Exodus 18 story about Moses in which he is beset day and night with cases to settle as the great prophet and his relatives come and visit him: Jethro, his father-in-law, and Sephora, his wife, and Gershon, his son. He does receive them gladly and then Jethro says, in effect, "Look how busy you are! You're going out of your mind if you don't get some relaxation. Tell you what: Why don't you delegate some assistants to share the work?" And Moses does; he chooses 70 men and they take part of the burden. Well, this looks so much like the puzzle pieces of Mark 3 in which Jesus chooses his 12 disciples that my guess is, originally, some Christian had simply borrowed the Exodus 18 story and made it read like this: Jesus is hampered with healings and teaching—as Mark 3 says—and his family comes to visit him and he would have received them gladly, then they would have said, "Don't you think you need some help here, or you're going out of your mind? Why don't you choose, say, 12 men?" And then Jesus would have done so and it would have been a happy ending; but Mark does not like the leadership group in the early church that traces itself back to the family of Jesus—the so-called "heirs of Jesus": James, Simeon Bar Cleophas, and others who lead Jewish Christianity. So Mark breaks up that story and has Jesus choose the 12 on his own initiative in the beginning of the story, and then has Jesus' family come because they think he's already gone crazy—presumably, they're going to take him home—and so Jesus is then made into someone who, like an early Christian martyr, must reject the concern of his family because they're unbelievers and don't realize it. So, in a martyrdom sort of a context, the way Mark has rewritten it, Jesus comes across as courageous and not sentimental, but it's fiction anyway you cut it. Jesus is depicted in Mark and John, especially, as a demigod on Earth who can say things you and I as Christians would not—like the "woes" in Matthew 23. We're not to understand, "Yes, that's what I ought to say as a Christian"; we're supposed to shudder and say, "Oh man, that's the voice of the Son of God that shakes the Earth." So the Gospels are only partly interested in showing a Jesus who's an example; they want to show you a godling who can terrify you, whom you need to worship.

LR—And also a patchwork of Old Testament stories—like the escape to Egypt, the persecution of Herod, isn't that true?

RMP—Yes, I was shocked when I naïvely read several books a few years ago in which authors tried to trace Gospel stories back to Old Testament stories. I knew that must have happened some, and as I read their books I thought that some of these comparisons were a little forced. But I made a list of the ones that seemed to me to be very plausible and when I was done I found that there was really no story in the Gospels, with the possible exception of one—the rich young ruler story—that didn't look like it hadn't been taken from the Old Testament and just reshuffled a bit with the names changed. I was just astounded. It really does seem to me that the Gospels are largely rewrites of the Old Testament.

LR—And in the Old Testament we see not only characters, but archetypes: Adam and Eve, Job, Jonah, Cain, Abel, etc. With the

attachment of archetypical facets to supposedly real and historical characters, haven't these characters obtained irrefutable status? I mean, even after Darwin, Adam and Eve are used as if
they were real historical characters, but at the same time as
symbolic archetypical ones. How can debate be possible with
religious people who use an ambiguous space-time criterion for
these characters?

RMP—It is a big problem. I was just having a debate on a podcast the
other night, and it was very frustrating because I was no longer in the
same ballpark, the same arena with the fundamentalist. I couldn't take
for granted any common ground. He would say, "Well, we know the
Gospels were written by eyewitnesses who saw Jesus." I'd say, "We surely
do not know that. There's no real reason to believe that." He said,
"How about the references to Jesus in the letters of the apostle Paul?" I
said, "You know—there are scholars that say Paul didn't write any of
these; they're filled with anachronisms. They must be from later on in
early Christianity." This guy just thought that was lunacy. I know why
he did, but it just would have taken me weeks to explain what I know
from critical scholarship. The Adam and Eve thing is a good case of
that: People are so frightened when they hear: "What? You mean there
was no Adam and Eve? It's all symbolical? How do I know Jesus wasn't
just symbolic?" Well, I hate to tell you but—he may have been! They
just cannot stand that. I understand it. They are just so indoctrinated,
they cannot entertain the alternative. So I don't know how you can
debate with them.

**LR—Among the "constructions" of the Old Testament were hell
and Satan. How did Christianity change it? It seems to me that
the doctrinal construction of hell and Satan is much more
refined in Christianity than in Judaism.**

RMP—Well, that's a matter again of which kind of Judaism you want
to look at. Satan became less important in what became mainstream
rabbinic Judaism, but there were many kinds of Judaism, and even
today, you can find some very conservative Jews who do believe in hell
and will tell you who's suffering what there. There are very conservative
Jews who view Jesus as a false prophet and say that he's boiling in ma-
nure in hell right now. So, they certainly believe in it. Other Jews would

say, "No, no, all right, the wicked won't inherit eternal life, but that's the end of them." Still other Jews would say, "Nobody's inheriting eternal life; we just want to live a good, pious life here." So it just depends on which Jews you have in mind. Hell and the devil were certainly vibrant beliefs in Judaism when Christianity began, so Christianity's mainstream gave more attention to these things than Jews eventually did. You see the same thing, for instance, with the idea that Jesus didn't die on the cross, that he escaped death and was replaced by someone else. Now, this was a view of some Christians—especially Gnostics, but other Christians too. But it died out of the mainstream after two or three centuries; and yet, it was still around, because when Islam began, it picked it up and made it a central belief. You have the same sort of a thing: The belief that Jesus didn't really die on the cross didn't begin with Islam—Islam got it from Christianity even though it was already a marginalized view there. Same sort of thing with hell and the devil, I think.

LR—When we speak of early Christianity, we speak also about diversity. What do you think of Walter Bauer's theories about early Christianity's geographical diversity? Was Catholicism a religious force that "won the day" by the truth of her message or by the force of her political and economic power centered in Rome?

RMP—I think the latter, and also, part of the success was that—I hate to say it, but sort of like Dostoyevsky says in "The Grand Inquisitor" section of *The Brothers Karamazov*—the kind of orthodox and Catholic Christianity that won out didn't leave a great deal to individual autonomy, and people really do like to be led like sheep. So that kind of "why-don't-you-leave-the-thinking-to-us" religion is very attractive to a lot of people. Bauer was right, and I think what we know of Catholicism indicates it was not even one of the earliest kinds of Christianity. I think it is a late fusion of elements from Gnosticism, from the mystery religions, and from the divine "hero-cult" where Jesus was a sort of Hercules, a kind of demi-god character. Catholicism is really just a late fusion of popular elements from these things. By late, I don't mean an hour, a day, or anything; I mean, already before the end of the first century. But I don't think that Jesus or any apostle taught that—assuming there was a Jesus!

LR—How important was the contribution of the early Church Fathers to the spread of Catholicism? Didn't they refine the doctrines of what is now "the" Catholic Church?

RMP—They were already institutional apparatchiks; they were already spin doctors for an institution—certainly one they believed in. Tertullian, Irenaeus, Justin Martyr, and these people in the late second century, they were either converts to—or grew up in—Catholic Christianity, and they were trying to fight off other kinds that were rivals, especially Marcionites, Gnostics, and Nazarean Jewish Christians. They didn't like them, but their own Catholic faith had already borrowed large elements from these three—whom they were trying to beat into submission, whether by argument or later (when Constantine came to power) by force, and they were pretty successful at it. If the Church Fathers managed to banish other opinions and vindicate Catholicism, it really did have to do more with politics, pressure groups, and things like that as to who "won out."

LR—Concerning Constantine—and just focusing on pragmatic issues—in his rise to power, why were Christians so important to him? Why would he need them?

RMP—I've read that he figured, here was an up and coming potential power bloc and it would be good to have them on his side as he was trying to consolidate his power against the other emperor. That could be, but there is good reason to believe that Constantine himself was born and raised a Christian and that he was simply trying to advance what he thought was the true faith. Naturally, he must have felt then that God was on his side to bring freedom to his people. He must have been a very shrewd politician and a ruthless one, but that doesn't mean he didn't actually believe it. I don't think he was an outsider who just saw a usable instrument in Christianity; I think he—sort of like Mike Huckabee in American politics—sincerely believed in a particular kind of Christianity, and he also sought power for what he thought were good reasons.

LR—What about his meddling in the Council of Nicaea? Was it plausible that the council could be controlled by Constantine when we have earlier reports of clergymen's courage against secular Roman power—the martyrs, for example?

RMP—I believe that it was Constantine's idea to call this council because there were such debates everywhere over the issue of the deity of Christ, the divine word, the nature of the Father and the Son; there were huge debates. We're even told that in Alexandria, down at the docks, the sailors would be in the taverns singing pro-Arian drinking songs—I would love to have heard that! Could you imagine the guys in the tavern hoisting their mugs of beer, "Oh-oh! He's *not* One with the Father!" [Laughing.] This was a big popular thing; so, Constantine said, "Look, let's get the thinkers together and settle this." I believe it was known that he was on the pro-divinity side; he supported Athanasius, but they really did have philosophical debates about this. Arius had his own draft of the creed ready and got outvoted. So it probably did have some strings attached, but I don't think it was necessarily a sham. The emperor said, "Let's get together and try to make peace" and they pretty much did. The Arians were excluded from the church but they did have an ongoing church among the Goths and the Vandals—people that eventually overthrew Rome; so I guess they got their revenge.

LR—One of the arguments that Christianity uses to validate its moral credibility is that it brought the message of love into a chaotic world dominated by pagan brutality and violence. Is this true? What were—if any—the real moral innovations that Christianity brought to the Roman world since it became the official religion of the empire? Were there any real improvements in slavery issues, women's rights, etc.?

RMP—It seems that there were. In fact, it's ironic to me when some people argue that Christianity had so little going for it in the eyes of pagans that Christianity's triumph must have been a miracle—and therefore, Christianity is true. That is so insulting to the early Christians and so ignorant because they did have higher moral standards. They would get together, in the first couple of centuries anyway, and take collections of money to buy the freedom of slaves. In times of plague and disease—of which there were many in the ancient Mediterranean world—even Julian the Apostate, the neo-pagan Roman emperor, said, "I wish we could get our selfish cowardly pagan priests to care for others like those rotten Christians do. Maybe we could get the same admiration." The Christians would refuse to expose infants at a time when people would say, "I got enough mouths to feed, especially female! If my wife has another girl baby, I'm never going to marry her off. Tell you what, just put the kid out with the trash." This is common; we have ancient letters of husbands writing their wives, telling them this. So there were two groups that mitigated this: one was pimps, who went around rescuing little girls and raising them to be prostitutes—which is certainly better than being dead! The other, Christians (and, of course, Jews, too). Christians were saying this to a culture that had exposed babies with no qualms. Christians, and Muslims after them, said, "No, no, no. You can't do this. You've just got to trust God to be able to marry them off." What happened when they grew up? The Christians did have more women and so they practiced missionary marriage. The Christian women would marry non-Christian men and eventually get them to convert. So that led directly to a demographic advantage for Christians—but it was a moral one also. Same thing about abortion: Early Christians were dead set against abortion; you read about the horrifying damnation awaiting abortionists in hell in the Apocalypse of Peter and the Epistle of Barnabas. They wouldn't abort kids, and they'd have more girls, they married them off, etc. And they didn't care if you're Christian or not, they would help you in a time of emergency. These were definitely higher standards—as some pagans actually recognized. So I think there's a real good track record and a lot for Christians to brag about there.

LR—Was that commendable moral behavior practiced by the different Christian sects—like the Gnostics, the Marcionites, the Ebionites, etc.?

RMP—That I just don't know. One thing we know about the Gnostics and the Marcionites: they were certainly sexually puritanical. The Marcionites were against divorce, if you were already married when you were converted. But they were so antiworldly that both the Gnostics and Marcionites said, "No, if you're married, that's pretty much fornication, there's no difference; don't have children to bring into this hell of a world." That strikes me as a little neurotic and a little pessimistic, but in a way, it's certainly strict morality at least.

LR—But we also have morality charges in Pauline Epistles— namely, some acts of deplorable moral behavior in different congregations. Was later Christianity more morally commendable than earlier Christianity?

RMP—I imagine it was better earlier simply because all sectarian groups, when they start out, are getting close to a 100 percent effort by everybody. Everybody seems to know that if they don't hold up their end of this thing, it's just not going to work. But if it does work, and it gets off the ground, in the second generation the members will begin to relax and assimilate back to the values of the surrounding society, saying, "What's wrong with that, with a little extra money, a little sinning here and there; you can always do penance." The earliest Christians, like in *The Shepherd of Hermas*, said, "If I'm lucky, I might be able to get a second chance to repent after baptism, but if not, I'm going to Hell." That's why Constantine waited to get baptized on his deathbed; he said, "I'm a believing Christian, but if I screw up after baptism, I'm damned." If you could even live in a religion like that, it showed you were pretty serious. Once you have an ongoing sacrament of penance, that's like just taking a bath every day. You're not taking it all that seriously anymore—"I can get forgiven anytime." So the later Christians were probably the more lax ones—and in fact, the Roman Empire only became as corrupt as it did once it was Christian. The earliest ones did have more of an equal role for women, but that subsided, and the reason we know that is we have the record of various church councils repeatedly trying to stop women's ministry: women should not baptize, women should not teach, women should not be deacons. You wouldn't be saying that unless there was a significant movement that allowed those things. Women did have more of a role—and again, that's what you would expect sociologically of a new religious sect. They all tend to be more egalitarian at the beginning, and then they fade back into the biases of the surrounding culture.

LR—The surrounding culture and into the power of centralized religion . . .

RMP—Yes. Alfred Loisy said, "Jesus preached the coming of the kingdom of God, but what came instead was the Church." That's kind of what happens. You expected to identify with this grand new institution, the messianic kingdom of God. That didn't happen, but human beings took charge and said, "Well, the next best thing would be a church run by us. What do you think?" "Yes . . . I'll sign on."

LR—But when you say that "Jesus preached the coming of the kingdom of God," in various passages of the Gospels, Jesus

performs miracles, casts out demons, heals the wounded, and so on, and yet he wants to maintain his abilities in secret—for example, in Matthew 17: How can someone who performs so many miraculous deeds in his life with such a degree of discretion no longer want to be discreet about his powers after his Resurrection? How can we deal with this intention?

RMP—I think probably Wilhelm Wrede was right in his book *The Messianic Secret*: Christians began to say that Jesus was already the messiah on Earth and did the things you would expect him to do—at least, what Moses and Elijah did—he must have healed people, fed people, raised them from the dead, and so on. But then, there were people who either remembered Jesus—if there was one—and said, "I don't recall anything like that." Or if there were people whose faith in Jesus was simpler: when they were getting into it nobody was mentioning any of these miracles—like the Pauline Epistles; they never mention Jesus doing any miracles or healing anybody. So there were people who said, "What's this? You're making Jesus into some sort of magician? No, no. When Jesus comes at the end of the age, *he will be the messiah then*, but he wasn't when he was on Earth; he was just preparing the ground." Well, poor Mark is saying, "Who's right in this? In any case, how can I get everybody together?" How about this: Suppose Jesus *was* the messiah all along and did the amazing works of the messiah but he managed to keep this quiet—except for a small number of people—and he wanted it to become known only after the Resurrection? Maybe that would explain why there are today Christians that had no idea Jesus was the messiah and there are others who rightly say, "Yes, he always was, but in secret." So this was a very clever way of reconciling these two christologies: "All right, Jesus was already the messiah, but it is understandable that some didn't know that, even some of his followers; but now we know, right?" So, I don't think again—even if there was a historical Jesus—that this was part of the history; this seems to me to be a clever rewrite. A similar example would be in the Gospel of Mark. Jesus is risen—he doesn't show at the tomb, though. But a young man there tells Mary Magdalene and the others, "Go, tell Peter and the disciples to meet me in Galilee." And it says that they fled in terror and didn't give the report because they were afraid. Then you think, but wait a second: Why would he tell such a story and what sense does it make? Well, it's a way of saying, "Okay, Jesus rose"; but it's a way of telling a new story about it that nobody else had ever heard. This means that the empty tomb story, of course, is a late product; Christians were telling it and a lot of Christians would listen to it and say, "Wait a second! I've been a Christian for years; how come I never heard of this in any Easter service? Where did you get this?" And they would say, "Oh, I can explain that: Jesus told them to tell the story but they didn't." Well—how do you know that, buddy? Mark knows because he made it up. Whenever you hear this kind of thing—"don't tell anybody about this"—you start wondering: wait a second, isn't this said just so somebody can say, "Yes, I know you never heard it"? It's like Gnosticism, for instance, or Sufism, or the Kabbalah, or any of these secret traditions in the religions. Those who advocate them say, "Nobody heard of this until a few hundred years after the founder, but that doesn't mean he didn't say it; he just said it to a few people and told them to keep it under their turban but now we can make it public!"

LR—And the new "mysterious revelations" help to boost and revive the religious message . . .

RMP—Yes. You're updating it and it also gives it the excitement that it once had since there is a new element.

LR—Concerning the religious message, the role of Peter in the Gospels always seems to me a little bit strange. He was Jesus' best companion, yet, witnessing Jesus' powers, he always stood amazed and confused about them, he betrayed his friend and teacher, and he even went fishing when Jesus died—assuming a defeatist posture. How could a man like this have had the capacity to spread the gospel, not only in his homeland but in Rome?

RMP—There are a couple of big problems with this, as you surmise. For one thing, Peter—though the number one disciple, the guy Jesus leaves in charge of the church—is such a moron throughout the book! Jesus says something fairly simple and Peter says, "I guess I can hit my brother after I forgive him seven times, so when number eight comes around . . . wham! Right?"

LR—Not only him but also the apostles.

RMP—Yes, James and John come in for a drubbing and then the others, generally, are made to be stupid. But why? There are two big reasons: Some of the stories come from Marcionite Christians who didn't like the Christianity descended from the 12—a type of Jewish Christianity—so, they're trying to make Peter, the prince of apostles, look bad. I think, for instance, the betrayal story is a fiction written up by Pauline Marcionite Christians to just totally discredit Peter and those who claim to have been taught by him. It's like today: If you don't like American Buddhism of a certain kind, the teachings, say, of Pema Chödrön's mentor, Chogyam Trungpa—a guy who wrote this fascinating book called *Cutting through Spiritual Materialism*, a really great book on Buddhism—somebody might point out: "Look, you don't have to take this guy seriously, he was a philanderer, he was an alcoholic, who cares what he thought?" Well, actually, in that case, it's true; but his teachings are pretty good anyway. But you can imagine, suppose he wasn't a philanderer or a drunk but somebody who didn't like him might want to slander him, and that, I think, is what happened in the case of Peter denying Jesus and also Paul persecuting Christians; I think these were both slurs.

The other reason someone might tell these stories about Peter—even somebody that liked Peter—is that these are like Dr. Watson stories in the Sherlock Holmes novels. Sherlock Holmes, the great detective, figures out the subtle clues and determines that so-and-so is the guilty party, and then Dr. Watson says, "I say, Holmes, how did you ever figure that one out?" Holmes says, "Elementary, my dear Watson," and then he explains. Why does he do that? Well, for the sake of the reader. He's got to have some way of having Holmes explain to the reader, and so he has a character in the story who asks what the reader wishes he could ask. Buddhism does the same thing. If they want to clarify something they will have the Buddha give a teaching and then his favorite but stupid disciple Ananda says, "Oh, well Lord, if that's the case, so and so follows, right?" "Hmm—no, Ananda. I'm afraid it doesn't. Here's the truth." It's an artificial ploy, it's a literary device, which means that none of this tells us anything about a historical Peter any more than the Holmes stories tell us about a historical Dr. Watson.

LR—So . . . Peter was made "ignorant" to benefit the reader?

RMP—Yes, that's right. It's kind of like the scribes and Pharisees in John's Gospel: They ask stupid questions just in case the reader has misunderstood, to give Jesus—really, John the evangelist—the opportunity to explain it a bit more. We would use footnotes, word balloons, or voiceovers, but they didn't have those luxuries.

LR—What about Peter's travels? Did he ever go to Rome?

RMP—There is no real archaeological or literary evidence to suggest that; it occurs in texts—like the *Acts of Peter*, the *Clementine Homilies*, and so on—that are too late to count. Now, we wouldn't doubt this—it's not out of the question that there could have been an apostle named Peter who would have gone to Rome, that's not an absurd notion—but the thing is, in the second century you already have churches competing with each other for clout. Their bishops wanted to be heeded far beyond the range of their own local church and the way to do that would be to say, "Hey look, you gotta listen to me because my church was founded by Peter (or Paul, or whomever); he taught the bishops they appointed and then they taught me." So these claims would mount up. For instance, in Antioch they would say, "We were the apostolic see of Peter; he taught our bishops, so you gotta listen to us." Well then, what would they say over in Rome? "That's pretty good, but I'll raise you one apostle: Both Peter and Paul came here to teach us." Since we know things like this were happening, you have to suddenly think: Wait a second! Is this really likely? It's very iffy, but that's not saying there wasn't a Peter. It's the same problem as with Jesus: It may be that there was someone, but he's been so thickly coded with legends and myths that it's now impossible to tell, really.

LR—What about the other apostles? Was their missionary activity also a part of myth?

RMP—It appears that it was. Walter Schmithals (a great New Testament scholar, sadly, recently deceased) believed there was a historical Jesus—he was conservative compared to me. He argued very convincingly that of the 12, there was only one who ever preached beyond Palestine, and that was Peter: He and Paul both assumed the burden of preaching the gospel outside Palestine. Schmithals says that the 12 were not constituted as a group in Jesus' lifetime. It was only afterward—because of the Resurrection appearance they shared—that they decided: "All right, Jesus is calling us to represent him"; but the 12 on a whole were simply to lead the church in Palestine. There's this early source, "Q" (the sayings found in both Matthew and Luke but not Mark), in which Jesus says, "You 12 will rule or judge Israel seated on 12 thrones." That must have been the big credential for the 12 for ruling the church in Palestine. You wouldn't make up a saying about "ruling the tribes of Israel" if you're talking about "world missions." That's why Paul billed himself as *the* apostle to the gentiles; that would have been ridiculous if all of the disciples were apostles to gentiles. That's why it didn't matter that he wasn't one of the original 12; the 12 were rulers of Christians in Palestine, but Paul was the apostle to the gentiles, and Peter is pictured as having a foot in both worlds. So the idea of the apostles spreading Christianity all over the world, that's just a Sunday school fantasy.

LR—Concerning Paul: Can you surmise the importance of Paul for the spreading of Christianity?

RMP—It's hard to say, because there's a lot of fiction that surrounds that as well. The book of Acts—I've been a member of the Acts Seminar, which is a sister group to the Jesus Seminar—and virtually everybody in that group studying Acts admits that "Yeah, this is simply a fiction; might be a partly historical fiction, but it's a fiction." Even the idea of Paul's conversion, as we read it in the book of Acts, is never even mentioned in the Epistles, and it looks so much like two other well-known stories—namely, the miraculous conversion of King Pentheus, who had first persecuted the religion of Dionysus and then was miraculously converted, became a believer, and was killed (just like Paul); and the miraculous conversion of Heliodoros, who was sent by the Seleucid emperor to steal the money from the Jerusalem temple treasury, but was prevented by the appearance of an angel that knocked him off his horse and blinded him until he was prayed over by pious Jews and converted to Judaism. Paul's story is so much like both of these well-known stories that it seems to me, "Yeah! This is fiction!" The first story is from Euripides' Bacchae, the second from Second Maccabees.

So, what else do we know about the man? Well, we don't know anything from the letters because they bear all kinds of anachronistic marks. Romans 11 seems to assume that the temple has been destroyed—something that happened only years after the traditional death of Paul. I think that the Epistles bear evidence of having come from after the time Paul is traditionally said to have lived; they deal with many issues that we usually think came up in the second century—baptism for the dead, celibate marriage, speaking in tongues, all kinds of things. The epistles seem to be patchworks where one writer will debate another: Should you speak in tongues: yes; should you speak in tongues: no. Can you eat food offered to idols: yes; can you eat food offered to idols: no. It appears like you have a kind of a digest of debate—almost like a blog—in First Corinthians; the same with the others. I don't believe we gain any information about Paul from this, either; so, what's left? Well, I think Robert Eisenman is correct in that Paul turns out to be a character that Josephus mentions, who we do find out about in the Bible, namely Simon Magus—Simon the Sorcerer, who, Josephus mentions, is hanging around with some of the same people: Bernice, Agrippa, etc.—and he was an ally of Queen Helen of Adiabene. Some of these stories in Josephus are heavily rewritten in Acts. So I think the historical Paul was Simon Magus and he would have preached Gnosticism, but whether he would have preached Jesus is another question; we are reading a Catholic-rewritten version of Paul.

LR—So, in your opinion, Paul was not such a relevant character? In the Paul that Nietzsche portrays *Of Paul* in his book *The Anti-Christ*, for instance, we see someone who's really the great booster of Christianity. Wasn't that so?

RMP—Well, everybody thought so then, even F. C. Baur, the great Tübingen critic. Baur began to crack this nut by saying, "All right, Paul didn't write any but the first four big Epistles." I think other critics are right who said, "No, he really didn't write *any* of them." In the time of Nietzsche, when the great scholar of Paul was F. C. Baur, he figured, "Yes, there was a Paul, who was an apostle to the gentiles and did the big thing spreading the gospel." It's post-Baur scholarship that has made me think, "I'm sorry, but not even that much is true."

LR—What about textual criticism? We see scholars like Luke Timothy Johnson asserting that Pauline stylistic characteristics in the Epistles could only came from a distinct individual, Paul.

RMP—Luke Timothy Johnson is both the best and the worst one to mention. He was once a very innovative New Testament scholar—and wrote a very good book on Acts—but he has come under the spell of this neoconservatism in Catholic scholarship and tries to take the most traditional view he can on anything. For instance, numbers don't mean anything, but it's very common to find that almost all New Testament scholars—except fundamentalists—would say that Paul did not write First and Second Timothy and Titus; probably didn't write Ephesians, Colossians, and Second Thessalonians. Well . . . not according to Johnson; he will come up with the stretchiest, spinningest arguments to try to show that Paul wrote the whole bunch of them, and he's simply trying to defend the old precritical tradition. There are other people, like Schmithals, who would say, "No, Paul didn't write those six letters, and scribes have made a mess of the ones he did write; they're all patchworks, albeit of Paul's writings." But you have to go further than that, as Darrell Doughty—my great professor at Drew—said: You look at any commentary on any of the Pauline letters and what do they mainly do? They're engaged in harmonizing. They say, "All right, Paul says this in First Corinthians, chapter 1; then in chapter 2 he gets into this whole different thing with no transition. What could he have had in mind, I wonder?" So they read into all kinds of things and when you step back for a minute, you realize that these commentators are just insisting that these are singular writings from one person; they don't seem to realize that if that were true, they just wouldn't read this way. I mean, only Philemon would! That's just one single page, and it does read like an individual letter from someone, but the rest of Paul does not. So I take issue with people like Johnson and most of the other Pauline scholars (Gordon Fee and others); these people certainly know their stuff, but they just seem to me to miss the forest for the trees. If you look at the comparative vocabulary—as Schleiermacher began to do in the early 19th century—you realize that whoever wrote First Timothy didn't write Second Timothy and Titus, but borrowed from them, and then you realize that these three letters have so much vocabulary in common with the Apostolic Fathers and so little with Romans, Galatians, Corinthians, etc., they simply cannot be by the same person. They have different uses of particles and prepositions, those little fingerprint kind of things that don't change throughout your life, like your favorite vocabulary. You realize then that whoever wrote Galatians did not write First Corinthians. So I think that for all of their minute scrutiny of the text and all their great knowledge—which I envy—I think they're just missing the forest for the trees; their whole effort is to try to prove that Paul *did too* write this stuff—when, it seems clear to me, he did not.

LR—Aren't these quests for historical biblical characters more of a "Vanity Fair" quest of scholars about their understanding of what Jesus, Paul, and lots of others, seem to be for them? How can we find reliability in history if different historians don't have a consensus about history itself?

RMP—What most people do is just to take a nose count. They just poll the delegation and say, "I have to assume that fair-minded people looking at the same evidence would agree with one another; so, if some nut like Price over here thinks differently, who cares? Maybe he's just hallucinating." I understand that, but it really ultimately doesn't matter. I feel like, if you are interested in the question enough to want to say something about it, you cannot go with what "most scholars say." You have to become one of them and make your own decisions; you've got to look at the issues and the data for yourself. This isn't that unusual; there are people who differ on all manner of historical questions outside of the Bible, because evidence for the remote past is fragmentary and ambiguous.

LR—If you had to name the most important books in challenging the Christian orthodoxy status quo and informing your thinking in biblical scholarship, what would they be?

RMP—The one that just absolutely demonstrates the lack of historical accuracy in the Gospels would be David Friedrich Strauss' great book *The Life of Jesus Critically Examined.* For a critical approach to Paul, among the real classics, the best ones would be Ferdinand Christian Baur's *Paul, the Apostle of Jesus Christ,* followed by a modern scholar, Hermann Detering's book *The Falsified Paul*—who makes the case that Paul was not the author of the Epistles, etc. With the Old Testament, I would say criticism really got off with a bang with Julius Wellhausen's great book *Prolegomena to the History of Israel*—which is still available, it's in print. Then, any of a number of recent books by Old Testament minimalists; for example, Thomas L. Thompson. I just read one of his called *The Mythic Past*—that might be the best one to read—where he shows that virtually all of the so-called history in the Old Testament is fiction—because archaeology just shows there never was any such temple of Solomon, or kingdom of David, or any of this kind of thing. That was a shock to me: I thought at least a good bit of the Old Testament after, say Joshua, was historical—but, no! So, I would recommend somebody that really wants a "baptism of fire" to read D. F. Strauss, F. C. Baur, Hermann Detering, Julius Wellhausen, and Thomas L. Thompson. That will pretty much nuke your assumptions.

LR—If someone becomes really interested in pursuing biblical studies, is it necessary to learn Greek, Hebrew, etc.?

RMP—It's blasphemy to say this . . . It's helpful to know any or all of those—and that kind of expertise can be a temptation. I mean, if anybody has the time and interest to do it, I say go ahead, and I certainly spent some years with Greek and did my own New Testament translations—but don't let that deter you because there are so many good translations to read and compare. Even more important are these studies that bring in broad perspectives and say, "Here's the evidence. How should we put the pieces together?" You can't really ignore that, and that, I think, is even more important. You mentioned Walter Bauer; there's another great book that says, "Okay. Here's all the evidence. I don't have any new evidence to put before you, but let's look at it in a new way," and suddenly you say, "Holy mackerel! The history of the church was totally different than I thought." Books like that are at least as important as the original languages.

LR—In Portugal, and perhaps in other nations as well, the rigorous study of religion suffers, in my opinion, from two main problems: the proliferation of bamboozle books—secret societies, "biographies" of angels and saints, astrology, tarot, power of the crystals, etc.—and the proliferation of academically biased books—in Portugal almost all of these are attached to a Catholic worldview. So, for Catholic—or just Christian—beginners, can you recommend some rigorous but also "Christian-friendly" books about historical biblical criticism?

RMP—I don't know if his books are available in which other languages, but Raymond E. Brown was certainly the greatest American Roman Catholic New Testament scholar. He was certainly way more conservative than I am—almost everybody is—but he had a genuine critical eye, argued in a fair way, and said things that would have got him burned at the stake in earlier centuries. But he was a devout lover of scripture as well as a keen-eyed scholar and biblical critic. So if you can, get a hold of any of his works like *The Birth of the Messiah* and *The Death of the Messiah*, or his commentary on John or his New Testament introduction—all big fat books with plenty of interesting material. Also, he was one of the main writers of the *Jerome Biblical Commentary* and that, I would guess, has been translated—it's been around for a long time. That has the same reverent, respectful, but genuinely critical eye trying to tell you, "All right, Moses didn't write the Pentateuch, but the Pentateuch is great stuff nonetheless." You wouldn't get the idea that he is someone trying to undermine your faith, some kind of communist or Satanist—because he certainly wasn't. So, if there's any access to Raymond Brown in particular or the *Jerome Biblical Commentary*, I'd say that would be an excellent way of helping somebody making the transition.

LR—Especially when somebody is still much immersed in a narrow view of theology. And concerning theology, isn't the element of contradiction the ingredient that makes theology a successful endeavor, allowing a multiplicity of interpretations? In the Old Testament, for example, you have God delivering the Commandment "You shall not kill" and in Exodus 32, that's exactly what Moses does to the children of Levi. How can a believer look at this and not notice the contradiction?

RMP—Well, that one—it's funny you bring that up—in one sense I don't think that is a contradiction. As I read the Commandments—which would seem to be aimed at common everyday life—they're saying: "You shall not murder." In fact there are a couple of words for *kill* used in the Old Testament; the one used there seems to mean "unwarranted killing of innocent people"—what we would call "murder." Killing in warfare or execution of criminals doesn't fall under that. As for the idea of killing those idolaters—of course we would say that's crazy fanaticism anyway, but *they* wouldn't have said that—technically, there wouldn't have been a contradiction. But when you point out Exodus 20 with the Ten Commandments, and then look at Exodus 34, you see Moses going back up Mount Sinai to get another copy of the Ten Commandments because he smashed the first one against the Golden Calf. If you look at all closely, only three of the Commandments match. The other seven are totally different! How can people read this and not worry quite a bit? What does that say about the inerrancy of the Bible? I read the Bible many times and just never noticed that, I don't know how, but that is a considerable contradiction. I guess people just focus on one passage at a time and don't ask questions.

LR—What about the "New Atheist" literature coming out from authors like Dawkins, Harris, etc.? Are they doing a nice job debunking religion or are they just smashing something without historical or philosophical background?

RMP—I have heard and read short materials by Sam Harris and a little bit of Christopher Hitchens's book, I've read various things by Dawkins—not the whole books yet though, so I may be totally wrong—but I'm a little uncomfortable with the approach they take in that they spend a lot of time ridiculing religious behaviors that almost everybody would ridicule. Bertrand Russell used to do this, for example in his famous essay "Why I Am Not a Christian," which I think is not very good. He saw some documentary about a Catholic convent where these nuns would take their baths in private, in their full regalia, for modesty sake. The reporter hears about this and asks, "Sister, no one can see you; why do you bother?" She replies, "Ah! But the good Lord sees!" Russell says that this lady is making God into a Peeping Tom! Well—true! But is that really an argument against Catholicism? Because there are some Catholic nuts? I know some atheist and secular nuts that take the cake. That kind of thing is funny but it's no real argument against religion. You really need to engage in the philosophical issues—and often they do—and you also need to realize that there are more subtle, intelligent forms of faith that do not rest on stupid arguments that fundamentalists use. So I think the New Atheists tend to paint with too broad a brush, but I'm still generally on their side: They are showing the danger that stupid religion poses to society and they are making some good points; I just wish they'd be a little less scattershot.

James Randi

James Randi was born in Toronto, Canada, in 1928. He is a stage magician and scientific skeptic well known for his challenges to paranormal claims and pseudoscience. Randi began his career as a magician, but upon his retirement he began investigating paranormal, occult, and supernatural claims. He was the recipient of a fellowship from the John D. and Catherine T. MacArthur Foundation in 1986, and his investigations of Uri Geller and other occult and healing claims was the subject of a *Nova* episode in 1993. His books include *The Truth About Uri Geller* (1982); *The Faith Healers* (1989); *Flim-Flam!* (1982); and *An Encyclopedia of Claims, Frauds, and Hoaxes of the Occult and Supernatural* (1997). Randi is the founder of the James Randi Educational Foundation, which offers a prize of $1 million to anyone who can demonstrate a supernatural ability under scientific testing criteria. The prize remains unclaimed.

Luís Rodrigues—Why did you feel the need to create a foundation dedicated to the study of the paranormal, the pseudoscientific, and the supernatural?

James Randi—Well, there's so much information out there available which is not true. What I call the "woo-hoos" (the people out there who believe in these things) have all kinds of sources and material that will tell them that these things are true, but they don't have any way of finding the truth. There are not many ways of finding the truth, and I want to supply that for them.

LR—Can you explain the "million dollar challenge"?

JR—It's been here for the past 10 years now, and it's simply an offer of one million dollars to anyone who can show that what they claim in the paranormal field is true. All they have to do is make an application, fill out the form. There's no money involved or anything like that. All they have to do is get the form notarized and send it in to us and we will negotiate a protocol which will prove—or not prove—the claim that they're making.

LR—How many applicants have tried to win the money since the challenge started?

JR—More than 400 from all over the world. Most of those 400 people didn't go through with the whole thing. They've made the application but they didn't fill it out properly or they didn't do something or other, they didn't tell what they can do under what circumstances. They seem to be remarkably either stupid or careless; they don't seem to be capable of making their statements clear.

LR—I read about some excuses made by claimed paranormal performers regarding your challenge. Some say they would never participate in such a test because they're not interested in the money, some say you are an evil spirit exerting bad energies and so on; with these kinds of excuses, don't you think that there will always be a rhetorical safe haven for the paranormal?

JR—Not unless you believe that. If you believe that someone's really seriously not interested in making an easy million dollars—and can take the money only in half an hour of work, to make a million dollars by doing what they say they do all the time. If you knew somebody who could play the violin, and I was going to give him a million dollars for playing the violin, what would you say if they said, "No, I'm not interested, I don't care about the million dollars, I won't play the violin"?

LR—Some faith healers, for example, excuse themselves by saying they're doing a pious job, that they don't heal for money and if they did, they would be doing "the work of the devil." What would be your answer to that?

JR—That's an excuse. If they don't want to earn the money, then, all they have to do is agree to give it to a charity—and they don't even have to name the charity; I will leave it up to them to send the money to the charity. Seems to me that if they could make a million dollars to pay for AIDS research or to feed hungry children somewhere in the world and they refuse to do that because they just don't care, then I think they're not very serious.

LR—Don't you believe in the hypothetical existence of a supernatural realm—a realm that is beyond the possibility of empirical testing or even verifiability?

JR—Well, I can't imagine such a thing. Can you think of any mathematical formula that can't be tested? Can you think of any question that simply cannot be answered if it has evidence to support it? No, I can't. Some people say there's no way to prove the existence of a god or a devil or any sort of thing. Well, these things by definition have certain properties and they should be easy to establish. These are all just excuses that these people make for not having the ability to prove their claims. I believe, and certainly if I'm offering a million dollars, I should think that would be enough incentive for them to come forward. Again, they can give to their favorite church or whatever they want to give it to—I don't care. But I don't see any reason for them not accepting the offer.

LR—Were you ever surprised by someone's magic trick—a trick so good that it made you think that something supernatural was going on—or have you never been surprised by that kind of performance?

JR—I wish I could say that I was surprised by some of them, but I've been around for many years, and I have seen just about every trick that I can imagine that anyone would do to try to fool somebody else into thinking they have psychic powers. Because of that, I think that I've seen just about all that they can offer. So, I would say that I can't be fooled; after all, I am a professional magician. I know how the tricks are done and I think I have enough experience to be able to solve all of them.

LR—You are notably famous for your exposure of faith healers like Peter Popoff, W. V. Grant, and Ernest Angley. Don't you feel that these victories are pyrrhic victories? Everyday the number of faith healers seems to grow exponentially and most people tend to see hoaxers as a small portion of rotten eggs in a basket full of honest ones.

JR—Well, pyrrhic victory perhaps. Yes, I think you have a good point there. But if you don't fight it, then you're doing nothing and you know that something is very wrong with the world. People are being swindled and cheated, their money is being taken, their security, their emotional security. I think that if you don't do something about that, if you don't offer some sort of solution and don't do something to fight it, then you're neglecting your duty to your fellow person in the world. We have to do what we can. I feel like somebody who has just seen an accident: I've seen somebody hit by a car, knocked up into the air, fallen on the road. I take that person out of the roadway and I offer to call for medical help—since I'm not a medical person myself, I'm not a physician. If that person, while I'm going to the telephone, decides to crawl back into the traffic, I think I might go and get that person one more time, but if he's determined to go back into the traffic and get killed, then I would leave him to it. I would only try, I think, twice to save the person's life. I think that anybody would try to save people from misinformation and these cheating operators out there who are trying to take their money, their security, and their sanity.

LR—Do you think you have enough media coverage to show your point, or do the "supernatural enterprises" prevent that from happening?

JR—I don't think the supernatural enterprises prevent that from happening, but after all, the media are in business to sell cars, cigars, aspirin tablets, or whatever they're advertising; they know that people out there are very, very fond of "woo-hoo" subjects and very much like to believe them. So they present a positive attitude—because that will sell their products. It's a matter of business. I'm not selling anything. I don't have anything to offer in the way of merchandise. I just have the organization for which I work—the James Randi Educational Foundation—and we work hard to make our money, to keep the organization going so that we can explain to people how they are being swindled. Other folks out there are always competing with us because they have an opposite point of view: They want to make money from the suckers, the dupes out there who don't know any better. We are trying to educate these people.

LR—Some television and radio stations devote part of their prime time broadcasting programs related with the paranormal—

astrology, communication with the dead, etc. Are these shows dangerous ways of manipulation or harmless means of consolation?

JR—They're not harmless. When someone's lying to you and trying to get you to spend your money or invest your emotional security in some sort of a cause, or a belief, or a claim of some kind, I think that's very dangerous. Lies are always dangerous. I don't think that they ever serve a positive purpose.

LR—How should a skeptic deal with these kinds of supernatural shows in the media? Disclaimer? Censure? Indifference?

JR—What they can do—and what I've always told them to do—is write letters to the TV stations. I used to write letters to PBS, for example. I used to subscribe to PBS and I used to support them; every year I would send them a check and it was money well spent, I felt. But now that I see that every time they do a fundraising they have Deepak Chopra, Wayne Dyer, and various people like these on that program . . . and they know what they're doing, they know that people will stay tuned and people will give money to PBS when they see these swindlers up on television. They will give money and that's what the PBS stations are all about. They have to make money, they have to have an income and they take full advantage of that. But I don't send them my money because they're misleading people by doing that.

LR—Some advocates of the New Age Spirituality movement use scientific terminology in conjunction with mystical ideas in order to claim avant-garde theories about the understanding of the universe—the "law of attraction" is one of those theories. In your opinion, why are people so receptive to these ideas?

JR—Well, they sound scientific because they use scientific words. They will use the word *vibrations*, they will talk about *quantum physics* constantly. They have no idea what quantum physics is all about—very few people do! Only scientists can really understand that sort of thing well. I have a bare inkling of what it's all about. They have no idea what a vibration is; they just think it's a mystical word that they can use—and they use it, of course. The public out there believes in it because they think that's scientific language—but it isn't.

LR—But if even scientists are not 100 percent sure about some theories and how they work, doesn't that leave some New Age thinkers with, let's say, a 1 percent possibility of using that lack of understanding to advance their own mystical theories as superseding those of conventional science?

JR—Oh yes; that's what they do. That's their gimmick. It's like selling quack medicine or selling an automobile. At least in the automobile case, you will actually get something when you buy it—whether it's a good price or not is a different matter—but with quack medicine you will get nothing, although it's exactly the same selling techniques: They lie about things, they exaggerate them, they don't care whether they're telling the truth or whether they're representing the facts of the matter. All they care is that people will send them the money.

LR—What do you think are the most dangerous actions practiced by these hoaxers?

JR—Most of the faith healers and the people who are offering cures of various kinds through vitamins and special substances, magnets, necklaces, and things like that—of course that takes people away from medical care. Medicine can't cure everything, we know that. Medicine is growing constantly and always developing, but there are some things that it simply cannot cure. People want cures. So, when the quack promises them that they will be cured, they immediately go to the quack. They celebrate that fact and they jump from one to the other because they're getting promises. Now, those promises aren't fulfilled; they aren't cured—but they have to die before they find that out!

LR—What are the main characteristics that a hoaxer must have to fool people?

JR—Well, the use of apparently scientific terms and the use of celebrities to support them. Tom Cruise, for example, supports Scientology, and Scientology has no more basis in fact than any other crazy crackpot theory. But, nonetheless, people will believe it if they see someone like Tom Cruise talking about it. "Look! That's Tom Cruise talking about Scientology! It must be true!" No. Not necessarily at all.

LR—Do you think that religion can live without displays of magic and healing?

JR—I think that the displays of magic and healing have always been part of religion. Look at the so called faith healers out there who strike people on the forehead. Now, what people don't realize is that this is carefully rehearsed. So, these are theatrical gimmicks. People like Benny Hinn do this sort of thing all the time and they do it all around the world. They get tens of millions of dollars in return for it—and don't pay any taxes on it.

LR—Many people still believe in the feasibility of some tricks—levitation, for example. Aren't magicians co-responsible for some excessive credulity concerning the paranormal?

JR—No. Because magicians never tell people that what they're doing is real. They simply say it's play acting. When you go to see David Copperfield, Penn and Teller, Lance Burton, or any of these famous magicians, you don't believe for a moment that what they're doing on stage is really supernatural, that they really do disappear or cause a person to appear out of nowhere. You don't believe that sort of thing. You understand that it's an illusion, the same as when you go to see *Star Wars* on the screen in the theater; those are motion pictures, television, video. You should have the common sense to understand this is play acting.

LR—In Portugal people have reported the so-called miracle of Fátima: A multitude have testified that they saw "the sun dancing." How can phenomena like these be explained without supernatural justifications?

JR—It's mass hysteria. Mass hysteria is very common. People often see things like that. I've known people who saw somebody hanging, for example, and then they saw the hanged man get up and walk away; the person's in the grave, and yet, they still think that's what they saw. People can be deluded, and they are deluded very, very easily. This is not unusual at all.

LR—What advice would you give to someone who's going to be "exposed" to a paranormal session (like spiritism, for example)? What are the main "procedures" to detect the hoaxes in those kinds of events?

JR—You can't do it. It's like watching a magician do a good magic trick. No matter how well prepared you are for it, you can't solve it if you don't know the trait, if you don't know the gimmicks that are being used. If you care to read our Web site, we have an encyclopedia up there that I wrote some years ago, and the whole thing is available free of charge on the Web site. You can click on any subject you're curious about that deals with the paranormal, and you'll find pretty good explanations of it. That can prepare people, certainly to some extent, to deal with these things, but don't ever think that you can go in front of a professional performer and figure out what they're doing. If they're good at it, they will have you fooled and you will stay fooled. You won't be able to solve it.

LR—Do priests and ministers behave like those kinds of performers?

JR—It depends what they're claiming. If they're claiming just to talk to God, anyone can talk to God. I can talk to anybody. I can talk to a post. I've got a cup of coffee here and I can talk to the cup of coffee. That doesn't mean anything. "Hello cup of coffee! How are you?" I don't have an answer, but I did speak to the cup of coffee.

LR—Not only do some people report speaking to God, but they also believe that he will come soon. How do you explain this expectation of the "Rapture"—the idea that Jesus Christ will come from heaven and will take everyone with him to his heavenly realm?

JR—It's a preferred belief. They're told this by preachers, by ministers out there who say the Rapture will come along any moment at all and they choose to believe in it. People live their own lives through and they will die like everybody else dies eventually and they won't see the Rapture; but, they will go satisfied that "Oh! I suppose you'll see the Rapture then! Okay. Well . . . I'll leave now; I'm going to die but I guess you will see the Rapture since you're much younger." This sort of thing has been going on for hundreds of years now! Hundreds of years in all different cultures around the world, and they're always promising something is going to happen and it never happens. Yet, people still believe in that.

LR—Do political leaders also believe in that stuff, or in their case, do they just use those beliefs in order to manipulate people?

JR—I don't know; you have to ask each individual. They all have their own delusions. Here in the United States, every political candidate has to profess belief in some sort of a god and they have to thank God constantly or they will never get elected. I know that it is quite possible that they don't believe in any god, or angels, or devils, or charms, or anything like that; it's possible they don't. But they have to say that they do because they know they will not get elected. People don't trust someone who doesn't believe in supernatural things.

LR—How do you feel about the fact that there's no life after death?

JR—I have no feelings about it at all. I don't believe there is any life after death; why would I be concerned about that? I've got it now. I'm 80 years of age and I expect to get maybe 10 years more out of it, if I'm lucky—and maybe more, who knows? I'm in reasonably good health and I expect to live for a few years more, but when my time comes, my time comes. I had a good life—Good-bye! I'm not worried about that at all.

Robert Sapolsky

Robert Maurice Sapolsky (born 1957) is a US scientist and author. He received his BA in biological anthropology summa cum laude from Harvard University and subsequently attended Rockefeller University where he received his PhD in neuroendocrinology. Sapolsky is currently the John A. and Cynthia Fry Gunn Professor at Stanford University, holding joint appointments in several departments, including biological sciences, neurology and neurological sciences, and neurosurgery. He has focused his research on issues of stress and neuronal degeneration, as well as on the possibilities of gene therapy strategies for protecting susceptible neurons from disease. Sapolsky also spends time annually in Kenya studying a population of wild baboons in order to identify the sources of stress in their environment and the relationship between personality and patterns of stress-related disease in these animals. He is the author of *Why Zebras Don't Get Ulcers, An Updated Guide to Stress, Stress-Related Diseases and Coping* (1994), which explores the effects of prolonged stress and its contribution to damaging physical and mental afflictions. His other books include *The Trouble with Testosterone, And Other Essays on the Biology of the Human Predicament* (1997); *Junk Food Monkeys* (1997); *A Primate's Memoir* (2002); and *Monkeyluv, And Other Essays on Our Lives as Animals* (2005). Although born into a devout Orthodox Jewish family, Sapolsky is an atheist.

Luís Rodrigues—Human beings are subjected to all sorts of social conditioning provided by the religious background in which they live. Can extreme fundamentalist religious practices and environments mold the average person's physiology in such

a way that he or she is no longer able to process the world in a conventional way? If so, can you describe that brainwashing process in terms of what it does to the brain?

Robert Sapolsky—Well, the easy answer is, of course a fundamentalist environment changes the brain, because any sort of environment does. What the specific version here is nothing but pure speculation. But here is what I would speculate if I *had* to come up with something. I think of extreme religiosity as, most deeply, a means to get easy answers to hard questions, and that indoctrination in a fundamentalist version of religion is an extreme case of this. If there is some challenging circumstance in life and there is the need to think, feel, reflect in a difficult way that might bring up some really hard conclusions (there is no god, there is no purpose, etc.), you always go for the easy version instead. In a very artificial way, a lot of this will then involve the frontal cortex. To be wildly simplifying, the frontal cortex makes you do the harder thing when it is right, instead of succumbing to the easier. This can be seen in the emotional realm; it's the frontal cortex that keeps you from doing something violent to someone when you're tempted. It works in the cognitive realm as well; it is hard for us to recite the letters of the alphabet backwards, and when instructed to do that, it is the frontal cortex that has to be working hard to keep you from falling into reciting the letters in the usual way. Thus, the ability to live within the framework of a fundamentalist religion that relieves one of the need to ever think/ feel the harder thing could very well involve a "weaker" frontal cortex (and what "weaker" means in neurobiological terms would be complicated). It could be that a weak frontal cortex is a prerequisite for becoming a devout fundamentalist or that becoming one causes some sort of atrophy of the frontal cortex; either could be possible. But again, I should emphasize that there is no evidence for this; this is pure speculation.

LR—Are some people more prone to religious belief than others? What does biology have to say in order to explain different predispositions to belief?

RS—Well, it is definitely the case that some people are more prone than others. But there are many different components to religiosity. As discussed above, the versions that lead one to be unable to do anything other than come up with the easiest answers may have something to do with the frontal cortex. The versions of religiosity that are very concerned with "metamagical features," spirits, speaking in tongues, communicating with the dead, and so on, have much to do with something called schizotypalism. The versions of religiosity that are all about ritual, order, practice have stronger parallels in obsessive compulsive disorder. So it depends on the type of religiosity. In all of these cases, I think there is a commonality, a strong tendency toward always taking the easier answer, toward metamagical possession, toward intense ritualistic behavior; all of these are potentially very disruptive to a normal life. But religion supplies a tremendous sanctuary, even a realm of reward, for people like this.

LR—Do the emotions generated by religious activities or any other spiritual involvement fill some kind of physiological need? I know this question might sound awkward but, can a liturgical Mass or a spiritualist session produce in the organism similar effects as those produced by, let's say, chocolate, tobacco, coffee, or even a powerful anaesthesia?

RS—Absolutely; some mixture of endogenous opiates, analgesia, dopamine.

LR—When talking about the brain, the question of free will always arises: Are our personality and our actions really a result of our will at work—as if our actions were the product of a "ghost in a machine"—or are we really just a machine running a predetermined program set in our neurons?

RS—My bias is that there is no free will, but the lack of freedom is not going to be explained by reducing us merely to a collection of genes, molecules, or neurons. Or to make my stance a little softer, if there is free will, it's in all the places that are not interesting, and the size of those places keep shrinking.

LR—"Power" and "energy" are recurrent concepts in the discourse of the New Age Spirituality movement, which says that there are no impediments against, for example, the possibility of levitation, telekinesis, or mind reading. What kinds of "energies," if any, does the brain deal with? Besides the

psychological effects of rhetoric, can the mind have the ability to exert control over anything or anyone outside the body in which it resides?

RS—I am not only not religious in the slightest, but I am not spiritual in the slightest either. Thus, I see no way to fit any of those phenomena into the world of science.

LR—The moral argument for the existence of God states that there are absolute standards for human morality; therefore, the immutable laws about what are the right and the wrong things to do could only come from an eternal lawgiver: God. What is your perspective about the notion of morality, its evolution through time in human brains, and the concept of the divine attached to it?

RS—There's not much for me to say about the latter part, given that I am a strident atheist. In terms of where the unique world of human morality comes from, I have two answers: (a) It isn't uniquely human, and our moral system, in both its extent and complexity, is on a continuum with other smart social primates; (b) there are lots of formal mathematical game theory models showing how you can evolve moral systems in a way that doesn't require an omnipotent organizer.

LR—Some say that the human mind possesses capabilities not yet discovered; this is the usual popular argument that people only use 10 percent of their brain potential. What do you have to say to that? Is this true or just a false argument used to justify God and the supernatural in whatever we don't know about the brain?

RS—For starters, the 10 percent business is a folk myth, with no basis in reality—it represents a misinterpretation of the results of some research in the middle of the 20th century. But as for the question: There are plenty of ways in which we understand behavior and brain function now that were beyond comprehension at earlier times, for which there was not even a framework for thinking about it. That is no doubt the case now as well, and there will be findings in the future that we can't even begin to imagine. But, functioning in the present, I see absolutely nothing in neurobiology that suggests that there is a god and the supernatural lurking in there in ways that we can't yet perceive scientifically.

LR—What is your opinion about the conflict between the theory of evolution and intelligent design—or more generally speaking, about the tensions occurring between a scientific worldview and a religious worldview?

RS—As for the specific conflict between evolutionary biology and intelligent design/creationism, there is nothing worth discussing there. Evolution, as a real, ongoing process has been demonstrated repeatedly, it is a "theory" only in the sense of there continuing to be ongoing uncertainty as to all of the mechanisms of evolution. There is no scientific basis whatsoever for anything in the creationist/ID world, and it has no business in any science classroom. But as for the largest issue of science and religion and whether they are intrinsically incompatible: I see how physicists keep deciding that they are compatible, and that God speaks through string theory or special relativity, or whatever. However, I don't see how a neurobiologist can accommodate both their scientific discipline and religiosity at the same time. But, despite my thinking that, there are obviously people who can.

LR—Having studied apes for a long time, have you ever felt that, with time and training, it would be possible for them to adopt practices resembling those we call "religious"?

RS—Nah, no way.

LR—A question about the future: Do you believe that it will be possible to control the brain in such a way that all its contents could be subjected to manipulation—including not only things like sexual orientation and memory, but mainly, the belief in God and in the supernatural?

RS—We already have the means to manipulate some of those things and we will acquire more in a crude sense. However, we will never be able to control it on a very precise level because of the intrinsic nonlinearities of how the brain works.

Henry F. Schaefer

Henry F. Schaefer III received his BS in chemical physics from the Massachusetts Institute of Technology (1966) and his PhD in chemical physics from Stanford University (1969). For 18 years he served as a professor of chemistry at the University of California, Berkeley, and was the Wilfred T. Doherty Professor of Chemistry and inaugural director of the Institute for Theoretical Chemistry at the University of Texas, Austin. Since 1987, Dr. Schaefer has been Graham Perdue Professor of Chemistry and director of the Center for Computational Quantum Chemistry at the University of Georgia, and in 2004, he became professor of chemistry, emeritus, at the University of California at Berkeley. In May 2010, the University of California at Berkeley hosted a large international conference in Professor Schaefer's honor. In demand as a speaker at hundreds of conferences, Schaefer's long list of awards and honors includes, recently, becoming a fellow of the Royal Society of Chemistry (London) in 2005. He was also among the inaugural class of fellows of the American Chemical Society, chosen in 2009.

Luís Rodrigues—What are in your opinion the most compelling arguments for the existence of God?

Henry F. Schaefer—I would point to three: First, I would point to the comprehensibility of the universe—the fact that using mathematical physics so many things can be explained and correctly predicted; thus the universe makes sense if there is a cosmic mind directing all these things. Second, I would point to the fine-tuning of the universe—the fact that if any one of the fundamental constants of physics is changed by even a tiny amount, not only do human beings not exist on this planet but neither does any other life form and, perhaps, the planet's not here at all. Third, I would point to the astonishing complexity of even the simplest living thing, the simplest self-replicating biochemical system. So, I think these are good evidences from science for the existence of God. They're certainly not mathematical proofs; I don't think God ever intended there to be mathematical proof of his existence.

LR—Your arguments for the existence of God rely on cosmology, mathematics, physics, and biology. These arguments would find general acceptance in a deist worldview, but in a Christian worldview, how does Jesus fit into this wider cosmic picture of creation?

HFS—Certainly these arguments I've just given you are not specifically Christian arguments. Now, we can talk about the Big Bang theory—which I think is correct—and from that, we would—if one's rational—conclude that whoever or whatever this god is, he is a transcendent being—that is to say, a being who occupies more dimensions than we human beings experience, in particular, at least one additional dimension of time. Otherwise, it doesn't make sense to talk about all the mass of the universe being concentrated in an incredibly infinitesimal spec with nearly infinite temperature pressure and all these things; this doesn't make sense without something coming before. Now, our time begins with the Big Bang, so the "before" must refer to some other dimension of time. Clearly, I think we are talking about a transcendent God, we're not talking about a god who is the universe or is part of the universe. When we really start talking about Jesus, we're talking about historical things, and so we have to consider historical evidence. That's fine for science as well; nobody was around 70 million years ago when the last dinosaurs were disappearing, but then we all believe dinosaurs existed from historical evidence. It's not unreasonable to use historical evidence to assess the validity of these events that took place 2,000 years ago.

LR—But when we're talking about the historical foundation for Christianity 2,000 years ago, we're talking about the Bible. Do you think that solely reading the Bible is enough for one to be a Christian and believe in its statements? What do you think about historical and textual criticism of the Bible—pursued by some scholars, for example, in the Jesus Seminar?

HFS—I think that the Jesus Seminar is a joke. These people are not serious scholars, and they're not pursuing an agenda that sensible people would pay attention to. They're just trying to get headlines by saying outrageous things.

LR—So, you don't believe in their historical assumptions?

HFS—No. I think the Jesus Seminar has no credence at all.

LR—Some theists emphasize the regularity and order of the universe, but they hardly claim a storm, an earthquake, a black hole, or a supernova as something orderly and beautifully designed by God.

HFS—No, I would disagree with such persons; I think these things are orderly and beautifully designed by God. That's my view.

LR—Why do you think God would design these things?

HFS—Well, if I could answer that question, I would be God—and I'm making no such claims [laughs]. I think earthquakes are beautiful; I mean, I've lived in California for 26 years of my life and it's fascinating to look at the sites of these earthquakes, these crevasses, and really be awed by the power of God.

LR—But why would an infinitely good God create destructive events, like tsunamis and earthquakes, that harm and kill human beings?

HFS—I think one has got to take a big picture of these things. I guess I can say this most simply by stating that it is clear that God's primary purpose in creating humankind was *not* to make them be perfectly working machines that never wore out. I think that's perhaps the place to begin. Suffering is part of God's plan for the universe, and I think that if one doesn't understand that a human life takes up a short period of time compared to eternity, then many things that God does won't make sense. But if you take the opposite view—which is that this is a testing period, if you like, for human beings, and it's just a small part of eternity—then many things that might be puzzling are not as much so.

LR—And here we arrive at theodicy: God and the problem of evil.

HFS—I take a strong position on that, and my position is simple: Everything that happens, ultimately, is the will of God—but oftentimes for reasons very, very different than human beings could imagine. No, I don't believe there are good and evil forces dueling for the destiny of the planet or anything like that.

LR—So, you don't believe in the forces of angels and the forces of demons?

HFS—They're all under the sovereign control of God.

LR—Some philosophers—namely postmoderns—think that we should abandon the ideas of attainable truth, attainable progress, attainable knowledge, and so on. How does a Christian answer these statements?

HFS—Well, I think it's better to answer as a scientist. We just don't agree with this. We think there is truth and that it can be found by scientific means, and we're not surprised that truth can be found by historical means and so on. No, most scientists don't accept the postmodern view at all. You probably are aware that there has been some controversy about this involving this New York University Professor Alan Sokal, who's written a spoof on postmodernism—you probably know this whole story. No, we as scientists don't put any credence in postmodernism. It doesn't have anything to do with being Christians. We're just scientists and don't buy it.

LR—Talking about science, you have your nemeses in science in figures such as Richard Dawkins. What are, in your perspective, the most relevant and the most incorrect arguments brought about by the New Atheists concerning religion and the existence of God?

HFS—Well, again, I take a pretty strong position on this. My position is that every human being intuitively knows that God exists from the simplest observations of the universe. So, when Dawkins tells me he doesn't believe in God, I don't believe him. I think Dawkins believes in

God, he just doesn't like God. The result of this suppression, of this truth of the existence of God, is a tremendous amount of anger. If you've ever seen Dawkins in action, or Christopher Hitchens in action, or the late Carl Sagan in action, or any of these outspoken atheists, there is a tremendous anger they feel, and that's because they're suppressing their own understanding that God exists.

LR—Do you think it's possible to find a common ground of understanding between atheists and theists?

HFS—No. There's no common ground on religious matters. Of course there are many areas outside religion for common ground: scientific, friendship, etc. My atheist friends and I rarely discuss God.

LR—If the respect for religious beliefs must be obeyed by nonreligious people, isn't the effort to maintain a separation between the secular and the religious a meaningless and unachievable prospect? I mean, where can we trace the frontier of separation between the secular and the religious? How does one know where that frontier is?

HFS—Well, I think everybody needs to respect everybody else. Nonreligious people need to respect religious people and religious people have to respect nonreligious people. I mean, I just think Richard Dawkins is wrong; I'm not wanting to put him in jail or anything like that. He's certainly free to express his own opinions in any venue he wants to.

LR—Do you think that a vision of ultimate meaning posed by most Western religions—which point to an ultimate goal called heaven or God—can be dangerous? In the most radical wing of Christian and Jewish fundamentalism, for example, the expectancy of a cleansing Armageddon or the Rapture can be very appealing. Do you think this is dangerous?

HFS—I don't think whether it's appealing or not is particularly important; I think whether it's true or not is critically important.

LR—So, do you think that a coming Armageddon or the Rapture are true prospects?

HFS—You know . . . I'm uncertain about the Rapture. I certainly believe—as orthodox Christians do—that Jesus Christ will return to this planet at some future time that I do not know. Beyond that, I think there's a lot of speculation and I wouldn't want to contribute to it.

LR—Very conservative Christians seem to be afraid of books; they think that the Bible is enough for them and no other way of achieving knowledge is required. What is your explanation for this attitude toward knowledge in conservative religious circles, especially in a developed country like the United States?

HFS—I certainly don't share those views. I'm a lover of literature and of history. I wish I had more time to go to Shakespeare plays and read novels of Charles Dickens for a third time instead of just having read them all twice. So, I'm not the right person to ask that question. I don't endorse any anti-intellectual activities.

LR—In your book *Science and Christianity: Conflict or Coherence?*, you often mention, as a justification for a theist vision of science, the commitments of other renowned scientists to a religious point of view—namely Christian. It seems the "argument from authority"—the experts leading or teaching the laypeople—looks inevitable: There will always be someone declaring they know what is correct, whether in science or religion. In that sense, what do you think can distinguish the epistemic attitude, whether in science or religion?

HFS—Both science and religion need to be testable. In science, a theory has a lifetime only as long as it appears to be testable. Once it either fails in the dialogue with observations, or its predictions just become such that there's no anticipation that they can be tested, it really ceases to fall within the mainstream of science. I think Christianity is testable too, in historical terms, so the historical dimension of Christianity is tremendously important.

LR—Some Christians use the Big Bang to justify God, but deny evolution. When they pick and choose in science whatever suits their religious views, isn't there the danger of transforming science into a subsidiary tool for religion?

HFS—I think that the Big Bang and biological evolution are two very different questions. Each one has to be addressed individually. I see little obvious relationship between the two. So I think these are separate issues that need to be addressed separately and it's not surprising that different people could come to two different views.

LR—What is your opinion about this polemic concerning intelligent design and evolution in the United States?

HFS—I think that more has been said about it than needs to be. I just don't see that discussion going anywhere. We have people pretty well entrenched on both sides and not very much listening to each other.

LR—So, what could be the final outcome of this question?

HFS—I think it's going to go on for a long time.

LR—Regarding the relationship between fundamentalist religion and science, I saw recently on television an Iraqi astronomer talking about "koranic science." Among his claims were that the Earth is flat and that the sun moves around the Earth. Although these claims look bizarre for someone living in the 21st century, how can Western civilization be regarded as being more scientifically advanced if similar ideas—for example, the idea that the Earth is 6,000 years old—are adopted in some Judeo-Christian denominations?

HFS—Well, it's not my position, so I'm not going to defend it. I think the Earth is 4.7 billion years old.

LR—In the age of capitalism, corporate labs and scientific institutes are increasing in number. In this context, can well-financed institutes engage in science with an ideological or religious agenda? If so, can reality be manipulated by social and economically empowered classes or groups?

HFS—Historically, there have been examples of that. I guess Lysenkoism in Russia, in the 1920s and 1930s, is the most obvious. That sort of thing is an example how ideology can drive science. There are other examples of this that are closer to more serious science. I would say that one of these is the steady-state hypothesis—the idea that the universe is infinitely old. I think the reason this idea was pushed so hard and for so long is that some atheistic scientists were terrified by the thought of a beginning. So there's an example where ideology kept the scientific idea afloat longer than it should have.

LR—Don't you think that the same objection could be raised against institutions with a religious bias? Here I'm thinking of the Discovery Institute, for example.

HFS—I'm not going to comment on the Discovery Institute. Like I said, these things have been over-discussed. It's not a debate I want to get involved in.

LR—Now on a more personal note: What are your expectations after death?

HFS—I'm expecting to be with Jesus.

Peter Singer

Peter Singer was born in Melbourne, Australia, in 1946, and educated at the University of Melbourne and the University of Oxford. He has taught at the University of Oxford, La Trobe University, and Monash University. Since 1999, he has been Ira W. DeCamp Professor of Bioethics in the University Center for Human Values at Princeton University. From 2005, he has also held the part-time position of laureate professor at the University of Melbourne, in the Centre for Applied Philosophy and Public Ethics.

Peter Singer first became well known internationally after the publication of *Animal Liberation* in 1975. Since then he has written many other books, including *Practical Ethics* (1993); *The Expanding Circle: Ethics and Sociobiology* (1981); *How Are We to Live?*, *The Ethics of What We Eat* (with Jim Mason, 1995); and most recently, *The Life You Can Save, Acting Now to End World Poverty* (2009). He is married, with three daughters and three grandchildren. His recreations, apart from reading and writing, include hiking and surfing.

Luís Rodrigues—Who, for you, are the most liberating ethical thinkers? Why?

Peter Singer—David Hume, Jeremy Bentham, John Stuart Mill, Henry Sidgwick, Bertrand Russell—I like their very clear, no-nonsense writing about ethics and politics.

LR—Do you believe in the possibility of creating a Universal Ethics Code like the Universal Declaration of Human Rights, but expanding it to environmental and animal issues? Is it possible to implement an "absolute ethic" that could take into account different cultural and religious contexts?

PS—I'm not sure what you mean by "absolute" here, but I do not believe ethics is relative to culture. So yes, I would hope we could produce some sort of code like that, although obviously at the moment it would not be possible to get agreement on how animals should be treated.

LR—The theologian Hans Küng has promoted the creation of a Global Ethic Foundation—a project that intends to promote a global ethic based on an ecumenical dialogue between different world religions. Being an atheist, how do you analyze this attempt to create a global ethic based on religious foundations?

PS—I don't agree with religious foundations for ethics, but there is common ground between the ethical views of the various religions, and also of those that are not religious, such as the Confucian tradition.

LR—People are confronted with personal ethical dilemmas everyday. According to game theory, their options result from the calculation of what their best self-interests are and the prediction of what other people's actions are going to be. In this sense, isn't religion a force that tends to balance the egocentric tendency that individuals have to promote their best self-interest?

PS—Yes, religion can be a force like that, but people can be altruistic when they are not religious too. I would like to encourage more compassion and empathy without encouraging religious belief, which can often lead to fanaticism and make problems more difficult to solve.

LR—Could you imagine a theocracy where the same ethical principles that you propose would be implemented? If that were possible, would you support that theocratic government (for example, cows are protected from slaughter in India due to religious principles)?

PS—I doubt that any theocracy would hold all the same views as those that I hold. And it is a mistake to believe that I think cows are well treated in India. On the contrary, I support euthanasia for sick cows, and in India that is often not possible. My views about animals are based on opposition to needless suffering, not on an objection to killing as such.

LR—Concerning the question of life and death, why do you think that people's desperate attachment to life—even the most degrading one—is always exalted unconditionally? Is the motive for that primarily religion or pure selfishness?

PS—Maybe it is a survival instinct that has an evolutionary basis.

LR—You state that the option to live or die relies on the utilitarian result. But, what if there's always a "winning side" that is not correspondingly morally right? You may say that a mother's option can prevail over a fetus; by the same token, can it be that the human preference can also prevail over other animal species? How can a secular ethics deny the principle that "might makes right"?

PS—Why should a secular ethic accept that principle? But a full answer to your question would require the development of a secular ethic— read any of the thinkers I listed in answer to your first question.

LR—You define the capacity to experience something as a quality that is ethically significant. So, the "consciousness of self" seems to be one of the parameters you most prize for an ethical valuation. But, being unable to scan the inner psychological depths of an individual and the future role that individual will have in society, what prevents you from committing an ethical mistake in your choice—for example, choosing to kill an "unconscious fetus" rather than a "conscious young Hitler"?

PS—I don't say that we should never kill a conscious being. If you could kill Hitler to prevent him murdering millions, you should.

LR—Some people tend to think of "ethics" as some kind of metaphysical objective and metaphysics as some kind of transcendental world (or a "noumenal realm"). This way of thinking obviously contributes to the concept of God as someone who's ultimately responsible for ethics and morality. Do you think it's possible—or desirable—to detach ethics from metaphysics?

PS—That depends how you define metaphysics. Everyone has some metaphysics, including, again, all those thinkers I listed above.

LR—If you had to convince a religious believer about the non-existence of God and the supernatural, what would be your main line of argument?

PS—The fact that there is so much needless suffering in the world shows that there cannot be a God according to the Christian conception: omnipotent, omniscient, and omnibenevolent.

Richard Swinburne

Richard Swinburne is a fellow of the British Academy. He was professor of philosophy at the University of Keele from 1972 to 1984, and professor of the philosophy of religion at Oxford University from 1984 to 2002. He has lectured at many universities in many countries. He is best known for a series of books on the meaning and justification of central religious claims, especially those of Christianity. His best known book is *The Existence of God* (1979, second edition 2004), which argues that the existence of the world, its conformity to scientific laws, those laws being such as to lead to the evolution of humans, humans being conscious, and other general phenomena make it probable that there is a God. His two more "popular" books on these topics are *Is There a God?* (1996, revised 2010) and *Was Jesus God?* (2008). He is currently working on a new book on mind, body, and free will.

Luís Rodrigues—Leo Strauss argued that Western civilization was built on two pillars: Athens and Jerusalem—reason and faith. Confronted with this choice, why did you choose Jerusalem?

Richard Swinburne—I'm not certain I did choose Jerusalem. I think Athens leads to Jerusalem. As you know, I'm a professional philosopher and I think there are good arguments for the existence of God. I think there are also good arguments for the particular detailed truths of the Christian religion; so, I don't find any conflict.

LR—How do you deal with the fact that some atheists, agnostics, or secular humanists may consider a theist philosopher to be a "lesser philosopher"? I'm remembering your polemics with Richard Dawkins, for example.

RS—Richard Dawkins is not a philosopher. He is an amateur from out-side philosophy. Most atheist professional philosophers think that *The God Delusion* was a pretty poor book; it wouldn't be the sort of book they would recommend to their students. He hasn't read the literature on the subject; he really hasn't. He's just read one or two little things, he may even have read three pages of Aquinas, and he's read a couple of popular books—including one of mine—but he hasn't gone into the subject very well, in my view. But of course there are, you're quite right, many good atheist philosophers in the Anglo-American world. Note that those who you say belong to Athens have disagreed with each other fundamentally on big issues and it's still like that today; one generation's minority becomes the next generation's majority. How to account for this? Well, firstly we are none of us perfectly rational beings; we are swayed by emotions, commitments to our own prejudices, not willing to lose face—I speak of myself as well as my opponents. Nobody's per-fectly rational—and nobody's perfectly clever. Some arguments take a lot of time to grasp and we have only a finite life, so some disagree-ment, I think, is going to be inevitable. But sometimes, also, we can convince each other; some philosophers and ordinary people who were theists become atheists, some who were atheists become theists. May the truth win.

LR—In your opinion, what is the major argument—or arguments—for the existence of God?

RS—I think there are strong arguments from the fact that there is a complex physical universe, and that every particle in the universe behaves in the ways codified by scientific laws—for example, every par-ticle attracts every other particle with a gravitational force proportional to the product of their masses and inversely proportional to the square of their distance apart. There's enormous predictable regularity about things, and that regularity is such as to produce human beings; most initial conditions of the universe and most laws of nature wouldn't pro-duce human beings. Further, human beings are conscious beings: no physical law can explain that; it's quite outside the kind of laws physics deals with. So, here are things which a priori, if there is no God, would be immensely improbable. How probable a priori is it that every parti-cle should behave in exactly the same way? But if there is a God, there's a reason why that should be the case, because God would be interested in bringing about good things—and we are good things. If we are to exist and be finite embodied beings—which is what our goodness consists in—then we have to be able to influence each other and influence the world, and we could only do that if things behave in regular ways. If whenever I put one brick on another it flew apart I couldn't build a house, or whenever I plant a seed and nothing happens I couldn't grow food, and so on.

LR—Let's assume that one of the best proofs for the existence of God is the existence of a physical universe, ruled by regular laws of physics fine-tuned for human existence. How can these laws have any significant divine and anthropocentric value? After all, they are the same laws that will dictate the end of life on Earth about a billion years from now when the sun will run out of hydrogen fuel in its core.

RS—We can often do evil, and so I would say it's an equally good thing for God to make us or not to make us; it's a risky thing. So he might just make some humans. But anyway, however many of us he makes, he could always make more. So even if we went on forever, it would be a complaint that there were not more of us in other parts of the world—and if there are, it would still be a complaint that there aren't yet more of us. However many of us God makes, he could make more of us and therefore, perfect goodness doesn't require that he will make any particular number of us. Anyway, the Christian doctrine is that although this world comes to an end, God has other plans for us—or for many of us—in another world. So, if he takes us from this world—which has its deficiencies (the harm we can do to us and the harm we need to suffer)—to a better world, that is no cause for complaint.

LR—If we are to destined to live in an eternal existence, then isn't this meaningless and gratuitous wandering in some kind of Garden of Eden (with no opportunity for human beings to continue to do what they did and continue to be what they were while alive) as bad as burning in hell?

RS—Two or three issues here: Firstly, I'm not committed to a literal Garden of Eden, though I am committed to the view that there was a first human being—that's pretty obvious—understanding by that, a being who had free will, a moral choice between good and evil. Now, humans made bad choices. But among the choices we all have when we make a bad choice is the choice of influencing others, and when humans start making bad choices, they make it easier for other people to make bad choices. It's a good thing to have significant choices for good or evil; every good choice we make makes it easier to make a good choice next time, every bad choice we make makes it easier to make a bad choice next time, and so we form our character. God gives us the opportunity of forming our character. He doesn't force heaven on anyone, he leaves it to us what sort of people we choose to become. Only good people would be happy in a life of heaven because heaven consists in the worship of God, helping God to forward His purposes, and if we are not good people, we wouldn't want to do that.

LR—You tend to see natural and moral evil as an opportunity that God gives us to exercise our moral duties and our formation of character?

RS—Indeed, yes.

LR—But what if, for example, someone chooses to die heroically in a war for his or her country? If we assume that some individuals must suffer so that others can benefit from their actions, isn't God discriminating against humanity by choosing those who are, so to speak, in the chorus, and those who are main characters in a grand cosmic play?

RS—First, we all have choices. The victims of the Holocaust, the victims of the Lisbon earthquake, they themselves had choices in their unfortunate situations; they had a choice of how to cope with it, whether to cope with it bravely, with or without bitterness, and that is a very great character-forming opportunity. This has been recognized by most people: When you're in a crisis, that's when you form yourself. Secondly, anyone who is—as you would say—a victim, is in fact the means of somebody else having a great choice. By their vulnerability, the Jews made it possible for Hitler and an enormous number of other Germans to have significant choices; and it's always a great good for me if I am the means of other people having great choices. So if human well-being merely consisted in being happy, then of course God would be wrong to let us suffer for the benefit of others. But if human well-being also consists in having enormous opportunities for forming our own character and being the means of other people forming their character, then I don't think the "victims" are very obviously total victims. It's a blessing to be in a situation were you can make really significant choices and you can be the means of other people having significant choices.

LR—So, according to the choices they've made, will some people live eternally in heaven and others in hell? Do you believe in the concept of hell?

RS—What I certainly believe is that people form their character on Earth. Many people—or some people—can form their character irrevocably; that is to say, they can make themselves such that they would cease to be open to good influences. Gradually, if people always choose the bad, they become no longer moral beings, and such beings would not be happy in heaven. God could still keep them alive, but if he did keep them alive, inevitably they would be in a situation where they wanted to hurt people; but God wouldn't let them hurt people. There's no point in providing opportunities for people to hurt others beyond this Earth; so inevitably, bad people would be unhappy. But in that situation, who knows? Perhaps God would eliminate them, I wouldn't know. What I do know is that if God is to give us really serious choices, he must allow us the choice of forming our own character permanently.

LR—Most theologians and theist philosophers try to absolve God of sending people to eternal damnation by putting the burden of guilt in the personal free choices made by those who are damned, as you've mentioned. But, to make an analogy with everyday life, imagine a drug addict and his most loving father: Do you think that in any moment, the father will consider that his son deserves the worst possible destiny for not having the capacity or the free will to abandon drugs?

RS—Oh no! I wasn't concerned with a situation like that. What I was concerned with is people who knowingly do what is bad when they could have chosen otherwise. Sure, there may be people who fall into drug addiction and who didn't really want to; they want to get out of it and they keep on trying. I'm not saying for a moment that God would send such people to hell; indeed not. Maybe nobody's in hell, but hell is a permanent possibility for people who choose deliberately, permanently to reject God.

LR—What about some acts of evil committed by ignorance?

RS—No, no. The Christian tradition has always maintained that it's only evil committed knowingly that is of any significance. Even Aquinas said that if anybody in hell was to repent, God would immediately take them to heaven; but, of course, he didn't think anybody would repent. Nevertheless, the point is even Aquinas thought that hell is for those who continue to reject God even though they could have done otherwise. If they do that, inevitably they're not going be happy in heaven and inevitably, they are going to want to do things God has every reason to stop them doing; so, they won't be happy.

LR—But imagine eternity for a moment: What will a person do or be in eternity if the endeavors that make a human life meaningful are condemned to disappear? For example, a good general will not have troops to command because there won't be wars in heaven, a doctor will no longer need to practice medicine because nobody becomes sick, there will be no artists because there will be no existential anxieties. What meaning does eternity have without the concerns that humanity has here on Earth?

RS—Well, fair question. Two points. First, the saints are supposed to be in heaven these days and they're supposed to be helping God in his work on Earth—hence we pray to the saints to ask them to ask God to help us. So being in heaven may involve helping God in his work. Secondly, the adoration of God, worshiping him and growing in the knowledge of him is a wonderful prospect. People like singing, and especially when it involves worshiping what is good; it is an immensely worthwhile thing to acknowledge what is good. It's immensely worthwhile to know more and more about it; and if God is omniscient, he can tell us ever more about the good and he can ever help us to acknowledge it. The pictures of heaven are the pictures of saints singing, though we don't need to take this literally: it's simply joyfully acknowledging the good. I repeat, it is an enormously worthwhile activity to give your best to acknowledge what is good; and if God is all he's supposed to be, it is enormously worthwhile to worship him—as well as help him in whatever further work he has in mind—in other universes, who knows?

LR—Isn't worshiping God a kind of "Sisyphus job"—a job where one is condemned to do for eternity the same kind of actions?

RS—Would you say that of some choir singing a great song?

LR—Yes . . .

RS—No, of course you wouldn't, and I dare say there are plenty of different songs for them to sing. Sisyphus's task was unpleasant because the task was unpleasant in itself, not because it went on forever.

LR—But if one doesn't like to sing on Earth, why would things change in heaven?

RS—Quite so, quite so, and that's just my point: That's to say, you've got to want to reverence the good; and if you don't want to reverence the good, heaven's not for you. It is great to recognize what is good and to acknowledge what is good, and to acknowledge that makes you something worthwhile.

LR—Do you think there are on Earth sufficiently pious people "entitled for that job," if I may say so?

RS—I wouldn't know, but Christians have always believed that there have been plenty of good people, like the saints. The Christian tradition has always been a bit ambiguous about the fate of intermediate groups, people who haven't finally formed their character for good or evil. The different Catholic and Orthodox traditions of Christianity have always recognized that. There is the Catholic doctrine of purgatory and the now somewhat unfashionable doctrine of limbo; and on the Orthodox side, they've always claimed that it's proper to pray for the departed and that implies that their state may not yet be fixed permanently. There's an intermediate stage: If we haven't formed our character on Earth, we may need another kind of existence to form it—one way or the other.

LR—What was, in your opinion, the most perilous moment for theism in the history of philosophy?

RS—Perilous moment . . . well, the strongest argument against theism has always been the problem of evil. I have my own theodicy—I think theism has always been a bit weak in developing theodicy and I've tried to do better. But concerning the history of philosophy, it is the case that

Kant wrote certain things which were enormously influential—especially in the continental tradition of philosophy. I think Kant's arguments are just bad arguments but, historically, their influence has been enormous. What Kant claimed is that he had shown that there could be no good theoretical arguments for the existence of God. Lots of people have thought that Kant showed that there couldn't be any rational proof of the existence of God—not even any good argument for the existence of God. He claimed there were three sorts of arguments for the existence of God, and that none of them worked. I think that all Kant's own arguments against arguments for the existence of God are bad arguments, but historically their influence as been enormous.

LR—Will metaphysics continue to be the safe haven in philosophy departments for those who defend a theist point of view? Or do you think that theist philosophers can—or must—develop their work in other fields of expertise?

RS—I think theism is a metaphysical doctrine in the sense that it's a doctrine about the ultimate causes of things, and therefore there has to be some sort of argument to show that it is probably true. If philosophy is to be of any use to theism and any use to rational people, certainly metaphysics must be done, and is central. But of course, lots of branches of philosophy merge into each other. Theism requires a view about epistemology—a theory of what makes a belief rational or justified or probably true. Theism has an ethics—or rather, any actual religion has an ethics—and therefore, issues about what it is for something to be good or obligatory and how we can show that it is, inevitably arise. Most questions raised by philosophy have some relevance to religion, I think, but metaphysics will be pretty central to that activity.

LR—You have a Christian theist perspective. Can you explain why it is so?

RS—I do not merely believe in God. I'm a Christian theist; I think the central doctrines of Christianity are probably true. I think the teaching of Jesus and the church which he commissioned, the central teachings, that is, are probably true and therefore my well-being consists in following them.

LR—So, how do you see some current forms of holistic spirituality—those that evolved from transpersonal psychology and culminate in the most recent New Age movements?

RS—Well, in order to discover what is good and worth doing, we can of course have rational arguments to start with, but I think we need help. If we are to attain what is most worth doing, we need help from God. I think that God gave us a revelation through the teaching of Jesus and the subsequent teaching of the church; and my reason for believing, and so for following that teaching rather than New Age psychology, is that I think God has shown that Jesus was God himself by the life he led and above all by the Resurrection of Jesus. That's why I trust it—not the only reason, but the central reason why I trust it—rather than anything believed by New Age psychology which, at any rate, seems to me not having great depth.

LR—What do you think provokes the most substantial "philosophical damage" in the Christian doctrine you defend: the undermining of orthodox Christianity from within the supernatural framework—one that, even maintaining Christ, uses him as just one more rhetorical figure in an inclusive pantheon of mixed gods, religious traditions, and spiritualities (I'm thinking of New Age gurus, psychics, some postmodernist thinkers, liberal Christians, etc.); or the undermining of Christianity from outside, based on a worldview that despises the supernatural (proposed by some atheists, agnostics, secular humanists, etc.)?

RS—Well, I think both undermine. I don't know which undermines more; probably the attacks from outside, yet both are influential. But if there is reason to practice any religion, that's because there's good reason to believe there's a god. And there is very good reason to believe there's a god of the traditional kind. A god of the traditional kind is going to be interested in humanity and in trying to help us, and if we've got any reason to suppose he has a particular revelation about his nature and how we ought to live, then we ought to take advantage of it. I think quite a number of forms of religion today are trying to have a totally secular morality together with some sort of reverence toward the supernatural; but these are trying to put together things that don't fit very well, because if you really take the supernatural seriously, then you think there's a reason to believe in a god who's going to help us a bit and that leads more to traditional religion.

LR—But astrology, for example, is a more ancient tradition than Christianity; so, according to that point, why wouldn't it be more legitimate?

RS—There are good arguments to show that astrology doesn't work.

LR—Change it to other religious traditions then: Hinduism, for example.

RS—There are many forms of Hinduism. Insofar as some forms of Hinduism believe in something like a god of the traditional kind, then I endorse it; but of course, most forms of Hinduism believe in many different gods and that seems to me a less probable hypothesis than the hypothesis of one God. We ought to look around for the religion that teaches the sort of thing which a priori we might believe such as one God to be interested in: reverencing the good and the true, helping other people, and so on. I think the Jewish tradition embodies all that. Above all, we might expect such a God to intervene in human history, share our suffering, and tell us more about how to live. Only one religion claims that he's done all that—or claims that it has any evidence that he's done all that—and that is the Christian religion; it claims that God suffered with us and showed us who he was by his Resurrection.

LR—But when we say that reason can inquire the different traditions, isn't reason inquiring the different qualitative manifestations of tradition? For example, the "best religion" may not be the one that best reflects "a god," but the one that has the best doctrinal construction, the one best written, the one with the best stories, the best myths.

RS—When we make our judgments on probability in comparing religions, I think that there are good arguments for the existence of God, so that means I'm going to go for a theistic religion. The main ones known to us in the West are Christianity, Judaism, and Islam. Only Christianity claims that God suffered with us and only Christianity claims to be founded on a super miracle—the Resurrection of Jesus—for which there is any substantial evidence. I think a God who makes us suffer—as clearly he does, for a good cause—ought to suffer with us, and the Christian religion is the only one that claims he did. Therefore, I think that is strong reason to believe the Christian religion rather than Judaism or Islam.

LR—Let's talk about the concept of "soul." How do you define soul, and why does the existence of the soul sound plausible to you?

RS—Well, we can define that term as we want, but what I'm interested in is the notion of a soul as an immaterial part of the human being. That is to say, humans consist of two parts: body and soul. The soul is the essential part, is what makes me "me," and that's the doctrine of soul I'm interested in defending; and of course, it's Plato's view and it's Descartes' view. Why do I think it's true? Well, knowing of what happens to bodies and their parts will not show what happens to me; the argument in essence is just that.

If you've read anything about the subject, you know I discuss this split brain experiment: Suppose some mad surgeon gets hold of me and says, "What I'm going to do to you is I'm going to take your brain out of your skull and I'm going to put half of that brain into some other body—from which the brain has been removed—and the other half into a different other body—from which the brain has been removed—and I'm going to take bits of your identical twin or your clone and put them together with each half of your brain so that we then have two conscious persons, each having half of your brain." Do you follow? The surgeon has taken my brain out, divided it into two and put half in one empty skull, half in another, and if that's not enough to make a conscious person he takes other bits from a clone or an identical twin so there are then two subsequent persons, each of whom has half of my brain. It's reasonably enough established that persons can exist without quite a bit of their brain. If quite a lot of my brain is destroyed, I can still be conscious and function; and if quite a lot of my brain is destroyed and other bits are provided, it would seem that there will be two conscious people, each of whom have half of my brain. Both resulting persons would probably behave much like I do and claim to remember much of what I did, and claim to have been me. Now, which of them is me? Well, there are just three possibilities: Either the person with my left half-brain is me and the one with my right half-brain is not, or the person with my right half-brain is me and the one with the left half-brain isn't, or neither are me. My point is: You wouldn't know which was me—even if you knew what has happened to every bit of my brain, and even if you knew all the experiences of both conscious people, you wouldn't know which was me. What that shows is that "being me" is not a matter of what has happened to the bits of my brain—because if it was, you would know which was me. But since you don't know, there's a further truth yet to be discovered, but no scientist could discover it because all he can know is what happens with bits of my brain. So there's a truth here, a truth which is quite different than the truth about what happens to the physical and what thoughts are being thought; only if you think I consist of two parts can you explain that—because the truth is the truth about what happens to the other part of me, which is of course, not observable.

LR—Do you believe God creates each new soul?

RS—Yes. All I mean by that is that there's not a physical mechanism for creating me and you. God gives to each body its own separate soul.

LR—Granting that a soul exists, and that God creates each new soul, why would he concede his creation to Satan every time one human being chooses to do evil according to his or her own free will? Is it a demonstration of love to create someone that you know has the probability of spending the afterlife in eternal torment?

RS—Well, no. But it's a demonstration of love to create someone who has the opportunity to get to love you permanently. I'm not committed to an eternal torment, but I am committed to the possibility of some people being eternally separated from God—and then either continuing to exist or being destroyed by God. If God has so arranged the universe that whatever I do can't affect my destiny and he's going to take me to heaven anyway, he is not trusting me with myself, and I think that is a deficiency of love. If you really love your children, you want them freely to choose to love you.

LR—But being God, you are omnipotent and have the omniscience to know what's going to happen to your children.

RS—No, no; that all depends how you understand divine omniscience. Omnipotence is the power to do anything logically possible—that is to say, anything that doesn't involve a contradiction—that's always been recognized. God being omnipotent can't make me both exist and not exist at the same time. He can only do what's logically possible. Similarly, omniscience should be understood as knowledge of everything logically possible to know. I believe that it is not logically possible for anyone to know what any future free agent will do, and therefore God can't do so: He takes risks with us. There are people in the Christian tradition who said what I have just said, although certainly the majority of the Christian tradition has held that an omniscient God knows infallibly what anyone will do freely, but I think that is mistaken.

LR—Why would God have the need to take risks with us?

RS—Well, it's an inevitable logical consequence of giving us free will to make choices affecting the sort of people we are to be. It is self-contradictory to suppose he could give us freedom and yet also ensure that we always be good.

LR—But why doesn't God allow us to exert that free will in heaven from the start?

RS—We have free will in heaven, but not free will to choose what is bad and evil. Free will has an enormous range in heaven, but by our own choices on Earth we can eliminate the possibility of ever choosing evil there. Each time on Earth we make a good choice, we make it a little less natural to make an evil choice next time. And so, at the end of our lives, if we have always chosen the good, willing evil is no longer within the range of our choice—or if it still is, but nevertheless we are really determined to make ourselves totally good, God will eliminate the possibility of our doing evil. The point of this Earth is to give us the opportunity to make ourselves the sort of people—if we choose to—who will naturally choose to do good.

LR—Why is it necessary to undergo this "internship" on Earth for obtaining the prize of an eternal existence with God?

RS—We clearly could be made naturally good—most Christians hold, for example, that baptized babies who die when they're babies go straight to heaven. There's nothing incompatible in supposing God could make someone naturally good, but it's good for us to have the choice of becoming a naturally good person or a naturally evil person.

LR—Turning now to science, how do you see the polemic between intelligent design and evolutionism?

RS—Well, it depends what you mean by intelligent design. I have no problem with the theory of evolution by natural selection in the sense that there are random mutations of genes producing animals which vary from their parents in different ways, and those that vary in ways which have a survival advantage survive. Among the features that have a survival advantage is intelligence, and that accounts for the development of humans. I have no problem with all that. That's God's way of bringing us about. There's no reason to suppose that, apart from bringing about consciousness—which I say is totally inexplicable scientifically—there's no reason to suppose that God interfered in the evolutionary process. I think it's a pity that a lot of American Protestant people think it very important to suppose that he did interfere in the process of evolution. He's arranged the world so that it's fine tuned eventually to produce us. Why would he need to interfere?

LR—If I'm correct, you are a proponent of inductive reason in order to defend theism. When you choose to elect inductive reasoning in order to defend theism, aren't you using a "logic of the gaps" in order to preserve the God hypothesis? In that sense, inductive reasoning seems to be for deductive reasoning what intelligent design seems to be for evolutionism, isn't that so?

RS—No, no, indeed not. There's no gap at all. That is to say, I accept evolution; I'm not saying there's a gap—apart from consciousness—in that. But the next question is: Why are the laws such as to lead to the existence of humans? And the answer is, because the laws of physics have a certain character; but then: Why do the laws have that character? And that's a point at which theism comes in: not to explain a gap, but to explain the normal process.

LR—Being a philosopher and obtaining from God after you die all the answers concerning the meaning of life, what are you expecting to do for all eternity?

RS—Well, let us hope I reach the right place at the end of life. I think that what we will do then is in God's hands. But the worship of God is a natural good for humans and it's a good which I anticipate sometimes when I attend church. God may also have other plans of worthwhile activities for me.

LR—Do you believe in alternative universes in which God also operates?

RS—There may be other universes yes, I don't know, but that's quite possible. And it's quite possible that those who die on this Earth have work to do in helping God with the development of another universe.

Thomas L. Thompson

Thomas L. Thompson (born in 1939 in Detroit, Michigan) is a biblical theologian who lives in Denmark and is now a Danish citizen. Thompson obtained a BA from Duquesne University, Pittsburgh, Pennsylvania, in 1962, and his PhD at Temple University, Philadelphia, Pennsylvania, in 1976. The focus of Thompson's writing has been the interface between the Bible (specifically the Old Testament) and archaeology. His *The Historicity of the Patriarchal Narratives* (1974) was a critique of the then-dominant view that biblical archaeology had demonstrated the essential historicity of figures such as Abraham and of biblical events such as the Exodus and the conquest of Canaan. *The Early History of the Israelite People* (1993) set out his conclusion that the biblical history was not reliable, a theme he continued in *The Mythic Past, Biblical Archaeology and the Myth of Israel* (1999). Thompson has been a controversial figure in biblical studies. He is closely associated with the movement known as biblical minimalism, a loosely knit group of scholars who hold that the Bible's version of history is not supported by any archaeological evidence so far unearthed, is indeed undermined by it, and therefore cannot be trusted as history.

Luís Rodrigues—First of all, why did you choose to investigate history—in particular, the scriptures?

Thomas L. Thompson—I began some 35 years ago. I was working on a dissertation dealing with the question of whether the biblical narratives of Genesis were historical, that we could speak of a patriarchal period in the Bronze Age. It was really in connection with that dissertation that I first became involved.

LR—You question some historical claims about the Old Testament, asserting that there's no evidence for a kingdom of Saul,

David, or Solomon, no evidence for a temple at Jerusalem in the early period of Jewish history, and so on. What are the main justifications of your assertions?

TLT—Well, the issue begins in the question of historical method and whether we have evidence. In my work on the patriarchal narratives back in 1974, I found that when we dealt with archaeological evidence directly, without consideration of the biblical narratives, the archaeological evidence and the written records showed a very, very different kind of history than that represented by the biblical narratives. That was carried through in the years following from the material from Genesis all the way through Second Kings. I have also argued that the Bible doesn't make any claims of being historical, and that it's only the effort to read them as historical material and to try to synthesize them with the archaeological material that creates a problem. With history, we write history whenever we have evidence, but that doesn't lead us to the Bible.

LR—Can we talk about a "theological conspiracy" to imprint historicity in the Bible?

TLT—Conspiracy is a hard thing to talk about because it's been going on for a century [laughs]. I would say it's a long habit to assume the Bible is talking about Palestine's past. This comes from a very old problem in biblical studies—especially in the study of Hebrew Bible: Unlike almost any other field, we don't have any history—or we didn't have any history at all, prior to the 50s and 60s, except from the biblical. In the pre–World War II period, scholars began to try to integrate the Bible into ancient Near Eastern history, and it was this movement that I began to oppose, and argued that we had to read the historical evidence that we were now getting from newly found inscriptions from the ancient Near East and from archaeological evidence to write our history, and we needed to separate that from the biblical narratives.

LR—What methods allow you and other scholars to interpret from a different perspective?

TLT—The method that I and my colleagues have been using were basically historical ones; that is: How do we write the history of the ancient Near East? The method of the previous generation was to try to write history by correcting or interpreting the biblical narratives on the basis of archaeological evidence. But they faced the difficulty that the biblical narratives were written in a much, much later period, mostly from the sixth century BCE or even later. When we tried to reconstruct the history of the Iron Age or the early first millennium or the second millennium, one had no written traditions about events in these periods, and the evidence from archaeology and the evidence from the inscriptions gave us a very different kind of history than we see in the stories of the Bible. The other side of this was that we were also trying to read the Bible inasmuch as we could to understand what the authors were trying to address, and what they were trying to talk about. I would say that if you compare the biblical tradition about Moses' laws with Plato or the way the biblical narrative is put together with some of the Hellenistic writers, you see that the effort of the biblical authors was not to write a history but rather to use traditional narratives to present and create an ethics.

LR—Can you describe what the "biblical minimalist school" is and compare its main contentions with those of other, "conventional," schools?

TLT—Well, first of all, the term "minimalist" is a term that has been given to us by those who oppose us [laughs]; it isn't entirely welcome because it seems to imply that you try to use the Bible as little as possible for writing the history. On the other hand, it also is appropriate, because I would say that the first premise we have is that we try to write history on the basis of evidence and on the basis of historical arguments. The biblical material doesn't give us evidence for the early periods. They only give us evidence for the time that they were written and for what people of that time knew about the past. They give us evidence for intellectual history, they give us evidence for the history of ideas, not for the history of events centuries before.

LR—Some detractors of this minimalist approach accuse minimalists of regarding history as some sort of postmodern interpretation: If the Bible is just a narrative, its deconstruction can be made in whatever way best suits the minimalist. Are these objections correct, or do you oppose them by saying that you're moving on the right path to obtain historical truth and that the other approach is wrong?

TLT—I think the latter is much more to the point. If you're going to try to understand what stories—or narratives, or traditional texts—are talking about, you have to compare them with similar texts; and in doing this, you find that these are fictive narratives which attempt to create an ideology, attempt to create a pedagogical form (such as we find in parables and allegories) for talking about ideals, about values; but they're not talking about history. I think you have to compare the biblical narratives with high literature—like Shakespeare or Boccaccio—and think what kinds of things such literature does. What it doesn't do is talk about the past in the way that a historian does. For a historian, you have to have evidence. You have to ask the question: Did it happen?

LR—In your books *The Messiah Myth* and *The Mythic Past*, you make reference to the mythological aspects of scripture. If those mythological aspects don't differ that much from the Egyptian or the Greco-Roman ones, why have Judaism and Christianity achieved a status of historicity that the others have not?

TLT—I think the status of historicity, which really was strong only in the very end of the 19th century and the first half of the 20th century, came at this point because Western scholarship as a whole began to identify truth with historical truth. This began—very ironically—in the whole Darwinian debate back in the 1850s, where the understanding of the origins of humanity and the origins of the biological universe were seen as opposed to the biblical revelation of the beginning of the world. Christian theologians began to defend, over against Darwinism, the notion that the Christian—or the biblical—view of the origins of humanity was historical. If you turn to theologians before the 1600s, you won't find this interest in history. There is an assumption that the stories were about a past, but there's no analytical or critical investigation for that kind of question.

LR—It comes from that period the chronological notion that the Earth came into being 6,000 years ago, isn't that so?

TLT—Yes. In the English-speaking world, it comes up with Archbishop Ussher, who gives a date for the origins of the world as 4004 BCE. Now, this comes in the latter part of the 19th century, and it's basically aimed at opposing the Darwinists in the debate over the truth of the Bible.

LR—What distinguishes Jewish religious culture from all other religious cultures in the Middle East in that time period? What led it to a monotheist framework—contrary to all existing syncretisms?

TLT—Well, this was a widespread development. Already by the late sixth, fifth centuries BCE, you have a movement—especially in Syria/Palestine—toward a kind of monotheism. I would say from the very latest Assyrian period, you began to see the "god of heaven" as a central religious figure—this was in Syrian literature Baal-Shamin, which means "the lord of heavens"—this was quite widespread and occurs in the Bible as "the god of heaven" or as "Yahweh, the god of heaven." You also find this same kind of concept in some of the classical philosophical literature of Greece such as in Plato and Aristotle. The idea of a united explanation of the world as a whole is taken for granted. I would say that this period (late sixth and fifth centuries BCE) witnesses the origin of monotheism throughout the imperial world—I'm speaking here of the ancient empire of the Persians and the Hellenistic Greeks. This is a very, very strong movement at that time. Judaism and the Samaritans, which begin in Palestine, are the best known Palestinian representatives of this philosophical movement. By the Roman period, Judaism and the Samaritans form the largest religious movement in the Western world.

LR—But aren't there also some early influences—for example, from the Egyptian pharaoh Akhenaton—pointed out as being a monotheist worshiper of the sun god Aton?

TLT—There are many close parallels that we can see between the kinds of things that Akhenaton tells about and what comes up in Late Bronze Egyptian texts, which seem to be in many ways monotheistic. There are many such texts from that period, but there is little continuity that we are able to trace between the Late Bronze Age—circa 14th, 13th centuries BCE—and the later period of the sixth and fifth centuries. In the sixth and fifth centuries, ideas of monotheism became dominant, whereas in the earlier period, it seems, as far as we know, largely limited to Egypt and of relatively short duration. In most of the ancient Near Eastern religious texts, one finds an understanding of a hierarchical structure of the world of the gods. All gods represent, in one way or another, the power of the most high—generally considered as a coherent, even unified whole. This is very old; this exists already in the third millennium BCE. Monotheism is not really opposed to polytheism: It rather tries to summarize it and rationalize it.

LR—Are the problems for the historical Abraham the same as those regarding the historical Jesus? As far as I know, at least

the historicity of some biblical characters like Abraham, Sarah, or Jacob can be evaluated by examining their supposed bodies in the Tomb of the Patriarchs at Hebron. Why isn't this done?

TLT—Well . . . you can turn to politics. The people who control the tombs—the Tombs of the Patriarchs—do not have the same critical interest that scholars do, and they would see this as blasphemous.

LR—But regarding the historicity of these characters, are their historical problems the same as those concerning Jesus'?

TLT—Yes, it is the same kind of question. The question is: Are we dealing here with a literary figure, or are we dealing with a figure of the past? If we assume that the narratives are talking about the past, then other issues of what is involved in this kind of literature—such as why the texts were written—become lost. But you are right: There's not a great deal of difference between the question of whether David existed or whether Jesus did, and I try to show in my *Messiah Myth* that these two biblical figures are intimately connected.

LR—Much of the Judeo-Christian tradition revolves around the temple at Jerusalem, which remounts to Solomon, its builder. What, in your opinion, are the motives that led to the creation of a mythic Solomon?

TLT—Here, as I understand the narrative, you have a development, a presentation of a narrative with three kings: One is King Saul who, as a human being, is portrayed and presented as a very good king. However, he was a king and his essence—as the narrative wants to present a king—is that he did what he sees was right. This, of course is his weakness and tragic flaw, because, in the theology that drives these stories, what is good is how God sees things, and so Saul is rejected. Then you have the figure of David, who goes through a very long history, involving both conflict and violence. In the end, David is seen as one who God chooses to love; but there's no peace, there's only conflict through the whole of David's life. Solomon is the third figure in the story and he's going to represent peace—shalom—that is what his name means: peace—Solomon. Shlomo is a name related to the Hebrew word *shalom*. So, Solomon's proper goal as king is to represent this ultimate peace that David could not win. Solomon is to be the king as God wants him to be. However, the first half of his life he does everything that is right.

When given the choice by God to have anything he might wish, he asks for wisdom rather than wealth. Now, if I can back up a moment, at the end of Deuteronomy—at the very end of the Pentateuch—you have a "law of the king" which foreshadows Solomon's story. Moses warns the people that when they choose a king, they must make sure that the king does not collect gold or silver, horses or women. In the First Book of Kings, when Solomon comes to the height of his power and builds the temple, he also builds himself a palace—which is three times the size of the temple and takes twice as long to build. He then, in his great fame, begins to collect wives—a thousand of them—gold and silver, and horses for his chariots and army. The rest of the story of Solomon is a story of his fall. So this story functions as a parable. You can speak of it in profound terms, as a tragedy, but it is also a narrative that tries to point out what kinds of human weaknesses always get people in trouble.

LR—Very similar to the story of the Tower of Babel, isn't it?

TLT—Absolutely! It's exactly the same kind of story, except that the Tower of Babel is a very short story and very limited, and Solomon's story is very complex; but it's exactly the same kind of story.

LR—No other culture produced so many prophets as the Jewish culture. What are the main reasons that lead to the rise of this prophetic tradition?

TLT—Ah, I don't know. I don't think the answer is really terribly historical; I think it goes into the question of one of the main storylines through the Old Testament, from Genesis to Second Kings, which is: "Why did it end up so badly? Why did God reject us?" In this storyline of rejection, they were warned by the prophets. But they hadn't understood when they were warned. I think the role of the prophets is really a kind of theodicy, if you will: an effort to try to justify God for destroying Jerusalem, arguing that he had sent the prophets to warn them what was going to happen, and so on. Isaiah plays a very central role, but also, the stories of First Kings and Second Kings—the prophets there, Elijah and Elisha, who constantly are telling the kings of Israel and Judah that what they're doing is wrong, and they must change. But they never do; they listen for a short period of time, but never more than a generation.

LR—Do you think that your interpretation of history undermines in any way the belief in God, the Judeo-Christian God?

TLT—Oh, that's a very, very difficult question, because it's a question about which there's great feeling. I don't think belief plays much of a role in biblical literature—I don't even think it plays much of a role in Judaism. I think that the biblical texts are philosophical discourses. I think you have as much belief here as you would have if you read Plato or Aristotle. It's not the central concern. The existence of God or gods is taken for granted, rather than based in a special kind of faith. Within the early Christian tradition, belief becomes very, very dominant and I think that comes first because of religious conflicts. The first conflict is between Samaritans and Jews about what the true Torah is—and what the true temple is—and then it's between Christians and Jews, and later between Muslims and Christians. The newer movement tries to surpass the elder in holding to the truth of the tradition. I think these religious conflicts that divide religions all represent in their own way the same tradition, but different aspects of the tradition. All really belong to a single religion. I don't think such competition about how one should believe is the best way of understanding the literature.

LR—How about Jesus? How do you see Jesus? According to your vision of history, who was he? Do you endorse the "Jesus myth hypothesis"—the theory proposed by G. A. Wells, Earl Doherty and others, suggesting that Jesus never existed—or do you believe in a historical Jesus?

TLT—I think Jesus is a figure of narrative. He is a figure who represents all of the highest values that you find in the Jewish tradition. I think he's a figure of messianic hope. There is an attempt in the Gospels to break the kind of never-ending story of failure the Old Testament gives to us, and I think there's some effort to break that with an ideal figure where you have a success, but of course, the success then has to be in terms of resurrection and the unknown future. But I don't think there's anything historical in Jesus.

LR—Jesus comes from a line of continuity of Jewish prophets: Isaiah, Elijah, John the Baptist, and so on; but what distinguishes him from all the others—a distinction that made him the center of one religion?

TLT—Well, he's not the center of one religion—at least within the Gospels, he's a Jewish figure. The religion comes later [laughs]. The new religion comes because of the conflict over Jesus as a figure. The Jews of the second and third centuries AD would not accept Jesus as a divine figure, as a divinely historical figure, and so there's a rejection there, where the Christians begin to develop a personality cult—if you want to use strong language—but understood in the sense of a historicizing what had been a narrative figure into a man who was also God. This was a creation of the third and fourth centuries. It's not in the Gospels.

LR—How do you see Bible studies in our contemporary society? Will biblical knowledge continue to be a matter for the elites while religious common practice will continue to be a matter for the broader population?

TLT—I'm afraid so. I'm very unhappy about that, but I think that the question of believing is something which is so strong, within the Western world at least, that as long as people's lives are hard, I don't think we are going to have a common ground between what you've called the "intellectual elites" and the broader population.

LR—Is there any way to diminish or minimize this lack of knowledge?

TLT—I think so, I think so very much; and I think one way of minimizing this is the effort to understand what's going on when people build traditions. We don't really have any trouble at all, for instance, with Danes understanding the Vikings and the stories of Vikings and things of this sort, stories within a mythological world, stories of the early gods of the North. But you have to come a long way into secularism before this can happen with success. Secularization is just beginning.

LR—What is your opinion about other scholars who don't reach the same conclusions than yours? Are they deluded? Ignorant? Biased? Unconcerned?

TLT—Well, hardly ignorant! They're very, very learned people. There are large issues at stake. Sometimes these scholars will hold conservative opinions because they cannot stomach the conflict. Conflicts over religion are very harsh. Some of my colleagues who are in Islamic studies have a very, very great difficulty in trying to speak openly about what they think, and the doubts that they have, and the concerns that they have, and also the positive things they have to say about the tradition because of the very great ignorance of religion that exists on a popular level. If we can succeed in furthering education about religion, I think that this will change attitudes very positively. I think myself that the Jewish-Christian-Muslim tradition is a very positive one, but right now, it's very dangerous.

LR—When strident atheists use some results of your investigations to refute theists, do you think your work is being misused or well used?

TLT—[Laughs.] Well, here of course we're dealing with anonymous atheists and it's something of a caricature; but to keep within that kind of caricature, I find the atheist believes far too much.

LR—So, you don't endorse New Atheist approaches to the history of religion?

TLT—No, I don't. Some of these proponents are very close colleagues of mine, but I would say that there's not much effort in atheism to understand religion. My own passion is to try to understand what these texts are saying, and also to try to clarify them, because what they are saying is something that is both very positive and also very necessary: to live with hope and to live with each other in a multicultural society—where some people believe and others don't. Understanding can help us in this. I find the polemics of a "caricatured atheism" basically distasteful; it's not very useful. I would say stronger things about fundamentalism.

LR—How do you see the future of biblical studies in Europe and the United States? What are its main challenges?

TLT—Well, in the United States, the main challenge is fundamentalism. There's a strong tendency within the states to avoid education. In Europe I see it as very promising, and I would say that in Europe the biggest danger is boredom; that is, a lack of engagement. There is too much willingness to see it as "this religious nonsense I don't want to hear about anymore." I think this is a mistake because we *are* going to hear about it, especially with the new migratory movements throughout Europe. This is a very serious issue that we have to face and we have to deal with—in a humanistic way. I don't think it's something that can be dismissed. Religion is far too dangerous to dismiss.

Neale Donald Walsch

Neale Donald Walsch has been called a modern-day spiritual messenger and a contemporary theologian. With an early interest in religion and a deeply felt connection to spirituality, Walsch spent the majority of his life thriving professionally, yet searching for spiritual meaning before beginning his now-famous conversation with God. His "Conversations with God" series has been translated into 37 languages, touching and inspiring millions of lives. In addition to authoring that best-selling series, Walsch has published 16 other works. In order to deal with the enormous response to his writings, Neale created the Conversations with God Foundation, a nonprofit educational organization dedicated to inspiring the world to help itself move from violence to peace, from confusion to clarity, and from anger to love. He is also founder of the Changing Change Network (www.ChangingChange.net), which seeks to assist people in using spiritual principles to deal with the political, economic, and relationship changes that mark modern-day life. Walsch's work has taken him from the steps of Machu Picchu in Peru to the steps of the Shinto shrines of Japan, from Red Square in Moscow to Saint Peter's Square in Vatican City to Tiananmen Square in China. He lives in Ashland, Oregon, with his wife, poet Em Claire. His personal Web site is www.nealedonaldwalsch.com.

Luís Rodrigues—What led you to deny religion and embrace spirituality?

Neale Donald Walsch—My observation that religion, the way it is traditionally taught, has not solved the problems of humanity. In fact, I have observed that in far too many cases, it has actually added to those problems. I searched deeply within my heart to see if I could discover and understand why religion was having such a negative effect on the world collectively when it seemed to have such a positive effect on individuals, separately. I couldn't understand how something that could do so much good for individual people could do so much bad for groups of people in various cultures and countries. So, I looked deeply at the teachings of the world's religions and discovered that those teachings were largely a doctrine of separation. I saw there what I came to call a "separation theology"—an idea that we are somehow separate from everything: separate from God, separate from life (in a sense), separate from each other (for sure), separated by time and distance and culture and beliefs, but not separated by desire. It seemed to me that all human beings desire the same thing: peace and safety, security and harmony, love and health, and abundance. Nobody wants anything different, and I have never seen a species of sentient beings so confused: If we all want the same things, how is it possible that we have not found a way to get it? This is the central question that humanity must ask itself: If we are so smart, and we are so evolved, and we are so religious, and if we have such a wonderful God—which all of our religions teach us—then how is it possible that we have not been able to achieve the simplest thing of all: peace and prosperity for everyone, safety and security for everyone, love and comfort for everyone, and compassion and understanding. Why is it so difficult for a species of advanced beings to create such a simple reality? That was the question that pushed me away from religion and toward spirituality, because I realized that the answer may not be in abandoning God but in thinking of God in a new way.

LR—Some traditional theologians say that the New Age Spirituality movements are incoherent and embrace all strange aspects of the paranormal—like UFOs, spirits, levitation, reincarnation, and so on. What is your answer for all those who say that these movements are nothing more than a mixed and contradictory set of beliefs?

NDW—I would say that the same thing is true of religion. If we don't see that our religions are a set of mixed and contradictory beliefs, then we are not looking at religion fairly. Clearly, some religions teach things that are totally unbelievable—a Virgin Mary, the appearance of saints and ghosts, the performance of certain miracles—that by anyone's measure would be considered paranormal. When miracles, virgin births, and other strange achievements and experiences are attributed to religion, however, that's acceptable; but when they're attributed to spirituality, that's crazy. I see how unfair that comparison is. If it's okay to talk about supranatural things under the umbrella of religion, then it's okay to talk about supranatural things under the umbrella of spirituality; you can't have it one way and not the other. The entire construction of the world religions is supernatural. It starts in the belief in a supernatural being called God—who no one has ever proven, who has never appeared, but who, nevertheless, apparently performs miracles in the everyday lives of people. If that's not paranormal, then what is?

LR—But imagine there's no God. Could it be possible to convey the same ethical values and messages proposed in your trilogy of books "Conversations with God" knowing that God did not exist?

NDW—Absolutely. So, too, it is possible to do so without religion in exactly the same way. Atheists have been doing that for hundreds of years. The Communist Party was an attempt to do that—although it did not do it well. So obviously, without question, your question answers itself. People have been saying that for thousands of years about religion; people have been saying "We don't need religion to create an ethical and moral society on the Earth," and it's true. We don't. But here's one thing we do need religion for—and for the same reason we need spirituality: Both religion and spirituality tap into a force and a source of invisible power—call it motivation if you will, or simple energy—that does in fact, and has been proven, to allow individuals and collections of people, whole societies, to produce specific outcomes, to create specific realities, and to experience life in profoundly joyful ways. This cannot be accomplished by a simple moral code of behavior. So people pray to God, or people use their spiritual understanding to bring into their lives a level of interaction with life itself that cannot be accomplished with the writing of a simple moral code, or a behavioral code, or a code of ethics. Ethics and morals don't produce miracles: God does. Ethics and morals don't create love in people's lives: God does. Ethics and morals don't produce understandings of larger things like what happens after we die—if anything—and what is the purpose of life: God does. So, a code of ethical and moral behavior can be functional and very practical, but it is not very inspiring.

LR—Isn't that vision of planet Earth as a cornucopia of abundance—offering the possibility of infinite goods and prosperity for everyone—a dangerous vision to offer especially when some strands of environmental economics see the Earth as a fragile ecosystem of finite resources?

NDW—I think that the statement contains its own answer. The fact is that we have sufficient number of resources—even though they are finite—for all the people if we simply distributed them according to religious or spiritual means; in other words, if we had charity in our heart and the highest good for all people as our common goal. We don't, at present. That is because there is a general sense of separation built into the world's religions and an absolute sense of separation built into the world's politics and economics, whereas in certain new spiritual traditions, the sense of separation disappears and the very message of the New Spirituality is a message of unity and oneness. So, the question is not whether the resources of the planet are sufficient to our needs: They are—we have enough food on the planet right now to feed everyone. We simply don't have the will to distribute that food in a way that gets it to everyone. We have enough wealth on the planet right now to make sure that no one lives in poverty, we simply don't have the will to share that wealth in a way that allows no one to have to live in poverty. It's not a question of supply, it's a question of will. What creates a will in the heart of humanity to produce particular outcomes is inspiration of a larger vision, a larger idea, a grander way of becoming human. These larger questions must first be answered. Who are we, really—I mean, as a being, as a species of sentient beings? Who are we? Where are we? What are we doing here and why are we doing it? These questions have not been answered by the human race—not collectively. Until they are, the human race will continue to go around in circles, trying to solve infinite problems with finite resources.

LR—Basic needs, like food, are part of the question, but what about luxury goods and other technological gadgets. For example, if everyone in China and India had an automobile, wouldn't that be an ecological disaster?

NDW—Of course it would, nobody says otherwise; "Conversations with God" certainly doesn't says otherwise. "Conversations with God" agrees with you. The problem is one of overemphasis on possessions and a lack of respect, ecologically, for the planet itself. The "Conversations with God" material agrees with everything you just said.

LR—How do we operate that shift of conscience? Don't you fear that your philosophy does sound very much like a set of good utopian intentions?

NDW—Of course! Of course! But every set of utopian intentions is what has changed the world. People don't change the world by talking about how terrible things are. People change the world by talking about how wonderful it's possible to make them. So we move step by step— and the steps may be small, but they are steps nonetheless—for that greater vision and that larger idea that you called "utopia." We will probably never get to a utopian society, but whether we get there or not is not the point: We must continue to head in that direction because the other direction brings no better things to us at all. Of course it's utopian, and of course it has difficulties in being fully implemented, but it's always the greatest idea that produces the largest outcomes. Albert Einstein once said, "If it's not impossible, there's no use even trying to do it." We must live the impossible dream; we must set for human beings the impossible goal, not those that are simple to achieve. Nothing is accomplished by doing what is simple to achieve.

LR—But utopias may set course toward very different directions: utopias designed to accomplish paradise on Earth for everyone, and totalitarian utopias designed to praise the elite— the chosen men, the chosen race, the chosen economic class, and so on. How do we find the right path to the first without making the mistake of choosing the second? History has often shown that humanity does not always make the right choice in that regard.

NDW—The human race is becoming far more sophisticated these days than it was 20, or 30, or 50, or 100 years ago. We are now able to see when a good idea has been warped, twisted, and distorted to serve ends that are not a good idea. No one, I don't think, would allow themselves to fall prey to the ideas of Adolf Hitler ever again, and perhaps, not even the misapplication of the ideas of Karl Marx. Communism, in its purest form, can make—for some people—a great deal of sense. Communism, in its purest form simply says: "from the capabilities of the capable is shared with those who are not capable, the fruits of the labors of all." It's a wonderful idea but it was distorted and it was twisted by those who would use it as a means of creating simple power and oppression; the ultimate utopia would include some of those ideas about sharing and communal living without loss of freedom.

You see, the key in any utopia is freedom. The key in any spiritual teaching and dogma is freedom. Freedom must be at the core of every teaching, of every dogma, and of every governmental system. When freedom is missing, you don't have true spirituality nor really the highest form of governance, but instead, a simple power play, somebody who wants power and others who are willing to give up their own power in order to have security or something else. But I don't think in the future there are going to be many people who are going to buy into that idea anymore, the ideas of Hitler or the twisted ideas of Joseph Stalin for instance; and for that matter, even of other people like George W. Bush—whose administration rapidly eroded and erased many of the freedoms of the United States in order that we might have security, and peace, and prosperity, so he says. So, there have been leaders throughout human history who have confused lack of freedom with the process by which prosperity and peace are attained. Those mistakes have always been made and I do not think that, as we get more and more sophisticated, human beings will fall to those temptations—although I could be wrong and you could be right. I wouldn't have imagined that George Bush could be elected twice. The first time, he fooled some people; but the second time, he simply scared them—and fear is a great motivator. So he scared the people into voting for him by telling them that if they didn't, things could get even worse and we would be attacked again and so forth.

LR—You said in one of your books that Hitler's going to heaven because there is no hell for him to be. I think I understand your point of view—it's a little bit like Socrates' point of view: Nobody does evil willingly and what we perceive as evil is nothing but ignorance manifested. But what I ask you is the following: If there's no hell, why then should there be a heaven?

NDW—There shouldn't be; there simply is. Heaven is not a place where one gets rewarded. Heaven is simply the place "that is." We call it heaven, we call it paradise, we call it nirvana, because it is a place where we are able to create and experience who we really are, in the fullness thereof. Heaven is not some distant realm that exists somewhere in outer space or somewhere in another dimension. Heaven is a three-part experience; it is an experience, not a place. The experience of heaven is divided in three parts: knowing, experiencing, and being—or what you would call: the spiritual, the physical, and the metaphysical. Those three aspects of the divinity itself, expressing through the process of life, are what the real heaven is about. So, heaven is not a place anymore than hell is a place. Heaven is simply a state of being; heaven is an experience, if you please. It is a way that we are and not a place that we are. The reason that there is a heaven is simply because that's what all "is"; everything "is" that. There's nothing that is not heaven—although we can experience it as "not heaven" because we have been given the creative power to do so.

LR—I would summarize your main ideas as "empowerment of the self"—as you said in one of your books: "Make the statement of your full self." With this idea, aren't you praising a morality for the extremes—to make the kind of people that Thomas Carlyle defined as "the hero"? According to that empowerment philosophy, you seem to praise much more the life of the excellent murderer and the excellent detective—because each one of them excel and fulfill themselves in what they do—rather than the life of the average indifferent Joe, isn't that so?

NDW—I don't see it that way. I think the opportunity that lies before all people is to, first, decide who they really are; decide how they wish to experience themselves—and this includes the average Joe—and then, to move into a demonstration of the expression and the experience of that: "Am I fair? Am I loving? Am I compassionate? Am I patient? Am I understanding?" These and other qualities are not available only to those who somehow become what you would call "excellent human beings," who do things extremely well. These states of being are open to—and achievable by—everyone, not just Mother Teresa or Martin Luther King or Gandhi, but Joe Smith, and Eduardo Rodriguez, and anybody else in the world who chooses to seek to attain these states of being. So, life is a wonderful process that allows us to, first of all, understand the blissful states of being, the blissful states of being that it is possible to attain through doing certain things in certain ways. And then, after we come to understand those blissful states of being, life is a process that allows us to actually attain them. That is, to act out in certain ways, that allow us to feel certain things about ourselves, about life itself, about each other, and about God, for that matter. That is the purpose of life, that is the wonder of life, that is the magic of life, that is the glory of life. Most people don't see life for the purposes for which it was designed, however, but that is the true opportunity and invitation that life offers for all of us.

LR—Can you describe your way of understanding the "law of attraction"? What are the reasons for its tremendous success?

NDW—The law of attraction is really what I called "a process of personal creation." It is using a fundamental principle of the universe; that principle states that everything in existence, reduced to its simplest level, is energy. Everything is energy, energy that is not standing still but in fact, is vibrating; and that is not vibrating identically, but that in fact, vibrates at differing rates of speed—or if you please, differing frequencies. If in fact, the "fuel of life" is the energy that is produced by the vibration—or frequency—of energy itself at different speeds—and we call some of these speeds "sound," we call some of these speeds "light," we call some of these speeds "physical objects"—if in fact this is the basis—I mean, the fundamental physical basis of life—and if that's true, then we have a mechanism, an actual mechanical device that can be adjusted and used. Just as you tune in the radio to receive signals of certain frequencies, you can tune in your mind, and even your experience; you can create an experience by tuning into the vibration of the experience that you wish to create. Or to put it simply: By thinking positive thoughts, you can create positive experiences in your life.

Incidentally, both religious and not religious people seem to agree on this fundamental point. A very famous American Christian minister in the 1940s, named Reverend Dr. Norman Vincent Peale, wrote an extraordinary book called *The Power of Positive Thinking*. Other ministers have written books about the power of prayer; prayer of course, is just a particular form of positive thinking. People who are not religious, who are not ministers, or rabbis, or ulamas, or clerics of any particular religion but simply philosophers, have made the same discovery. So we are clear that from time immemorial people have noticed that, as you think, very often that's how you experience your life. Émile Coué, a French physician actually—he wasn't a minister at all—he was aware that in World War I, when he would go into hospitals and the wounded soldiers would say, "I'm gonna die! Doc, I'm gonna die!" and he would say, "Don't think that way! Don't think that way! You're not going to die! You're going to get better! I promise you're going to get better!" and the patients that took his word for it, more of those actually survived than those who didn't believe him. He was so impressed by this in World War I, noticing it, he said, "Isn't that interesting? People who believe it when I tell them they're going to live, live—a higher percentage of them, do—and people who don't believe me, die—a higher percentage of them, die. So he developed a famous approach to life called autosuggestion and he taught his soldier patients to use autosuggestion; he taught them to say his famous phrase, which now has become world famous: "Everyday in every way I get better and better." He instructed his patients—the soldiers in those army hospitals out in the field—to say this to themselves at least a hundred times a day; 20 times in the morning, 20 times in the early afternoon, 20 times in the afternoon, 20 times in the evening, 20 times at night. He assured them that it would produce spectacular results—and incidentally, it did; thus was born a process called autosuggestion. The man behind this was Émile Coué, a French physician in World War I—and he's not the first person. Of course it goes back thousands of years actually; way, way back to the dawn of human history and as recently as the movie *The Secret*, more contemporarily.

So we see that throughout the span of human history, human beings have understood that their thought, for whatever reason, has powerful influence and a powerful impact on their daily lives. Now, I've given you the reason: The reason is that "Like attracts like." In this matter of energy, it is like a magnet: Like attracts like; if you think positive thoughts, you are actually sending out—because the physical body actually sends out—energy patterns through the power of thought. We already know that energy creates patterns that can be measured (lie detector tests have demonstrated that to us). So we find out that we are all simply transmitters. Human beings are transmitters, and they're receivers as well. They're transmitting and receiving stations; they transmit certain energies in the form of their thoughts and ideas and they receive—or draw to themselves—energies of a similar, if not identical, nature. So a person who thinks positively and joyfully all of his life, I'm not saying that every single solitary thing is going to turn out wonderfully in that person's life, but I will say that he'll have a life of greater joy, happiness, and abundance than someone who thinks negatively and pessimistically all the time. So I would describe the law of attraction as a fundamental law of physics which says, essentially, like attracts like.

LR—Why do you think that what's operating here is spirituality rather than psychology—or even mass psychology?

NDW—It is. It is mass psychology! The question is not the way you pose it. The question is: Because it's mass psychology, why does that eliminate God or spirituality as part of the process? Suppose that mass psychology and spirituality were one and the same—I don't see those two things as being mutually exclusive. It is mass psychology! Of course it is! You would be a fool not to see that. But do we not imagine that God would use mass psychology as a marvelous tool with which to equip human beings to create the reality they would prefer?

LR—Isn't the law of attraction then the closest thing we can get to William James's pragmatic way of dealing with religion? If it works, and if it makes you feel good, nobody cares how it operates or if it's true. Don't you think that's why no scientist takes "New Age physics" seriously?

NDW—What is your question?

LR—My question is: If scientists don't take this physics seriously, if they disagree with it, what legitimacy do most New Age thinkers have in order to claim that vibrating strings or energies can be controlled by one's will?

NDW—Well, first of all, I will disagree with you that no scientists recognize it; that's number one. That's a broad-based statement that is simply and patently untrue. There are many scientists, legitimate scientists—Dr. John Hagelin for instance, who's a world renowned physicist, would disagree with you completely on that statement—so, Dr. John Hagelin and many other physicists who are starting to put together superstring theory and so forth, would hear you say what you just said, "no scientists agree at all," and they would say, "Excuse me; I'm a scientist and I agree." And there are many, many physicists, I'm not talking about one or two or three, but hundreds of physicists and scientists who agree. So, first of all, your question is based on an absolutely and patently false premise that science does not agree. Now, if you have said to me, "Some scientists don't agree," then I would say "You're correct." But "No scientists agree"? Patently false. So, the question is a question that's loaded with inaccurate information. Now, having been asked a totally inaccurate question, I will answer it anyway. The fact that some scientists don't agree does not mean that it's not true. Many, many people did not agree on certain things until they were proven beyond the shadow of a doubt. But what right does spirituality have to talk about superstring theory, or vibrating energy, or frequencies, or the law of attraction? The right that spirituality has to make those claims is the experience of people. Always is the experience of people. People have always experienced reality before science has proved it. I'm going to repeat that so you can really get it: People always experience reality before science proves it. That's what makes science try to figure out what's going on. Science is merely the effort of human beings to explore what they already see happening and to try to explain it. Newton saw the apple drop on his head and then he tried to figure out the law of gravity. It's not true that apples never fell until Newton created the law of gravity. Apples fell all the time, long before Newton was born. So, things happen and then science attempts to explain them. It isn't that science explains something and then things happen, and the same thing is true here. The law of attraction is working and science has not yet been able to explain it. So, by that means we should say it's not happening? Of course it's happening; just as apples have always fallen before Newton created the law of gravity.

LR—In book two of "Conversations with God," you praise Rudolf Steiner's Waldorf Schools learning methodology. Don't these schools discard mathematical and scientific approaches to the world in favor of more expressive and emotional approaches to it? We see many more Waldorf students in drama, poetry, and the arts in general, rather than in astronomy, physics, chemistry, and the like. For you, is it more important to know the world or to express oneself in the world?

NDW—First of all, I think that Waldorf students are found more frequently—but not exclusively—in the arts and in the expressive forms of creativity because Waldorf students are encouraged to get in touch with—from the very beginning of their learning years—the esoteric side of life rather than the simply factual side of life. But I don't think that Waldorf students are any less intelligent with regard to the factual side of life. I think Waldorf students are, generally, at the top of their class; they usually have no problem getting into any college anywhere—as a rule—and they generally wind up knowing as much about physics, astronomy, and chemistry as the average person would anywhere. But they are inclined—I would agree with you—to spend the days and times of their lives in artistic and esoteric pursuits, because this is the aspect of life that they have been opened to, far more profoundly than the average pupil in the average school—where esoterics and the foundational basis of life, the expressive arts, the feelings, emotions, and the natural beauties of life are not emphasized, much to the dismay of future generations.

We are at a loss, I believe, to express ourselves with the beauty, the wonder, and the joy of life in these days and times as we did in the days of the Greek philosophers, or the days of the Renaissance in Italy, and in other former times in our collective human history, when far more value was placed on beauty, wonder, ethics, and morals, and far less value on mathematics, simple science, and mechanics—how the world works. I would argue for both: I would say that we need a balance, but an equal balance between the two. A look at the mechanics of life, a deep understanding of it, an appreciation of it, and a use of those mechanics to make life even better and better for all of us, for sure. But also, a look at the artistic side of life, the nonmechanical aspects of our experience, the aspects of beauty, truth, and harmony in all things, the integrative process by which life in fact creates itself through the use of the creative tools I've described earlier, and the fundamental and foundational basis of all of life which transcends the mechanics, transcends the physical, and tends to rise to the metaphysical. So, I think that in the future, schools will do both with an equal balance, and then provide the true genius of the human species who will understand the mechanics but also apply the ethical, moral, and philosophical standards to the use of those mechanics—which would stop them from being used for our own self-destruction.

Currently we have a very privileged species which understands the mechanics of life all right, but doesn't understand life itself, its purpose, and its function; therefore, we are like children playing with matches— and we are self-destructing, obviously, wherever we look. Knowing the mechanics of life, knowing chemistry, biology, science, mathematics, and technology does not guarantee that we're going to be elevated or highly evolved beings. As a matter of fact, without the metaphysical, ethical, and moral component to life, we will not only fail to be evolved beings, we will probably self-destruct—like children playing with matches.

LR—Can values like morality and beauty be taught without reference to the esoteric, God, the spiritual, and so on? Are atheists handicapped in their ability to feel?

NDW—I would not say that. I don't think it's necessary for you to keep on coming back to the same question. I don't think that it's necessary to believe in a supreme being or a super power in order to come to a place of deeper appreciation of the beauty and the ethical constructions underlying the mechanics of life. I am suggesting to you, however, that people who believe in a power greater than us—or in the sum total of the power of all of us—to be focused and applied with intention in particular ways, can often produce consistent and predictable results that are not open to people who simply don't believe that such a power exists. So, I don't know that it's a question of anyone being handicapped per se necessarily, automatically from the outset, but I do think that when people believe in something larger than themselves, even larger than the collective of all of us, when people allow themselves to embrace the notion that there is some overriding element or aspect to life that even reaches beyond the limits of this planet, out into the solar system, into the galaxy, into the universe itself, if you please; that there's something going on here fundamentally and powerfully evident by simply looking at the night sky; that in fact we—having to admit our humility—can't explain, do not fully understand, but can use even as we are invited to use it by that power itself.

So, I think that it would be a specious argument to say that such a power does not exist. One merely needs to look at life beyond the end of one's nose; one merely needs to look into, as I said, a night sky to conclude that, you know what? There's something we don't fully know here—the knowing of which would probably change everything. There's something bigger than us here, something far more powerful at play than simply the human mind. The human mind may in fact explain many of the things that are going on here in day-to-day life, but one look down a microscope—at the microcosmic universe of cellular intelligence—or one look up through a telescope—at the macrocosmic universe of universal intelligence—leads us to quickly conclude: There's much more going on here than meets the eye. Or as wonderful William Shakespeare put it so perfectly: "There are more things in heaven and earth, Horatio, than are dreamt of in your philosophy."

LR—What were the major influences that led you into your spiritual path?

NDW—My mother; then, probably Dr. Elisabeth Kubler-Ross and her writings; a wonderful science fiction writer named Robert Heinlein—who opened my mind to possibilities through the deft use of science fiction—Paulo Coelho who, likewise through his writings, expanded my inquisitiveness and my ability to wonder, "Gee, I wonder if that could be true . . . I wonder." The great philosophers—you've mentioned Socrates yourself earlier, Plato and all of those wonderful dialogues from the days of the early Greek philosophers—were a great influence in my journey; and then, the lives of people who have made an extraordinary difference in contemporary times on this planet: Gandhi, Mother Teresa, Lech Walesa, Martin Luther King Jr., and others I could name in all the countries who have stepped forward and become larger than life in their willingness to move mountains, to change the course and direction of human history. These people have all inspired me and I've read biographies of many of them. When I read those biographies I look inside and between the lines: What is it that drives the engine of their experience? What is it that produces such a sure and certain faith in the outcome—if they will only persevere, and persevere, and yet persevere one more time. So those are the people that have inspired me and played an enormous influence in my life—beginning with my mother, who had an unshakable belief in God.

LR—Have you ever felt tempted to curse God for some of your life's misfortunes?

NDW—Well, of course, who hasn't? [Laughs.] Of course I was. I cursed God, I cursed life, I cursed myself, I cursed whatever was in the way.

LR—Life not going the way you've wanted: Was that a disturbance in your belief in God?

NDW—Yes, it certainly was.

LR—How did you deal with the fact?

NDW—I just simply changed my mind about that as a result of a supernatural experience that I had—which you surely know about; it's written in "Conversations with God," Book 1. When I had my own personal encounter with the divine, I obviously, quickly, and naturally changed my mind.

LR—We've mentioned about Socrates, Martin Luther King Jr., Mother Teresa . . . what about you? Do you see yourself as someone who's a philosophy and theology popularizer or, rather, do you see yourself as an original and illuminated contemporary prophet?

NDW—I wouldn't use the word *prophet*, but if you'd used the word *messenger*, I would have said "yes." I don't know that I'm original; I would strike the word original. I don't think that Socrates was original, I don't think that Martin Luther King was original; I think those people merely came with an urgent and earnest articulation of nonoriginality. [Laughs.] Martin Luther King would be the last person to say that his ideas were original, but they were certainly urgently expressed with a wonderful ability to articulate and a way of representing ancient ideas that made them feel fresh—and more importantly, made them feel possible. So the great articulators throughout human history are people who have taken old ideas and made them feel newly possible. If you ask me if I was that person, I would say yes; that's the person I strive to be.

LR—Some philosophies and religions (namely Eastern) portray attachment to the material world and the inner desires of one's own will as the prime motives leading to suffering. Spirituality—in the idealist or dualist form—then appears as a solution to mitigate this human condition. Is it really necessary for a fulfilling human being to feel always happy about reality, even if that implies a distortion of it in order to correspond to one's own perspective?

NDW—[Laughs.] One's own perspective is all there is. There's nothing else. So I don't know if it's "distorting reality"—I think it's creating it.

There is no such thing as Reality with a capital R; there is no "objective Reality" that one has to then distort to fit one's own personal perspective. The process works the other way around: One's personal perspective creates one's individual reality, and objective reality does not exist in the universe; that is, 10 people can see the same thing and will give you 10 different ideas about what they saw. So we're pretty clear that objective reality does not exist, but subjective reality certainly does; subjective reality is not the result of one's distorting objective reality but, in fact, of one's creating one's impressions of the reality that one is viewing in order to meet with one's highest expectations and goals, and grandest notions and ideas. As an example, a person like Gloria Steinem in the United States might have looked at the objective reality and said, "Women are being debased in this country, they're not being properly valued, they're not being treated equally and they probably never will, that's just the way things are and nothing can be done about it." Or she could have looked at the same reality and said, "With the proper application of my skills, my insights, my abilities, my talents, and my energies, this entire situation can change. I, singularly, with the work I'm going to do in the world, can ultimately create equal pay for women, voting rights for women—in all organizations, not just in the government—and other forms of equality; it may not take a week, it may not take a month, it may not take a year, it may take much longer, but I can do this." Now, that's her reality and as wonderful John Kennedy said when he expressed to the world his idea about tomorrow: "All of this may not be accomplished in the first 100 days, nor even in the first 1,000 days, or even perhaps in our lifetimes, but let us begin."

LR—You say that there is only one's own perspective; granting it so, that personal perspective may be well oriented or badly oriented by others—and often, by agents who have nothing to do with that person's life: We have the mass media, spin doctors, and the like who manipulate reality and lead masses. Do you agree that there are distortions of reality that are not chosen by the person who lives it?

NDW—Of course I agree with you. Those are people who don't know who they really are, who don't know that they have the power to create their own reality, subjectively. Those are people who do not deeply understand the things you and I are talking about even, much less embrace the notion that they have the ability to step away from the ideas that others would foist upon them—and force upon them—and to create their own ideas instead. Of course it happens, it happens all the time.

LR—Those are people who can easily be manipulated. How can they be protected from the manipulators?

NDW—The challenge is to raise the level of the collective consciousness. This is the last and final frontier. You know, the old *Star Trek* TV show used to start off with the words "Space, the final frontier." It's not the final frontier, with respect to the late Gene Roddenberry, who wrote those lines, it really should be: "Consciousness, the final frontier." So when we raise collective consciousness—which is the task now before humanity, this is the final task before humanity—then the masses will not be so easily swayed, because more and more individuals will begin to understand, through the raising of their consciousness, what is so, who they are, why they're here, and what they can do about it.

LR—Aren't some New Age thinkers neglecting the world's real problems by camouflaging reality? I will give you an example . . .

NDW—You don't have to give me an example: The answer is yes. Of course they are; that's the point of my book *Happier than God*. I make that exact point. Of course they're encouraging people to ignore the world's problems by camouflaging them in all sorts of hairy, fairy, fluffy, New Age gobbledygook which has no relationship to what's going on on the ground in day-to-day life. I couldn't agree with you more; so, we have to stop it. I've been asking my New Age friends to stop it for quite some time now; stop it! Don't stop talking about higher realities, but stop talking about them in such a way that it makes it look as if everything is perfect, everything is wonderful on the Earth because, guess what: It's not!

LR—But shouldn't they be giving the example of that "ground proximity"? I've been visiting some New Age thinkers' Web sites and most of them prefer to schedule workshops and paradise trips to pleasant places to talk about spiritual and terrestrial utopia. Why don't these thinkers take people to face reality and change it—for example, instead of making cruises in the

Mediterranean, why not visit city slums, take them to meet nongovernmental organizations (NGOs), or even take them to visit third world countries with urgent health care needs?

NDW—Because of what's practically possible. It's far more practical to talk to people where they are than to drag them by the scruff of the neck to where they're not. If you want to engage the services, the dedication, the commitment, and the willingness of, let's say, a handful of wealthy people—20 or 30 wealthy people—to do something about the slums, the ghettos, and the places where people are oppressed, what you do is gather them where wealthy people feel the most comfortable. Then and there, using their language, in their environment, you impress upon them the need to use some of their wealth—at least—to solve some of these problems. But you don't invite the queen of England to step off onto the shores of Darfur and walk the battlefield, or step off into the fields of Haiti where children are dying of starvation everyday, or walk down the slums of Los Angeles to see if she could do something about the racial inequalities in the United States. No, you talk to the queen of England in her palace and you expect that she's a bright enough person to understand that these things are happening without having to step right in front of them and that she could use her good offices to good effect, to change some of those conditions. And in fact, that's exactly what happens: The people of the world—whether they're royalty, political leaders, or simply very wealthy people—have made enormous contributions to solve these kinds of problems. Bill Gates, who created Microsoft, does not have to walk among the dying tribes of Darfur in order to know that it makes sense to send $50 million to ease the suffering there. So it doesn't necessarily follow that if a person does not physically walk among the suffering he cannot understand that it's taking place. So, why certain people have cruises to the Bahamas, or spiritual renewal retreats at these fancy resorts, is to attract the very people who need to have their eyes opened—and their hearts open as well. In order to do that, you create an environment where they feel comfortable; once you get people in an environment where they feel comfortable, then you make them feel uncomfortable [laughs]. Every messenger knows this.

LR—Do you have that experience? Do you know people who felt change after that kind of trip and who manifested the desire to change their way of life?

NDW—Of course. Many people have gone on my Alaska cruise and have come back and joined The Group of 1000, or joined Humanity's Team, or sent large contributions, or have their whole idea of who they are and why they're here changed. Of course that's true—otherwise, people wouldn't do those things, or people would not continue to offer those programs or to present those ideas in the ways that they do. Nevertheless, all true spiritual teachers approach people at every level; they don't simply do cruises to the Mediterranean or to Alaska exclusively—they may do one or two of those once a year. They also may do one or two programs in the ghettos—or at least, invite people who are from the ghettos to come to their retreats at no cost, absolutely free. They will talk to people in between as well—not the very wealthy, and not the very poor—but the vast middle class in between. True spiritual teachers talk to people at every area on every level of the human spectrum—I know I do!

Phil Zuckerman

Phil Zuckerman is a professor of sociology at Pitzer College in Claremont, California. He is the author of *Society without God* (2008) and *Faith No More* (2011), and the editor of *Atheism and Secularity* (2010).

Luís Rodrigues—What are the factors that can best explain high rates of disbelief in various nations?

Phil Zuckerman—I think there are always special circumstances in every country, idiosyncrasies that are unique to every nation, every culture; so, there's always going to be a variety of issues that make this question very complex. But if we take a step back and try to make some general explanations, I think the most useful one is that which is proposed by Norris and Inglehart in their wonderful book called *The Sacred and the Secular*; they really do show, with a lot of data, that the truth to the matter is that when countries are peaceful, prosperous, democratic, have enough housing, jobs, medicine, education, and there's not a lot of war and crime, people have good health care and health insurance, these countries tend to be the more secular—or the less strongly believing. The countries that have the most war, poverty, disease, corruption, crime, and insecurity, these tend to be the most religious or devout. Now, it's not absolute—there are always exceptions because human societies are very complex things—but in my opinion, if I had to pick one answer to that question, I would go with that one.

LR—The standards by which utilitarian levels of development are measured can be questioned by theists who may say, "Okay, atheist Swedes or Danes may be richer, organized, less

corrupt, have more social justice, etc., but theists—like the Brazilians—though they have none of that, are more extroverted, seem more happy, have soccer, samba, beaches, hot weather, and so on." How can an atheist justify that his or her own set of values, used to measure quality of life, is the preferable one?

PZ—Measuring quality of life is always subjective. There is no absolute standard necessarily upon which everyone can agree. For example, I may believe that a good society is one that allows women to vote, but someone in Saudi Arabia may think that's a bad society; I may believe a society is good that is vegetarian, but someone from a meat-eating culture may disagree. Of course there are always going to be disagreements about what makes for a good or healthy society; it's a subjective question. What is a good car? What is a good computer? What is a good husband or wife? There's no absolute answer to this; so, all we can say is that it may not have to do with happiness necessarily.

For example, we know that poor people have much lower suicide rates than rich people. I'm not saying that it's necessarily related to how happy people are—I mean, I think the music in Brazil is much better than the music in Scandinavia; the weather in Brazil is nicer than the weather in Scandinavia [laughs]. Of course there are these differences, but as sociologists, we want to measure certain standards—and by standards I mean widely accepted indicators of a healthy society. For example, rates of poverty: Maybe some people like poverty! Who's to say poverty is a bad thing? But at least we can measure how many people have enough to eat, how many people go hungry at night, how many people have access to medicine and health care, how many people have access to a house. If you go to the streets of Calcutta in India, every night you will see tens of thousands of people living in the streets with no home. Are they happy? Although I doubt it, maybe they are; maybe they love sleeping in the street. It's not about happiness as much as it is about these somewhat standard measures of well-being: Are there bombs going off? Is there murder? Is there a democracy? These can be measured. Now, that doesn't mean just because a country has a good democracy, good health care, good housing, and no war, that doesn't necessarily mean it's great on every measure; maybe people are miserable, or lonely, or bored, or have bad music to listen to. While I do believe that Brazil has wonderful music and happy people, they also have terrible poverty, children living in the streets with no school, no health care, no housing; life is very hard for a lot of people and I think that helps explain a little bit about why they turn to religion for comfort. There are a lot of studies about the growing evangelical movement in Latin America—in Brazil, in Central America—and a lot of these people that go to these evangelical churches are going because they have nowhere else to go for help. If you can't afford a doctor, you go to the church and ask the priest to pray for you; if you have no access to medicine, at least you can ask Jesus for help.

But again, I don't think it's always that poverty causes countries to be religious and wealth causes countries to be secular; I don't believe that at all. I simply believe that the correlation is strong. So that means, most of the time, the more secure, democratic, and peaceful nations are the less religious, and the more poor and corrupt are the more religious. But that's not all of them; it's just a correlation, it's just a pattern—and of course, there are some countries that aren't in that pattern.

LR—What do you think people expect most from religion and belief in God? The pure and simple perpetual maintenance of life (even in a supernatural realm)? Some sense of life's meaning? The idea of belonging to a community with shared beliefs? Of these, and other, factors, which do you think carry the most weight?

PZ—There's no one answer to that and I think it's different in different cultures, in different societies, and in different times. I don't think there is one single universal reason people are religious. And you have to separate belief in God from being part of a religion: Many, many people are involved in a religion and they don't necessarily believe in God. I myself am involved in many religious things but it's not because I believe in God. So, we have to separate religion—which refers to rituals, and songs, and food, and celebrations, and prayer—from belief in God. Often they go together, but not always. I know many people who are Catholic—involved in their Catholic church—but they don't believe in God; I know many Jewish people who are involved in their Jewish religion but don't believe in God. I even know some Mormons who don't believe in God.

So it's not always the same; but even if it were the same, what do I take as the most important? I think it is different for different people.

For some people, belief in God is a comfort in their life; it gives their life meaning, it gives them a sense of purpose, it gives them a sense of being loved, it gives them a sense of being forgiven. For some people, God and religion are about community and being connected to other people in a meaningful way, in a moral community where they can feel as though they're part of something and part of a plan—that is God's plan manifested among a community of believers. I think that that is the most beneficial aspect of religion: the community aspect, the sense of belonging that it gives to its believers. Some other people are religious and believe in God simply because they were taught to; it's just the way they were raised. I think many, many people believe in God or are part of a religion because that is all they know: their parents, their grandparents, their friends, their uncles, their cousins, their neighbors, and so on. I strongly believe that we are shaped to a large degree by our culture, our society, and our families. So if we are born into religion, it's very likely we will stay religious.

LR—A kind of militant atheism seems to be increasing today— namely, in the so-called movement of the New Atheists. Is this a marginal and confined intellectual response to religious fundamentalism or does it have the capacity to grow on a popular scale? From a sociological standpoint, what do you think will be the impact of this movement?

PZ—I don't know. It's too early to say. In a way, you're asking me to make a prediction about the future—which, I think, is something religious people like to do [laughs]. I do believe, however, that there are a lot of people who didn't care about religion, didn't think about it, didn't worry about it, so they weren't very strong in their atheism and in their secularism, but two things changed that: the first was 9/11, and the second was the presidency of George W. Bush. I think these two things were a bit of a wake-up call. A lot of Americans—I can't speak for other people around the world—who were not interested in religion suddenly became aware that religion was not going away and that it was affecting the world in a negative way. So I think they responded to the New Atheists in a way they wouldn't have, maybe 15 or 20 years ago, but today there is an awareness that religious fundamentalism is affecting the world, it was affecting our government here in the United States under George W. Bush, and I think a lot of people—who were not strong atheists—suddenly became fans of the New Atheists because they spoke what they were believing or thinking and didn't really care to say until now. The other thing I will say, though, is that I'm not quite sure what a militant atheist is. Every atheist I've ever talked to always says the same thing: "I don't care what other people believe; I just don't want them to force it on me." Now, that's not what militant *religious* people say. Militant religious people say, "You must believe in our religion or we will hurt you or you will go to hell." The threat is either "now"—among Muslims in Saudi Arabia or Iran, if you don't accept Islam, you're in big trouble—or the threat is in the future. An evangelical Christian will say, "You have to accept Jesus or you're going to hell." Atheists don't condemn people to hell and, as far as I know, atheists don't want to take anyone else's rights away; they just don't want them to impose religion on their children. When we talk about militant atheists or fundamentalist atheists, I have a problem with those terms because, in my opinion, a fundamentalist Muslim or a fundamentalist Christian wants to make society Christian or Muslim and wants everyone to adopt these beliefs, whereas a militant or fundamentalist atheist simply says, "You can have your beliefs; just keep them private and don't force them on us." I think that's a big difference. Now, there may be some atheists out there—like Joseph Stalin—who want to destroy people's right to be religious, but those people are insane and I don't think they represent even 1 percent of most atheists.

LR—Stalin is often quoted as saying, "When one man dies, it is a tragedy; when millions die it's statistics." Don't you think people tend to associate this lack of emotional attachment with secular and atheistic governments?

PZ—Definitely. I think the Communist dictators really gave atheism a bad reputation. There's no question Stalin was an evil man and it's very unfortunate that he is so closely identified with atheism. People have hated atheists for at least 2,000 or 3,000 years. If you read the Bible, Psalms 14, verses 1 to 3, you see that whoever wrote the Bible says that "the fool hath said in his heart, there is no God. They are corrupt, they have done abominable works, there is none that doeth good." If you read the Koran, there are many passages that say bad things about atheists. So I think that, even if we didn't have Stalin, people don't like atheists. That's because, I think, for the last 5,000 years, the people that have been in power have claimed their authority based on God; so when you have people who don't believe in God, that's a threat to the people who use that claim to be in power. If you think about people like Joseph Stalin, how many people in history, how many rulers and kings, have done horrible things in the name of religion or God? It's so far in the past that people don't think about it. If you read Adolf Hitler, he said many religious things but people don't seem to associate Hitler with Catholicism. He was very much a Catholic and he believed very much in God, and yet that didn't seem to discredit Catholicism. The Catholic Church, in fact, didn't even condemn Hitler, and yet nobody blames the Catholic Church.

LR—In an article in the *Cambridge Companion to Atheism*, you make a distinction between "organic atheism" and "coercive atheism." Can you explain the difference between these forms of atheism?

PZ—Yes, it's very simple. I would consider coerced atheism—or forced atheism—when a dictatorship takes over a country and then makes atheism the official policy, enforces it, and, by law, closes churches and forces people—as best they can by threatening them with prison, fines, and torture—to not be religious. This is exactly what happened in the Soviet Union. There's a wonderful book called *The Plot to Kill God* by Paul Froese, where he shows how ruthless and how brutal the Soviets were in trying to destroy religion. Now, that is obviously a forced atheism, and the reason I called it forced is because it's coming from the top down; it's the government in power, the dictatorships in power, the fascists in power that are forcing it on the people. So, we can't say that the people are becoming atheists; it's simply the government above them that is forcing it on them.

I call organic atheism a situation where in a free democratic society people simply become less religious over time on their own. No one is forcing them, no one is making them, there are no laws against religion, there are no punishments; it's just that simply people stop believing as strongly in God—or in God at all—over generations, not because they're forced to feel this way, or threatened to feel this way, but simply because they lose their faith—for whatever reason. I would argue that in Albania, in China, and in the Soviet Union, to give just three examples, you have a sort of forced atheism, whereas in the Western

Europe—the Netherlands, Belgium, Scandinavia, United Kingdom, and so on—it's more organic. People just aren't going to church anymore, they just don't believe anymore, and no one is forcing this—it's just happening freely. The truth is, when you have a fascist dictatorship that is atheistic, that doesn't necessarily mean that people under them really stop believing. It just means they have to pretend.

LR—Can we establish the same analogy regarding theism and religion? I mean, can we talk about a coercive religion and an organic religion—or do you think that religion is always coercive?

PZ—That's a good question. You know, I've never thought about it but I would agree that sometimes religion is coercive and sometimes it is organic. Certainly we know many examples throughout history where people were forced to convert to Islam, or people were forced to convert to Christianity, but we also know of certain instances where people took it freely and naturally. I don't think Buddhism, for example, was forced on anyone at the end of a gun. I'm not as good on this because I'm not an historian of religion, but I do believe that, yes, you could talk about religion the same way.

LR—How can societies achieve organic forms of atheism?

PZ—You know, I ask myself this question all the time. I don't know if it can come about by people making fun of religion, I don't know if it can come about by people arguing rationally against religion—because after all, religious belief is irrational, so how can rational arguments win? If people believe in things that are irrational, you're not going to be able to convince most of them with rational arguments; nevertheless, you can try. Every now and then, in my own research, I have inter- viewed many people who were religious and then their own intellectual thinking about things got them to lose their faith. I think that the only way to bring about organic atheism is to make society stable, peaceful, and healthy. The other thing is, of course, education: We just have to repeatedly speak the truth about science, evolution, the laws of physics, and eventually people will come to it. But there is no magic solution and I don't really know if we can ever get rid of religion; maybe it is too important to people, maybe it speaks to people on an emotional and psychological level that is hard to get rid of. And I don't necessarily think we need to get rid of religion: I just don't like the dangerous versions of religion.

LR—One factor that can prevent that from happening is the constant lobbying of religious groups in the political sphere— and here I'm recalling as an example the enormous influence exerted by the megachurches and religious denominations located in the so called Bible-belt in the United States. Isn't this close relationship between politics and religion something that helps inhibit organic atheism?

PZ—I think you're right. We have to keep a good separation between the government and religion and we need to have a good separation between church and state; I think that's very important. But it's not a guarantee. The United States has a constitutional separation of church and state, and yet we have a very strong religion. In many parts of Europe, they have a government-funded church, and yet the religion is very weak. So it's not so easy to say. I agree with you, that we shouldn't have megachurches calling the president every week, telling him what to do, but . . . what can we do?

LR—Is the question really a matter of separation between church and state or the separation between the state and the economic power behind the churches?

PZ—I don't know. That's a good question. I've never thought of that; it's not my area.

LR—Theists may assert that although some secular countries may have better welfare systems and social conditions, these systems are nevertheless purely artificial: They are state dependent, lacking the "human factor," the social solidarity and the friendly human ties that theistic societies have. Can you comment on that?

PZ—I think it's possible that that's true, but that's not my experience. When I lived in Scandinavia—which has the most extensive welfare system in the world—I felt that there was tremendous social solidarity. I felt that people had a very strong sense of caring for others, taking care of other people, and a very strong morality—that no one should be hungry, no one should be homeless, no one should freeze out in the streets. So I suppose what they're saying is possible—that it is a bit bureaucratic, soulless and heartless—but in my experience, that was just not what I found. I find that heartlessness much more abundant here in the United States, where people don't care about the suffering of other people. Maybe in their churches they care, but in terms of their fellow countrymen, they don't care if someone has no health insurance, they don't care if someone has no access to the hospital. So I hear what you're saying and I hear the criticism—that perhaps it seems like this state bureaucracy and there's no heart and maybe in a church group there's much more personal interconnection—but I felt that people in Scandinavia had a very strong social solidarity, a sense of belonging, taking care of each other and taking care of their fellow human beings.

LR—So how do you see the criticism that attempts to portray atheists as immoral, as individuals who have no basis or justification to support any kind of morality?

PZ—It's just totally absurd, and there's no social science to support it. It's a superstition and it's a myth. The myth that atheists are these cold, immoral, evil people is simply untrue. There's no science that supports this—and in fact, quite the opposite. If you're just following the Commandments of God, you're not moral—you're just obedient. To be truly moral, you must be an atheist: An atheist is choosing between right and wrong because it's right and wrong, not because they're following orders from a God of the sky. So, in fact, if you are a believer in God, you have no morality; you're simply obedient. You do not choose between right and wrong, you follow commands, you follow orders. That's not morality. Morality is choosing between wrong or right, using your own compass, using your own heart to decide, regardless of the consequences. A religious person simply follows orders, and I've never heard of that as being described as moral.

LR—How do you think secularism will evolve worldwide in our contemporary society?

PZ—I think the problem is that of birth rates: Secular people have not so many children, religious people have a lot of children, and religious fundamentalists have 20 children! So, the more religious people there are, the more children they have; the less religious they are, the less children they have. I believe that it's simply a matter of birth rates. Religious fundamentalists simply have more kids and secular people don't. So, I'm very pessimistic about the future of the world on that front. We will just have to wait and see.

Index

About the Author

LUÍS F. RODRIGUES was born in 1976 and is an architect in Lisbon, Portugal. With a BD and an MD in architecture and urban planning, he has written about urban planning for local newspapers. He started investigating religion several years ago by studying ancient Egyptian hieroglyphics and the history of religion in Portugal. He presented a paper at the first gathering of the Portuguese Association for the Study of Religions and has finished writing a history of atheism in Portugal.